Templates for Authorship

TEMPLATES FOR *Authorship*

AMERICAN WOMEN'S LITERARY AUTOBIOGRAPHY OF THE 1930S

WINDY COUNSELL PETRIE

UNIVERSITY OF MASSACHUSETTS PRESS
Amherst and Boston

Printed in the United States of America

ISBN 978-1-62534-552-3 (paper); 551-6 (hardcover)

Designed by Deste Roosa
Set in Adobe Garamond Pro and Futura
Printed and bound by Books International, Inc.

Cover design by Rebecca Lown
Cover photo by LiliGraphie,
"Old Letter with Vintage Handwriting—Grunge Background." © Shutterstock.com.

Library of Congress Cataloging-in-Publication Data
Names: Petrie, Windy Counsell, author.
Title: Templates for authorship : American women's literary autobiography of the 1930s / Windy Counsell Petrie.
Description: Amherst : University of Massachusetts Press, 2021. | Includes bibliographical references and index. |
Identifiers: LCCN 2020019503 | ISBN 9781625345516 (hardcover) | ISBN 9781625345523 (paperback) | ISBN 9781613767979 (ebook) | ISBN 9781613767986 (ebook)
Subjects: LCSH: Women authors, American—Biography—History and criticism. | American prose literature—Women authors—History and criticism. | American prose literature—20th century—History and criticism. | Autobiography—Women authors—History and criticism. | Biography as a literary form—History and criticism.
Classification: LCC PS366.A88 P48 2021 | DDC 810.9/9287—dc23
LC record available at https://lccn.loc.gov/2020019503

British Library Cataloguing-in-Publication Data
A catalog record for this book is available from the British Library.

A portion of chapter 1 was previously published as "The Shifting Self: Edith Wharton's Renunciations in A Backward Glance," in *a/b: Auto/Biography Studies* 14, no. 2 (Winter 1999): 204–22. Reprinted by permission. A portion of chapter 5 was previously published as "Resisting Dismissal: Working-Class Women in the Popular Fiction of Edna Ferber and Mary Roberts Rinehart," in *Modernist Women and American Social Engagement* (Lanham, MD: Lexington Books, 2019), 21–43. Reprinted by permission. Portions of the text were previously published as "Grace King," *American Writers: Supplement XXVIII,* ed. Jay Parini (New York: Charles Scribners' Sons, 2018); "Gertrude Atherton," *American Writers: Supplement XXIV,* ed. Jay Parini (New York: Charles Scribners' Sons, 2013); "Edna Ferber," *American Writers Supplement: XXIX,* ed. Jay Parini (New York: Charles Scribners' Sons, 2018); "Carolyn Wells," *American Writers: Supplement XXVI,* ed. Jay Parini (New York: Charles Scribners' Sons, 2015). Cengage Learning Inc. Reproduced by permission. www.cengage.com/permissions.

CONTENTS

PREFACE

This project was born years ago from a serendipitous library shelf-reading expedition. I was looking for a hardbound copy of Edith Wharton's autobiography so that I could view the original illustrations in it. (And before I go any further, let me exhort readers of this book to do the same. There are many wonderful photographs of these authors in the original hardcover autobiographies that could not be reproduced here for a host of reasons but are well worth contemplating.) Once I arrived at the correct shelf, I started scanning for Wharton's book, but the books surrounding it arrested my attention. As I scanned the titles, I discovered autobiography upon autobiography by American women writers, many by authors I had never heard of in my years of undergraduate and graduate study. I had always been an enthusiastic student. I did all the assigned readings. So why had I never even heard of so many of these women writers?

And so it began. I started reading those adjacent autobiographies, and then I realized that to really appreciate and analyze them, I would have to learn a lot more—about the writers, about their lives, and about their careers. Very slowly, year after year, I took on the project of reading anything by or about these women that I could get my hands on. More than once, I lamented that most of them had lived very long lives and enjoyed prolific writing careers that stretched across four or more decades. It took me two and a half years to tunnel through Gertrude Atherton's massive oeuvre. Mary Roberts Rinehart's work enlivened the next two, while Carolyn Wells's took only a zippy thirteen months. My reading on Grace King was slowed down by a cross-country move. Finally, after two more pleasant years reading my way through Edna Ferber's short and long fiction—and watching all the Ferber films—the book began to gel.

However, what made it finally come together was not only my sense that the autobiographies were taking part in a larger conversation, nor was it the fact that so few women's literary autobiographies were published in the decades preceding the Great Depression that the bumper crop I found on those library shelves initially seemed to have sprung from nowhere. The foundational work of book historians as well as recent work in celebrity studies allowed me to explore and identify how the 1930s marketplace for autobiography was both created and influenced by cultural assumptions about women's authorship. However, it was a question I was asked by an American literature student that truly galvanized my efforts to publish a study of this group of autobiographies. She approached me after class and asked if all early twentieth-century American women writers had been depressed or suicidal. I was flummoxed. Where had she gotten that impression? Then I thought about my syllabus, with its reading list not too different from the ones I had been assigned as an undergraduate. I realized we had just read *The Awakening, The House of Mirth,* and *Quicksand,* all essentially stories of women's failure to thrive. We want to teach our students to have spunk, grit, and resilience, but when it comes to literary modernism, we have inadvertently created what I've come to mentally label the "canon of women's despair." We have not provided our students—especially the aspiring female writers among them—with a balanced perspective, with stories of women writers who endured, survived, thrived, and, yes, even enjoyed their work. Those stories, with their spunk and grit and resilience, need to be passed on.

Beyond further illuminating both a watershed moment in women's literary autobiography and a fascinating decade in American literary history, I hope this book allows its readers to get to know these twelve writers, especially those whose reputations have been oversimplified, their work neglected, or their significance dismissed, particularly by elitist or sexist criticism of the 1940s, 1950s, and 1960s. I hope readers can catch a glimpse of these writers as individuals, as I came to do as I read their stories. I hope readers will truly see the range of opportunities that these women created for themselves in context—not from our perspective of nearly a century later but from theirs. They represent an impressively wide range of choices within the available templates for authorship of their time. Some of them worked doggedly and without encouragement at their writing for decades before publishers took an interest. They confronted rigid norms of female conduct, beauty, and health. Some of them struggled with mental illness, while others suffered from debilitating physical fatigue that resulted from a combination of domestic and professional labor. These women were tough, much tougher than their autobiographies acknowledge that they had to be. They were talented, but they did not always know how to name their gifts in ways that would stick. They were funny but afraid of being laughed at. Getting to know them has convinced me that the important work of recovery—both of American women's writing and women's history—is far from finished.

This project would not have been possible without the generous assistance I've received along the way. First, I would like to thank Susan Goodman for starting me on this path with a graduate seminar paper and for entertaining my shifting and expanding vision over the years. I also owe a debt of gratitude to Bonnie Scott for raising important and lingering questions about the gender of Modernism. Azusa Pacific University's Office of Research and Grants provided a Faculty Research Grant that sponsored much of my archival research and funded two writers' retreats which were essential to this project's development. Some of the material on Edith Wharton in chapter 1 has been reprinted by permission from an article I wrote long ago for *a/b: Auto/Biography Studies*. I am grateful to my administrative assistant Holli Morrow Tubbs, who not only made space for me to do more of my own work but to do better work. To my children, thank you for the summers when we played and played while this work progressed at a snail's pace, and for the last couple of summers when you have been so understanding of my drive to see this thing through. And, finally, to my husband, Kyle, who has heard me rehearse this project verbally more times than I can count, your unfailing support and encouragement make all the difference to me every day.

Templates for Authorship

Introduction

American Women's Literary Autobiography in the Depression-Era Marketplace

IN A December 1940 letter to Ethel Smyth, Virginia Woolf made her now-famous declaration: "There has never been a woman's autobiography." There are a number of interpretations we might assign to this provocative statement; however, we certainly cannot take it literally, as it was penned at the end of the most prolific decade women's autobiography had yet seen, including the publication of a significant number of women's literary memoirs. In America, this bumper crop of 1930s autobiographies included Margaret Anderson's *My Thirty Years' War* (1930), Mary Roberts Rinehart's *My Story* (1931), Mary Austin's *Earth Horizon* (1932), Gertrude Atherton's *Adventures of a Novelist* (1932), Grace King's *Memoirs of a Southern Woman of Letters* (1932), Edith Wharton's *A Backward Glance* (1934), Charlotte Perkins Gilman's *Living of Charlotte Perkins Gilman* (1935), Margaret Deland's *If This Be I* (1935), Harriet Monroe's *A Poet's Life* (1938), Edna Ferber's *A Peculiar Treasure* (1938), and two veiled autobiographies, Gertrude Stein's *The Autobiography of Alice B. Toklas* (1933) and Carolyn Wells's *The Rest of My Life* (1937).

This diverse group of texts owes its existence to an unprecedented Depression-era demand for American women's literary autobiography.

While, as Peter Conn has documented, the biographies of long-dead famous American men were popular reading in the decade, the autobiographies of famous living women, including Eleanor Roosevelt, Amelia Earhart, and Margaret Sanger, were more sought after than those of their living male contemporaries in the 1930s.[1] And when we narrow the field from women's autobiography in general to women's *literary* autobiography—defined as the official autobiography of a successful writer in other genres—the results are even more striking: only one official literary autobiography by an American woman was published in the 1920s (by Kate Douglas Wiggin). However, at least a dozen of them were published in the 1930s, an astonishing growth rate that suggests women's literary autobiographies were published in rates far outstripping the growth in the 1930s market for autobiography in general *and* for women's autobiography in particular. This project examines the market forces that created this unprecedented and as yet unduplicated decade of growth in the demand for and production of American women's literary autobiography, and analyzes the cultural conditions that influenced the composition, publication, and reception of these texts.

DEPRESSION-ERA MARKET FORCES

As the Depression developed in the aftermath of the stock market crash, American publishers, even those who resisted the notion of publishing as a commercial enterprise, were forced to fall in line with new ways to make books profitable. Starting in the late 1920s, experienced publishers like Frank Nelson Doubleday led the transformation of the industry from a genteel, scholarly vocation into a commercial trade. In a memorial essay about Doubleday, popular novelist Christopher Morley called him "the first of a new era of book publishing—which he visualized foremost as a business, not merely as a dignified literary avocation."[2] By 1935, book clubs, bestseller lists, and price-cutting were among the techniques that publisher Frederick Stokes denounced in other houses, even though he was increasingly forced to utilize some of these tools himself. Cheap reprint series also proliferated throughout the Depression: by 1939, Doubleday Doran had six such imprints, including one that reissued Gertrude Atherton's *Adventures of a Novelist* for a dollar only two years after its original publication. Bestseller lists became more important than ever during this time, as the acquisition of "headline authors" was a good way for a publisher to stay in business. The success of the Depression-era startup of Farrar and Rinehart particularly demonstrated this model. These two young employees of Doran's (one of them the son of popular writer Mary Roberts Rinehart) did not like the changes brought on by the 1927 Doubleday-Doran merger and left to form their own publishing house in 1929. Because of the stock market crash, the new firm's odds for survival seemed very low, but the new enterprise quickly acquired "one of the most impressive lists of headline authors," which spread itself out over several strong categories, including the bestselling historical drama *Anthony Adverse,* a new mystery from Mary Roberts Rinehart, and some well-chosen literary classics. According to John Tebbel's *History of Book Publishing in the United States,* Farrar and Rinehart's carefully curated list may have made the difference between their success and failure; the story of Farrar and Rinehart's early years proves that for Depression-era publishers, choosing the right books mattered more than using modern methods to market them.[3]

In the financial climate of the 1930s, there were several categories that became relatively safe bets for publishers, and literary autobiography could potentially be marketed within all of them. Histories of book publishing record the convergence of three significant market trends in Depression-era sales: nonfiction, nostalgia, and self-help books and success stories. Book historians have recorded a notable rise in the publication of nonfiction during the American Depression, but the 175 percent increase in the publication of biography between

1920 and 1940 is particularly striking. Sales records also reveal that autobiography had a strong appeal for Depression-era readers; many of the books near the top of the cumulative bestseller lists for the decade were autobiographical, including two of the bestsellers: Grand Duchess Marie's *Education of a Princess* (1931) and Clarence Day's *Life with Father*, humorous reminiscences that were published as short stories in the magazines between 1931 and 1934 but were collected into a book in 1936. In 1934, Gertrude Stein's veiled memoir, *Autobiography of Alice B. Toklas,* also became a bestseller, occupying the lists alongside the *Autobiography of Box-Car Bertha.*[4] By 1935, the trend toward autobiography risked becoming a popular joke: book reviewers found themselves awash in a sea of autobiographies, and Carolyn Wells, a popular mystery writer and humorist, made fun of herself for cashing in on the market in the first chapter of her 1937 memoir. Wells's anecdotal assessment of the 1930s preoccupation with autobiography has also been confirmed by recent scholarship: in *Men and Women Writers of the 1930s: The Dangerous Flood of History,* Janet Montefiore labels the "thirties memoir" a distinct species of twentieth-century British autobiography.[5] Montefiore's study includes many English World War I memoirs, like Vera Brittain's 1933 *Testament of Youth.*

Because of the rapid cultural change sparked by World War I, American writers and readers had also become deeply preoccupied with the past.[6] The onset of the Great Depression only intensified this preoccupation, and advertisements—not only for books but for countless other products—indicate a fervor of nostalgia in the 1930s.[7] Gordon Hutner's *What America Read* documents the historical novel as one of the four most prevalent types of middlebrow fiction in the decade, while James D. Hart's study *The Popular Book* asserts that the popularity of books like *Goodbye, Mr. Chips* demonstrates that the cynicism which had dominated popular fiction in the 1920s had been replaced by sentimental nostalgia in the 1930s.[8] Peter Conn's *The American 1930s: A Literary History* records that not only authors but also visual artists "found in the past a means of responding to the dislocations of the present moment," making the 1930s "among the busiest of all decades of historical pictures" as well as historical novels.[9] In 1934, the prevalence of biographies led scholar Mark Longaker to coin the phrase "Men who read little else read lives."[10] While Longaker's study examined the growth in the production of biographies about American presidents, pioneers, and inventors, artists' autobiographies were also desirable in this market, including Frank Lloyd Wright's 1932 autobiography, which focused on the creative genius and personal drive behind his innovative architecture. Literary biographies also proliferated throughout the decade, including three studies of Edgar Allen Poe and five books about the life of Emily Dickinson.[11] Similar market principles provided a spur to the publication of American literary autobiographies, including those of Theodore Dreiser and Lincoln Steffens in 1931, and Langston Hughes in 1940. Even young authors like F. Scott Fitzgerald wrote autobiographical reflections on their writing careers thus far for the booming market: Fitzgerald's "Echoes of the Jazz Age" appeared in *Scribner's* in November 1931.

Many of the Depression era's bestselling books appealed to more than one of these three dominant trends: for instance, biographies like Clarence Day's *Life with Father* (1931) and the semi-autobiographical *Little House on the Prairie* series by Laura Ingalls Wilder also had strong nostalgic appeal, while works like Dale Carnegie's (1936) *How to Win Friends and Influence People* sold well as a nonfictional, autobiographically based self-help book that revealed its wealthy author's formula for success. From the standpoint of Depression-era publishers, obtaining the autobiography of a well-known, older American author must have seemed like a way to cash in on all three trends—nonfiction, nostalgia, and success story—in a single acquisition.

Pressed by their publishers, some of these women were reluctant autobiographers. For instance, by 1930, Charlotte Perkins Gilman had written to Zona Gale complaining that publishers *only* wanted an autobiography from her—and nothing else.[12] The facts support her claim: Gilman's 1929 mystery novel, *Unpunished,* went unpublished in her lifetime. Market demand was such that highbrow, middlebrow, and lowbrow publications were willing and able to pay significant fees to serialize or excerpt many of these autobiographies. Magazines could afford to pay more because their sales had suffered less than book sales in the Depression: David Welky calculates that 3 billion magazines were sold in the year that marked the nadir of the economic crisis. In 1933, *The Atlantic* ran a series of autobiographical excerpts, including the draft of Wharton's first chapter of *A Backward Glance* as an article entitled "Confessions of a Novelist" in April, and excerpts from Stein's draft of *Autobiography of Alice B. Toklas* in the May, June, July, and August issues. Competition among popular women's magazines for women's literary autobiography resulted in a $50,000 deal for Mary Roberts Rinehart to serialize her life-story in *Good Housekeeping* in 1931, $25,000 from *Ladies' Home Journal* for Edith Wharton in 1933, and the same amount from *Women's Home Companion* for Edna Ferber in 1938. Because the literati—herself included—looked down on magazines like the *Journal* as the repository for inferior writing, Wharton hated the idea of serializing her work in the popular magazine, but her sales between 1930 and 1934 had brought in a small fraction of her pre-1930 royalties and her financial obligations had not lessened. The money the *Journal* offered—equivalent to almost half a million dollars today—must have been irresistible. To make matters worse, the *Journal* regularly spoke out against both divorce and divorcees in the 1930s, which may partly explain the muffled treatment of Wharton's divorce in *A Backward Glance.*[13] Other writers were also facing sudden crises brought on by the crash: Rinehart and her husband had recently lost most of the financial portfolio they had been building for decades, so the serialization of *My Story* in *Good Housekeeping* provided a way to recoup losses quickly. When Gertrude Atherton first signed with Horace Liveright in 1922, she had saved his publishing firm from financial crisis, but by 1930, the situation was reversed: Atherton was living in reduced circumstances, being importuned by friends like Carl Van Vechten to write her life, and in need of the money that Liveright's lavish publicity machine would help provide.[14] By the time Mary Austin signed a contract for her autobiography, she was exhausted from giving frequent lectures for speaking fees ranging from $100 to $150; Houghton Mifflin arranged elaborate publicity for *Earth Horizon* and pleaded with Austin to send in the chapters faster.[15] Carolyn Wells had pitched the notion of writing an autobiography to her editor—and been rejected—in the 1920s, but by 1935 everyone was clamoring for her life-story, saying she "owed it to [her] public."[16] Another important woman writer of the period, Zora Neale Hurston, refused requests for her autobiography before she eventually capitulated, publishing *Dust Tracks on a Road* in 1942.

These literary autobiographers were a diverse group in many ways. Some were high-modernist, others decidedly middlebrow, occasionally venturing into pulp; some were poets, others wrote literary fiction, sensationalism, mysteries, comedy, romance, drama, journalism, critical commentary, or any combination of the above. Together, they represented every region of the United States from New England to the South, Midwest, Southwest, and West Coast. They came from every kind of family: Wharton hailed from the legendary "first 400" of New York society, while Gilman inherited the strict vocational legacy of New England Puritan intellectuals. Rinehart, Austin, and Wells came from middle-class merchant families of varying stability, Ferber was the daughter of financially struggling Jewish immigrants, and Stein hailed from a more financially stable Jewish background. Both King's and Monroe's fathers were lawyers who believed in educating their daughters just as well as their sons. Both men had fared relatively well when they were young but lost much of their financial standing as their daughters grew up. When they were working as professional writers, these women lived in every kind of domestic arrangement, some remaining single, several marrying young and then divorcing their husbands, a few cherishing traditional nuclear families or long-term lesbian partnerships, and others celebrating peripatetic global lifestyles. Several of them—and their careers—were impacted by disability: Gilman's autobiography reveals her long struggle with depression, Austin's discusses her developmentally disabled daughter, and Wells's deafness spurred her intense engagement with the world of books from a very young age. The two things that these women all had in common were lengthy careers as writers and the financial motivation to publish autobiography in the 1930s.

Although not all of these American writers were of Anglo-Saxon backgrounds, they could all "pass" for white if they chose. Edna Ferber's autobiography relates stories of outing herself as a Jew at dinner parties when other guests made anti-Semitic remarks. Both Ferber's work and Stein's discuss racism and boost ethnic and cultural pluralism as important qualities for being an American. And while whiteness is an assumed norm in most of these autobiographies, both Margaret Deland and Mary Austin address the issue of white privilege in their texts, as chapters 3 and 4 demonstrate. Unfortunately, there were no literary autobiographies published by African American women writers in the 1930s. Jesse Fauset and Nella Larsen never published life-writings. Zora Neale Hurston's 1940s autobiography demonstrates similar narrative techniques as the 1930s texts do, especially in her rhetorical evasions and subversion of expectations, and Hurston's sage observations about the genre seems to wink at the other twelve texts, as I discuss further in the epilogue. We cannot be certain as to why Hurston waited until the 1940s, but perhaps she was avoiding "official" autobiography by publishing "unofficial" forms of life-writing in the 1930s. In that decade, she wrote both the cross-genre combination of ethnography, travel narrative, and anthropology that is *Tell My Horse* and the semi-autobiographical novel *Their Eyes Were Watching God,* which reflects on her passionate but brief third marriage and utilizes her memories of the time she spent in Florida lumber camps, including a notorious hurricane that occurred in the region. It could also be because Hurston did not have a problem publishing her other texts in the 1930s, unlike writers like Gilman, who found autobiography her only available option, or Margaret Deland, who was starting to be viewed as out of touch. Hurston's work was still cutting edge enough for American modernism, and she may also have wanted to get some distance from her *Mule Bone* dispute with Langston Hughes before she spoke directly about her life. Hurston also seems to have waited until after Hughes's *The Big Sea* appeared in 1940 to venture into the autobiographical marketplace, and to have used every evasive maneuver that the rest of the women in this group did, with the result that Hurston fans—accustomed to more boldness in her other work—are often disappointed by *Dust Tracks* today. However, in frustrating its readers, Hurston's book is certainly well-aligned with American women's literary autobiography of the era. Possibly the risks of writing literary autobiography, already steep for women, were multiplied by the color line that constantly confronted Hurston wherever she went in the United States, resulting in more years of hesitation for her. Because Hurston's work rhetorically dovetails with the others, and because, coming right after the 1930s, it offers a sort of coda to the conversation between the group of twelve texts that inspired this book, the discussion in my epilogue is founded on Hurston's central autobiographical metaphor.

Despite the vast differences in their backgrounds, lifestyles, and career trajectories, most of these Depression-era autobiographers had about thirty years of experience crafting written characters, plots, images, arguments, and impressions, which enabled them to respond to readers' demand for nostalgia for the past and anxiety about the future. Due to 1930s market conditions, these texts were both sold and reviewed for their historical value, which was a way to appeal simultaneously to readers' urge to focus on nonfiction and to their nostalgia for the prewar, pre-Depression, American past. For the autobiographers themselves, writing a personal view of "history" gave them authority in two ways: it legitimized their personal opinions as worthy of public consideration, and it allowed them to conceal things they wished to keep private by placing themselves in the background when they chose to do so. In offering women's lives as glimpses of history, their publishers were reading the literary marketplace quite accurately. Many reviews emphasized the value of these 1930s memoirs as portraiture of times gone by in order to recommend them to readers. One review of Gertrude Atherton's book thriftily declared that he found her autobiography to be of more "permanent value" than any of her fiction.[17] Other reviewers, though they did not like Atherton's book, felt compelled to admit that "it [contained] much of value" nevertheless.[18] Critics called Mary Austin's *Earth Horizon* "a record of the frontier" and a "saga of America," underscoring its historicity, while reviews of Wharton's autobiography bore titles that focused on historical instead of personal worth, such as "Mrs. Wharton Recalls an Era" and "War and Peace."[19] Ferber's *A Peculiar Treasure* was recommended to readers for revealing the "American background; the pioneer spirit which has been building America for 300 years," and Deland's "Civil War memories" were highlighted as the "most interesting parts" of her story.[20]

ENDURING TRADITIONS AND NEW TEMPLATES

Part of these autobiographers' emphasis on historical events and their corresponding hesitance to publish the details of their private lives may have stemmed from the dearth of female role models in the genre of literary autobiography. Before the 1930s, life-writing by female writers in America or Great Britain mostly took the form of diaries, travel journals, and autobiographical fiction. Patricia Meyer Spacks comments on the dearth of women's literary autobiography in *The Female Imagination:* "Relatively few women have asserted themselves unambiguously as shaping artists in the act of writing about themselves; even Anais Nin, whose self-glorification as an artist and as a woman parallels Isadora Duncan's, publishes diaries rather than formal autobiography."[21] The hesitation Spacks notes goes back to the 1800s: many Victorian female writers recoiled from the idea of publishing their private lives. In Great Britain, George Eliot was repulsed by Harriet Martineau's autobiography, and Elizabeth Barrett Browning decried the "vanity" of the process. In fact, none of the major nineteenth-century British or American woman novelists wrote official memoirs.[22]

When nineteenth-century women did write autobiography, it was often with a sense of trespass and a fear of judgment. According to Valerie Sanders's work on Victorian autobiography, female autobiographers felt compelled to write on "feminine" topics like charity projects, family life, or literary soirees to evade accusations of conceit and preserve notions of female modesty perpetuated by the "Cult of True Womanhood."[23] Anna Cora Mowatt's *Autobiography of an Actress; or, Eight Years on the Stage* (1854) declares, for example, that "there seems a degree of egotism in the constant use of the first person singular. . . . For any consequent trenching on the borders of good taste, I hope to be pardoned."[24] In 1854, an anonymous author dedicated *Memories of a Grandmother by a Lady of Massachusetts* to her "dear children." She wrote that she hoped the public would excuse her for "indulging" herself in both telling her story and including a portrait in the frontispiece, since she had been told throughout her childhood that little girls should not be seen *or* heard, a rule that Margaret Deland's 1935 *If This Be I* recalls as part of her nineteenth-century upbringing as well.[25] This anonymous "grandmother" seems to have correctly interpreted the situation: nineteenth-century autobiographers like Annie Besant were "reprimanded" for their "egotism" by reviewers, and even biographers of women tended to apologize because their subjects had "done or said something to be talked of."[26] So strong was the ideology of feminine modesty that women autobiographers in the late nineteenth century often avoided writing about their adult lives: in Catharine Maria Sedgwick's posthumous *Life and Letters* (1871), the story ends when she is fourteen, and Lucy Larcom's *A New England Girlhood* (1889) concludes when she is twenty-eight, just before her forty-year writing career really began.[27] These writers chose to follow feminine tradition by emphasizing their private lives; even though they were writers, they avoided any discussion of their literary work, so their texts can hardly be considered literary autobiography at all.

Even activists wrote surprisingly mild autobiographies in the nineteenth century: first-wave feminists and women's suffragists like Elizabeth Cady Stanton and Frances Willard wrote as "wives and mothers," offering advice to other women and eschewing the idea of self-promotion.[28] Estelle Jelinek, in her broadly researched volume *The Tradition of Women's Autobiography from Antiquity to the Present,* suggests that women like these, who were publicly known as activists, wrote autobiographies to counterbalance their notoriety and demonstrate their "femininity." They produced texts that were "startl[ingly] soft[er]" than their previous work, emphasizing domestic identities and womanly duties.[29] However, Linda Peterson has theorized that the dominance of domestic tradition in nineteenth-century women's autobiography was partially shaped by male editors who categorized, marketed, and published texts with their own notions about gender categories in mind. Peterson explains that memoirs were often edited to highlight the autobiographers' roles as model wives, mothers, and daughters, contending that the "feminine" tradition women thought had been handed down to them by women was in fact molded largely by men.[30]

Since they had barely any models for women's literary autobiography, these 1930s writers tended to borrow from other preexisting models to frame their autobiographical personas. For instance, activism had been a strong and enduring template for female authorship and for women's autobiography for a good half-century by the time these women wrote their life-stories. Although it may seem counterintuitive, the activist template for authorship was, in fact, one of the more familiar ones for female autobiographers in the early twentieth century, and autobiographies of female activists serve as prime examples of the rhetorical tensions involved in women's life-writing at the turn of the century. Martha Watson's study of Frances Willard's, Elizabeth Cady Stanton's, and Emma Goldman's activist memoirs examines both the preexisting and intratextual rhetorical situations within these memoirs, discovering how an autobiography that is too overdirected to one set of readers may set itself up to fail with another.[31] Among the 1930s literary autobiographers in this study, Gilman and Deland rely most heavily on the social activism template to frame their life-stories, while Mary Austin and Harriet Monroe borrow a bit from it, redefining their activism as literary and regional. The activist template long provided women autobiographers an opportunity to be outspoken, as the boldness of their voices was deflected by their claim to be speaking on behalf of silenced others.

While the proportion of male to female editors had not changed much by 1900, the Progressive era inspired a pragmatic curiosity in American readers, so women's autobiographies that were purportedly written solely to be useful to society became the dominant trend. In this spirit, a few female writers joined activists and actresses in publishing autobiography. Most of them focused on writing as an exciting professional opportunity for women. Journalist Elizabeth L. Banks offered her memoirs as a window into her experiences as a "newspaper girl" in 1902. Popular writers Elizabeth Stuart Phelps and Ella Wheeler Wilcox also wrote Progressive-era autobiographies but, in step with the times, focused exclusively on writing as a career option for women rather than on their private lives. According to Jelinek's timeline of women's autobiography, more women's memoirs were published during the Progressive era than at any other time until the 1930s. In the 1900s and 1910s, the women's club movement was at its peak, the suffrage campaign was gaining momentum, and the "woman question" was spurring public discussion in every area of print culture. Reading these texts allowed women to explore broader possibilities by living vicariously. For example, Jane Addams's *Twenty Years at Hull-House* (1910) allowed readers a glimpse into a world they might never have been aware of otherwise.[32] However, traditionally feminine self-portraits had not disappeared in this new climate, and most Progressive-era women's literary autobiographies still hearkened back to nineteenth-century feminine gentility. For instance, *Marion Harland's Autobiography: The Story of a Long Life* (1910), Ella Wheeler Wilcox's *The Worlds and I* (1918), and Kate Douglas Wiggin's *My Garden of Memory* (1923) highlight the domestic rather than professional aspects of their lives. Even so, Houghton Mifflin, who printed Wiggin's *My Garden of Memory*, considered it an "experiment" to publish a woman's literary autobiography at all.[33]

Notably, professional women who published literary memoirs that did not clearly fit into either the activist or domestic traditions paid a price for their innovation. For instance, Mrs. Humphrey Ward's 1918 autobiography, *A Writer's Recollections*, is one of the first women's autobiographies whose title proclaims that it is a *literary* autobiography (note that Harland's, Wilcox's, and Wiggin's titles elide their identity as writers). The reception of Mrs. Ward's book suggests why literary autobiography did not attract more female authors. Her largely self-effacing *Recollections* were panned by reviewers in 1920: one declared that Ward was "egotistical, and morbidly introspective, but secretive," and used the "cosmetic art of fiction" to "make the appearance of a heroine."[34] While the reviewer's query about the "truth" of autobiography is relatively typical, its terms of critique are clearly sexist. Apart from the question of how many male literary autobiographers have applied a little fiction to their life-stories without being accused of using "cosmetics," it is easy to see that the position of women as *literary* autobiographers was still precarious well into the twentieth century.

The twelve texts under consideration here reveal that literary autobiography remained a conflicted genre for women throughout the 1930s. Jelinek's brief consideration of women's literary autobiography in the early twentieth century notes the "self-consciousness" and "striking lack of confidence" the texts demonstrate compared to the memoirs of other women artists, such as dancer Isadora Duncan's *My Life* (1927) and sculptor Janet Scudder's *Modeling My Life* (1925).[35] Jelinek speculates that a career in literature should have given these women more confident voices, but this assumption may be overlooking the disjunction between cultural expectations of women writers in the nineteenth and twentieth centuries. Works like Mary Kelley's *Private Woman, Public Stage: Literary Domesticity in Nineteenth-Century America* explore how the generation of women writing while these 1930s autobiographers were growing up (including Harland, Wiggin, and Wilcox) generally portrayed writing as an occupation that did not violate ideals of domestic femininity.[36] With nineteenth-century women writers who rarely wrote autobiography as their only female models, the writers in this study ventured into largely uncharted territory when they published written accounts of their lives. Those who were divorced, including Wharton, Austin, and Gilman, were really navigating uncharted territory and faced reliving the painful scrutiny and gossip that their divorces had originally triggered. It must have been tempting to avoid the entire issue, as the public debate over marriage and careers for women had actually reintensified under the economic strain of the Depression. Perhaps sensing this precariousness, Susan Glaspell, an accomplished author in her own right, published a 1930s biography of her husband and marriage instead of a true literary autobiography, sharply contrasting the bold, intimate memoirs published by activists like Emma Goldman and the more confident autobiographies of popular heroines like Eleanor Roosevelt and Amelia Earhart.[37]

Texts like Goldman's, Roosevelt's, and Earhart's sold well because of their authors' individuality and notoriety, conditions that are essential to what early autobiographical theorists Georges Gusdorf, Roy Pascal, and Phillipe Lejeune term the "autobiographical impulse." Lejeune predicates both the composition and reception of any autobiography on the "prior notoriety of the author . . . [and] the mode of production of the published text."[38] However, many feminist and postmodern scholars have criticized these assumptions for locating the autobiographer's authority within his or her public life and within a coherent, published text. Sidonie Smith's theory of women's autobiography demonstrates that the notion of a "unitary, bold, indivisible autobiographical 'I'" has been traditionally gendered as "male," while Domna Stanton's "Autogynography" defines the female autobiographer as a "female subject trying to assert [herself] in a system where [she is] defined as [an] object."[39] The fact that women often feel less comfortable with their position as autobiographers is reflected in Margo Culley's discovery that female autobiographers refer to their gender in their titles much more often than men do, at a ratio of ten to one.[40] This disproportionate gender referencing in autobiographical titles highlights both the sense of generic trespass and group subjectivity with which female autobiographers have had to contend throughout the history of the genre. Julia Watson points out that "bios-bias," or the assumption of the autobiographical authority through accomplishment and public experience, is particularly prejudiced against women autobiographers who frequently do not tell traditional narratives of individual achievement, while Helen Buss explains that "the less individualistic sense of the self is more obvious in women's texts, because they have never been permitted a traditional *bios*."[41]

However, as a subgenre, literary autobiography is founded on the achievement and individuality of the writing subject. Thus, the autobiographers in this study composed their texts from an awkward, double perspective: though they had written for decades before their autobiographical privilege was assured, they had very few female models within the genre of literary autobiography. They had lived and written as both resistant female objects *and* privileged literary subjects. As professional writers, these twelve women had assumed the "autonomy," "authority," "individuation," and public achievement that are fundamental in theoretical definitions of traditional, or "male," autobiography.[42] For example, in *The Autobiography of Alice B. Toklas,* Gertrude Stein records feeling "terribly touched" when a friend's comment made her "realize that some time she would have a biography," because the comment implied that her work would become successful and Stein would become so prominent that the public would want to know more about who she was.[43]

Lejeune first differentiated the literary biography from other types of biography and autobiography in his definitive study, *On Autobiography,* a category that William Howarth has labeled poetic and problematic.[44] Lejeune examines the influences brought to bear in framing a famous life through assumptions about "literature." However, as he acknowledges, one era's assumptions about literature are bound to be different from another's, so one of the most effective ways to read literary autobiography is to read it in relationship to the assumptions of its time. Lejeune observes that "the texts making up the corpus of a genre such as it functions in a given age, have engendered one another and can, from a certain point of view, be seen as the transformation of one and the same text."[45] Since Lejeune's seminal work, autobiography written by established authors has been examined as a unique category of its own but not often within the confines of a focused literary era. Additionally, very few books have examined women's literary autobiography in particular, and those that have focused either on the eras preceding the twentieth century or following World War II. In this category, Jeanne Braham's *Crucial Conversations: Interpreting Contemporary American Literary Autobiographies by Women* includes an important chapter on "Self-Authorization" in literary autobiography.[46] Even when they are evasive, these 1930s literary autobiographies are all bold acts of self-authorization, conducted as public conversations with one another and with cultural norms.

Cultural expectations about women's roles, literature, and autobiography were rapidly changing as these autobiographers composed their texts. Since "the rules for writing about one's own life [as a woman] may have been changing as the nineteenth century slid into the twentieth," these autobiographers faced an unprecedented plethora of options, including the implicitly male "successful public figure" model, a feminine tradition bound by the rules about gentility and modesty with which they had grown up, and riskier new options for self-exposure, exemplified by texts like Mabel Dodge Luhan's *Intimate Memories.*[47] Linda Peterson's observation that "some women autobiographers may avoid female literary tradition," and others "may self-consciously evoke multiple traditions," can help us understand the complexity of these 1930s female literary autobiographies.[48] These writers had worked hard for historically "male" privileges, such as public status, financial independence, critical respect, and personal freedom, but they had also been either constrained from or condemned for their ambitions because of their gender. Writing literary autobiography provided them with a chance to assess the costs and benefits of being a female writer in the early twentieth century, and reading these texts provides us with an opportunity to better understand what those costs and benefits were. All these texts tell stories about how being women affected and inscribed their quests for *author*ity, but some were more candid about this than others. As Barret Mandel has rightly observed, the "tone, style, and organization" of an autobiography can often reveal more than its "content."[49] Under pressure to choose how much to conform to or diverge from tradition, it is no wonder that these authors make such careful rhetorical decisions about substance, style, and delivery.

MECHANISMS OF MODERNISM

In addition to negotiating the traceable schisms within women's autobiographical tradition, these authors were also confronted by the intensifying gendered binaries of modernism by the time they were composing their texts. Modernist literary discourse often positioned masculine/artistic/high culture as a cluster of overlapping markers of literary quality standing in embattled opposition to a cluster of threatening literary "others," particularly feminine/middlebrow/mass culture. This rhetoric reverberates in the voices of male writers throughout the 1920s and 1930s. For instance, in 1921, Joseph Hergesheimer wrote "The Feminine Nuisance in American Literature" for the *Yale Review*, calling for more authentic masculine voices in American literature. Hergesheimer, who would narrowly lose the Pulitzer Prize to Edna Ferber four years later, depicts an ongoing power struggle between the genders to gain literary ascendancy in his essay. "For some years," he writes, "the support and reading of novels have been surrendered to women. . . . Literature is being strangled with a petticoat."[50] Book history does indicate that by the 1920s, women writers had sold in numbers remarkably larger than ever before.[51] Although the increase in female readers largely corresponded to the growing number of women who were attending college, the success of books such as Pearl Buck's *The Good Earth* were often appropriated as evidence of the female/popular, male/artistic binary in literature.[52]

Hergesheimer's fear of the growing strength of female authors and readers was part of a larger cultural and literary backlash that has been described in various terms by historians and literary scholars. For instance, historian James R. McGovern built a case for what Elizabeth Ammons terms a "virility response" as a reaction to the "feminization of American culture" in the period traced by Ann Douglas's study of that name.[53] This response, which frequently expressed itself in criticism of writing by and about women, was particularly virulent in the 1920s and 1930s. Unfortunately, Hergesheimer's dramatic manner of characterizing the debate was not uncommon. Elaine Showalter delineates how some young male writers of this period voiced their complaints about the purported emasculation of American fiction in violent terms. While these concerns likely had more to do with a sense of competition than a concern for literary values, unconventional women writers who refused to follow feminine traditions either in their fiction or their lives, such as Gertrude Atherton or Margaret Anderson, were particularly reviled. For example, Showalter explains that works such as Nathanael West's 1933 novel *Miss Lonelyhearts* reflect this violent dislike in its vision of male/female literary competition.[54] In one scene, disillusioned newsmen gather to lament the number of women writers, especially the new group of them who do not use the more genteel "Mrs." designation but instead have three names (such as Charlotte Perkins Gilman or Mary Roberts Rinehart). The newsmen conclude that "what [the women writers] need is a good rape." West faults the mass marketplace, and female success within it, with this inexcusable statement. His characters, he writes, "were aware of their childishness, but did not know how else to revenge themselves. At college, and perhaps for a year afterwards, they had believed in literature. . . . When they lost this belief, they lost everything. Money and fame meant nothing to them."[55] West's fiction here delineates the binaries and battle-lines being drawn in the modernist masculinist perception of literary production: college is where young men believe in Literature (capital L), while popular fiction (largely by and for women), tainted with sentiment, money, and fame, results in angry disillusionment.

Although studies such as Catherine Turner's *Marketing Modernism between the Two World Wars* have demonstrated that the elite, male, highbrow artist of the modernist period was more rhetoric than reality, the ideal of the artist as technically innovative, free from domestic entanglements, and above concerns with money and fame was definitely a common ideology in the 1930s.[56] In *My Story*, Mary Roberts Rinehart recalls the power of this ideology: "The theory was that the true artist lived and expressed herself only in her art. . . . Above all, she must be free."[57] Rinehart wryly observes that married mothers like herself—especially married money-making mothers—were automatically excluded from consideration as "serious" writers. She offers herself as a model of compromise, becoming a pioneer in what we now call "work-life balance." As we shall see, a number of these autobiographers attempt to revise this solitary, highbrow, "artistic" template in some way, but Edith Wharton and Grace King seem to have pursued this artist template in their texts almost exclusively. Throughout their careers, the phrase "serious writer" had come to indicate writers to whom artistic concerns were primary, but the phrase was also used as a critical tool to segregate one or two women from the herd of "women writers" whose purposes and products were presumed to be less pure. Elizabeth Ammons notes that nearly all of them "refused to identify with the popular white women writers who had dominated the fiction market in the United States throughout most of the 19th century." Ammons demonstrates that many women writing at the turn of the century actually defined themselves antithetically to the sentimental, domestic, or romance traditions, in order to disassociate themselves from "women's fiction."[58] These authors seem to have internalized the idea that there was scant room for women in the "serious" category of American literature to varying degrees. Wharton believed that to be seen as "serious," she had to eschew sentimentality, and "must not write as if she were a woman."[59] Literary criticism in that era usually selected a few women writers to praise and left the others to languish in groups in chapters describing sentiment, hysteria, rebellion, or mannishness, depending on whether the critical weapons were being launched against the old guard or the New Woman. Friends remembered Atherton and Austin exchanging claims to be the greatest American female author, and they each must have read at least some of the many pieces of criticism which claimed that honor either for them or for Edith Wharton.[60] Joseph Collins's 1924 work *Taking the Literary Pulse* provides one example: he selected Wharton and essayist Agnes Reppelier as "our country's most precious literary ornaments" while lumping

Cather, Stein, and Hurst as "adventurers" seeking "novelty."[61] Susan Koppleman astutely points out that the male critics sometimes pitted women against each other, "by comparing, favoring, or encouraging women/women attacks."[62] In this climate, women writers were likely to distance themselves from other female authors. The impact of this trend reverberates throughout the texts in this study: Austin declared that she had "outgrown" her mother's books at a young age, while Atherton, Gilman, King, and Monroe located their origins as writers within the libraries of their male ancestors and friends. Other women writers of this literary generation also tried to distance themselves intellectually from other women: Willa Cather's criticism often displays a "sweeping contempt" for other women authors. Cather was, in fact, insulted at being selected to be in *The Women Who Make Our Novels,* a 1918 collection of evaluative life-works essays about both established and emerging American women writers by ubiquitous fiction editor Grant Overton, who parlayed his editorial connections into publishing a number of similar books and anthologies of reprinted material. Cather did not like to be included in such gendered collections: she dreaded being named as one of the "authorines."[63]

Perhaps in fear of being relegated to the dubious status of authorine, these writers eyed each other warily—feeling themselves to be in competition for both critical reputation and popular reception. However, they were not as isolated from one another as their autobiographies might imply. For instance, Austin attended Atherton's literary salon in New York, and Carolyn Wells paid tribute to Mary Roberts Rinehart's work in her critical volume *The Technique of the Mystery Story.* Atherton's autobiography notes that she and Rinehart had participated in Sam Goldwyn's Eminent Authors program at the same time.[64] Monroe introduced Anderson to potential supporters and contributors for her *Little Review,* which became perhaps the most notorious of the American "little magazines" purveying the new frontiers and experimental work of literary modernism. Atherton, who had been a local feminist heroine to Alice Toklas when she was growing up in San Francisco, hosted Stein and Toklas when they visited the United States for Stein's 1934 lecture tour. But Atherton openly criticized Wharton's major work, *The House of Mirth,* probably because she considered Wharton her most formidable rival. Publicly, Wharton hardly acknowledged the existence of any of the others, although they were compared to her often enough in literary criticism. It was probably irksome to Wharton when Rinehart quipped in *My Story* about their common struggles with Hollywood adaptations of their novels. And when these women did have relationships with each other, personal loyalty often took second place to literary reputation. For instance, Austin and Gilman formed a sympathetic alliance early in their careers, but they each criticized the other's artistic vision in their autobiographies. Sadly, most of these authors distanced themselves from other women in their public statements, and much of their fiction centers on lonely, exceptional female characters like *The House of Mirth*'s Lily Bart, Mary Zattainy in Atherton's *Black Oxen,* Ferber's traveling saleswomen, and Mary Austin's "Walking Woman." Like their creators, these characters are isolated either by sexist interpretations of their behavior or by their inability to relate to the lives of other women.

As writers like Ernest Hemingway, F. Scott Fitzgerald, and William Faulkner gained esteem in the 1920s and 1930s, masculinity became a de facto prerequisite for "serious" art and literature. Bonnie Scott's *The Gender of Modernism* definitively demonstrates that the notion of genius was "unconsciously gendered masculine" in modernist criticism.[65] Several of the autobiographers in this study wrote fiction that revealed the pretensions and gender inequities of elite, highbrow concepts of art and the artist.[66] But there were female artists who either bought into this notion or used it to separate themselves from other women. For example, Willa Cather, herself harshly criticized by Hemingway, constantly differentiated between women's attempts and male achievements in her literary criticism, commenting once in an article assessing women authors as a group that, given the choice, she would "much sooner pick up a book by a man than by a woman."[67]

This implicit gendering of artistic genius as male undergirds Hergesheimer's entire argument in "The Feminine Nuisance." There, he envisions a masculine triumph in the literary marketplace: when authentic male voices are finally appreciated, a "new and inviolate body of American literature will be established."[68] His language echoes one of the most frequently articulated sentiments of high modernism: that Art be above and beyond the influence of the feminized mass audience—"inviolate" because it cannot be compromised by the whims of the market. Steps had already been taken to construct this "inviolate" (read "male") body of national literature in England. Gaye Tuchman's study *Edging Women Out: Victorian Novelists, Publishers, and Social Change* concludes that near the end of the nineteenth century, British women writers were more and more excluded from the realm of "high" literature. I suspect that quantitative analyses of the formation of the early twentieth-century American canon would reveal similar dynamics.[69]

Aware of this gendered binary, many of the women writers in this generation were uneasy about the ways in which their work was being categorized or discarded with the formation of the academy.[70] According to Thomas Strychacz's *Modernism, Mass Culture, and Professionalism,* American universities were firmly established as a "legitimizing agent" for writers in the modernist period.[71] However, in the case of many women writers, universities often acted as a "delegitimizing" agent: Rinehart's *My Story* noted that her sons were disappointed when they went to college and were taught that their mother was only a popular professional writer. It must have been satisfying for them when she was awarded an honorary doctorate from George Washington University in 1923.[72] However, by the 1930s, American women writers were generally disincluded by the newly forming academy: one 1935 college textbook entitled *Major American Writers* includes no women at all.[73]

The twelve literary autobiographers under consideration here were not ignorant of the mechanisms of modernism. Their life-writings reveal their awareness of the importance of the academy as a legitimating agency: *A Backward Glance* corrects the most commonly made academic diminutions of Wharton's work, Atherton proudly cites a university professor's praise of one of her works, Gilman expresses her indignation that a nearby college did not welcome her as a speaker, and Ferber and Wells muse about their legacy hopefully, noting that one or two of their books were taught in college classrooms. Realizing that the academy had started closing ranks on them as they neared the ends of their careers, these authors defended their contributions to American literature in their autobiographies.

The American academy's judgment was also supported and influenced by the little magazines that prevailed between 1912 and 1932. Little magazines often worked to promote the "new," "highbrow," or "experimental" (most often masculine) literature from contamination from the "domestic," "sentimental," "traditional," or "popular" (categories to which most of the autobiographers in this study had been relegated by the 1930s), and to provide the authors who wrote in them a medium for work that was "too esoteric or intellectual" for the American public.[74] These literary journals "provided [less popular] writers with an increasingly elaborate infrastructure and sense of community."[75] While the majority of little magazines were edited by men, two of the autobiographers in this study, Margaret Anderson and Harriet Monroe, published memoirs about the struggles of editing literary magazines in this era: Anderson's *My Thirty Years' War* relates the vicissitudes of running the *Little Review*, and Monroe's *A Poet's Life* extrapolates the purposes and policies of *Poetry* magazine, which she founded and edited from 1912 to 1936. Magazines like these often defined themselves by distinguishing who was producing new, innovative literature and who was not. While they may have provided a safe haven for modernist writers frustrated with the pursuit of commercial success, little magazines often excluded the work of American women authors who had established their careers decades earlier. As chapter 5 demonstrates, only Harriet Monroe's *Poetry* remained open to less avant-garde work by women as high modernism took a firmer hold in American literature, and Monroe was heavily criticized for her pro-woman editorial decisions throughout the 1920s.

As the 1920s gave way to the 1930s, the mechanisms of modernism began to increasingly exclude women writers.[76] Literary history reveals ample reasons for the anxiety of American women writers in the 1930s. In addition to being largely excluded by the literary critics and college professors who were effectively forming the American canon, the upcoming generation of women writers suffered periodic bouts of suppression and decline. Calling them the "Other Lost Generation," Elaine Showalter delineates the frustration, fragmentation, and silencing of younger women writers in particular.[77] But while older female writers still held a wide audience, they suffered the diminishment of their critical reputations. Wharton, not liking what she read in 1920s reviews and criticism of her work, started to privately worry about "forestall[ing]" the influence of "things people are going to assert about me after I am dead" in the years leading up to the publication of *A Backward Glance.*[78] Both she and Willa Cather were scorned by the new literary establishment as "decorous relics" in the 1930s.[79] Because of their lengthy careers, many autobiographers in this study were facing the same sort of ageism: by 1941, the second half of Margaret Deland's autobiography was rather condescendingly dismissed as a "gentle woman's gentle book" written by "a very old lady."[80] The rapidly forming "great divide," as Andreas Huyssen terms it, was not just gendered in literature but also generational.[81] Critically relegated to their aging "public," these writers' success had become a double-edged sword: it gave them power in the public marketplace, and thus an economic appeal to publishers, but it also sharpened the lines of the gender binary that associated women writers with mass culture rather than with "Art." As they composed their texts, these autobiographers all knew that their literacy legacy was on the line. In writing to the power-brokers of their time—those who controlled the mechanisms of modernism—these authors faced a conundrum that female autobiographers have faced since Teresa of Avila: "composing a version of the past that will argue for a desirable future."[82]

CELEBRITY CULTURE

For these authors, securing a "desirable future" for their work must have seemed unlikely, as conditions were not auspicious for women trying to build literary legacies in the early twentieth century. Marysa Demoor's collection *Marketing the Author: Authorial Personae, Narrative Selves, and Self-Fashioning, 1880–1930,* traces five female British authors from this generation and their attempts to "control their public image by creating a self." Demoor finds that almost all of them—with the exception of Virginia Woolf—failed to do so, because the public either overrode their projected images with other popular narratives about them, misunderstood their intentions, or just forgot about them once they were no longer in the press. Demoor concludes that women's "association with mass consumption problematized the position of the aesthetically and intellectually ambitious woman" in the early twentieth century.[83] Like their British counterparts who made such unsuccessful attempts to control the public's perception of them, these American women writers were all subject to the scrutiny given to female celebrities throughout their careers. This culture of celebrity surrounding American women writers had been growing since these women began writing, though not all of them relished it. At the outset of her writing career, Grace King noted in her journal, "The writers of the present day, the Americans I mean, seem rather to wish to be an *art* rather than artists. No sooner do they get a little reputation from writing than they hasten to confide to the entire public all they know about themselves. Their thoughts, feelings sensations, mode of life . . . what they eat, drink, and wear during the process, trying always to exemplify some theory or theorum."[84]

By 1930, the various "theorums" King decries had resolved into four primary templates used to categorize and label different types of women writers in public discourse: (1) the artist or "serious" writer, (2) the activist, (3) the professional, and (4) the celebrity. While many writers intentionally utilized one of the first three templates to frame their work, the celebrity template for authorship was apt to interfere with writers' attempts at self-definition. King presaged this in her journal, expressing her fears that the publicity machine with its "openness" and "frankness" would do both the writers themselves and the world in which they existed a "great wrong."[85] The public interest in personal details about professional female writers that King describes led to the publication of books like the 1903 volume *Women Authors of Our Day in Their Homes,* which contained interviews and photographs of twenty-seven American writers. Later works like Grant Overton's 1918 *The Women Who Make Our Novels;* 1922's *The Women Novelists* by R. Brimley Johnson; and *The Genteel Female: An Anthology,* which Alfred A. Knopf published in 1931, demonstrates the intensifying interest in women writers in the first few decades of the twentieth century. In these same decades, growing public interest in authors and authorship had resulted in the expansion of the "Books" section of the *New York Times* as well as the launch of both the *Saturday Review of Literature* and a new Books section for the *New York Herald Tribune.*[86] To fill these additional pages, the "profile" became a staple of magazines and newspapers, and well-known writers often found themselves "profiled" with or without their permission.[87]

Other American phenomena, like the ladies' amateur arts association movement, peaked at the same time and were fed by the same curiosity. By the 1920s, many women's clubs had invested in building huge clubhouses to accommodate the crowds that writers like Mary

Austin or Charlotte Perkins Gilman drew.[88] Public curiosity about the women's lives led to greater and greater levels of detail: for instance, the public eagerly imbibed tidbits about writer-celebrities like Edna Ferber and the other authors who formed the Algonquin circle.[89] Throughout the 1920s and 1930s, publishers' memoirs or biographies (including that of Wharton's publisher, Charles Scribner II, and Atherton's, Horace Liveright) gave yet another glimpse into literary circles. These books often contained anecdotes about what it was like to deal with these women and other well-known writers "behind the scenes." The proliferation of publicity in all these forums reflects a greater trend in the literary marketplace, an increasing public curiosity that Carolyn Wells decried as an appetite to know all the "petty details of the life of a celebrity."[90] Thus, very few authors wholeheartedly embraced the celebrity template in their literary autobiographies. Popular writers who were photographed often, like Edna Ferber and Mary Roberts Rinehart, wrote autobiographies that overtly downplayed their celebrity status. And, as chapter 2 demonstrates, when Gertrude Atherton and Margaret Anderson did write autobiographies that emphasized their notorious celebrity, it produced some dramatic results and negative reactions.

Because of Depression-era shifts to more visual advertising and promotion methods for books, this increasingly intimate scrutiny of the lives of writers had reached a new peak by the time these women were composing their literary autobiographies. Even biographical dictionaries printed physical descriptions and domestic details along with typical catalogues of each author's works. For instance, *Living Authors,* published in 1931, reports on the name of Dorothy Parker's dachshund, describes Agnes Reppelier's "fine head, crowned with vigorous gray hair" and Gertrude Atherton's "pale gold hair," calls Zona Gale "as beautiful as any girl could be," describes Edith Wharton as "exquisitely dressed . . . with a kind of air," and refers to Mary Austin's "jam-borees," which is what she called the bouts of canning she indulged in between novels. Such intimate details, especially about physical appearance, occur more frequently in the chapters about women authors than about men, with the exception of flamboyant figures like Carl Van Vechten.[91] Entries about male writers such as Upton Sinclair do not include significant physical description or domestic detail.

These literary "portraits" suggest the tenor of public interest in women authors in 1931. Apparently, readers expected to be allowed greater intimacy into the private worlds of women writers—an expectation which demonstrates that the conditions of composition were still quite different for female and male autobiographers well into the twentieth century. The difference may account for the "striking lack of confidence" and "self-consciousness" Jelinek notes in this group of texts: the self-consciousness may be grounded in a suspicion that opening a limited portal into one's private life and thoughts might be met with other voracious demands for more details or with condescending, sexist responses. Lejeune characterizes autobiography as a "'collective agreement' reached between authors and readers through the intermediary of the publishers," both "a mode of reading as much as it is a type of writing"—one wherein the author and reader implicitly agree to certain conditions. These conditions create what Lejeune calls "The Autobiographical Pact" including the "referential pact" in which autobiographers "claim to provide information about a 'reality' exterior to the text."[92] But by 1931, there were so many versions of each of these women in circulation in press releases, gossip columns, society pages, and newspapers, and it already would have been difficult for readers to distinguish which preexisting narrative was closest to reality. Just as they have for other genres, the horizons of expectations for autobiography have changed over the centuries, and the public's reactions to these women's autobiographies demonstrate that 1930s readers held a new "tell-all" expectation transported from celebrity culture. Indeed, many readers complained that the autobiographies in this study did not tell enough, especially when compared to memoirs like Mabel Dodge Luhan's *Intimate Memories* or Emma Goldman's *Living My Life.* Editors and critics alike noticed and lamented this fact in all these books. Mary Austin's editor wanted her to "elaborate" on the "skimpy" second half of her manuscript. At one dinner given in her honor, she even felt the need to apologize for her omissions of any "romantic affairs" in *Earth Horizon.*[93] Some of Wharton's reviewers noticed that she was holding her readers at a distance, and it is true that Wharton's unhappy married life and her one passionate love affair form no part of her story. Often, the intimate details of these women's private lives are either deferentially hidden or lurk behind a facade of false bravado. Their discomfort with their position as female autobiographers who came of age in an era in which they were taught to be discrete, and then wrote memoirs half a century later to an audience who demanded intimate details, is readily apparent. Read in that light, the innovative narrative rhetoric their autobiographies use to hide or elide certain intimate details about their lives can be read as a form of resistance to the marketplace.

VISUAL DISCOURSE AND VERBAL DEBATE

Due to the combined pressures of public curiosity about authors and fierce competition for sales, pictorial publicity was especially emphasized in the 1930s book market. By 1933, publishers had switched from "drab and wordy" descriptions of the books on their lists to advertisements that were every bit as flashy as those for any other product. Newspapers carried advertisements for all manner of books, and photographs of the authors were a key tool in such advertisements.[94] In 1936, one astute observer compared the press surrounding the release of a new book to that of a Hollywood film.[95] Advertisers used photographs so prominently that in a good many cases, the image took up more space on the page than the preview or review of the book. As Marta Banta has demonstrated, any woman "who elected to advance a body of social and political principles was compelled to resolve the question of how to embody those values pictorially." For instance, suffragettes often used glamorous pictures to combat their public perception as harsh, strident, or "mannish." In contrast, early twentieth-century pictures of female judges and leaders in the temperance movement usually wore professional garb in photos, dressing for their work instead of for a male gaze, desexualizing their images, sometimes defeminizing themselves to claim their places in a "man's world."[96]

Authors were not exempt from this visual scrutiny. In fact, Christopher Wilson has compared the "rage and fretting" about the caprices of fame by authors in that era to that of a "modern rock star."[97] In such a climate, these authors learned to exercise control over their public images, and they tended to use the same pictures or poses over and over again as publicity shots, either to reinforce or to contradict public discourse about them. For instance, Gertrude Atherton, who referred to herself as an "intellectual siren," was adamant about being photographed in off-the-shoulder gowns until she was nearly ninety years old. Likewise, Mary Austin rejected an Ansel Adams photo of her because, as she explained in a lengthy letter to him, it did not convey "the energetic index . . . an upright and forthgoing quality" she was looking for.[98] Austin did not want the public to see her fatigue or frustration: she feared losing their confidence, and thus their attendance, at her lectures. Gertrude Stein's famous cross-dressing photographs both embodied her critique of gender as a performance and established her iconoclastic celebrity brand. But Stein was not the only author who used visual discourse to craft a unique brand. Most of Edna Ferber's publicity photographs are sleek and professional looking, the clothes she wears in them as tidy and well-coordinated as her stories. But, although she shared Ferber's intense work ethic, Mary Roberts Rinehart looks like a movie star in many of her publicity shots: she is glamorously draped in lush fabrics or furs, with dramatic eyebrows and Clara Bow lips. While the photographed Ferber looks as if she could sit right down and start writing or head out on one of her legendary long walks, Rinehart's photos embody readers' dreams of what a successful female writer's social life would be like.

Naturally, all these authors carefully selected images for the frontispieces of their autobiographies. On the first page of her autobiography, Mary Austin is dressed as for her role as American Sybil and earth mother: her hand rests contemplatively on the side of her chin, she is swathed in a large shawl, and a large piece of Native American jewelry hangs around her neck. She faces the camera directly, claiming authority by gazing back at the viewer, as female judges did to assert themselves in photographs of the same era. In her frontispiece, Charlotte Perkins Gilman seems unaware of the camera, gazing calmly away from it. This serene portrait reflects the theory her autobiography proposes, that one's "living" or inner reality is entirely separate from one's "life" or outer reality. However, there is a fascinating visual/verbal tension that these photographs create within many of these texts. For instance, Wharton's frontispiece photo mixes the direct, measured gaze of a judge with an elegant pearl choker necklace and luxuriant furs. However, the text of Wharton's autobiography rejects both femininity and fashion. Edna Ferber selected a very unusual photograph for the frontispiece to her autobiography. Rather than the professional, sophisticated publicity portrait she usually used, there's a picture of Ferber as a little girl, her hair in fuzzy pigtails, wearing a bonnet tied with a huge bow, fanning out her long, crinkled skirts. She is either dancing or about to take a bow—it's hard to tell which—in front of heavy floral curtains on a busy floral rug. It is unsophisticated, unprofessional, and naive, the opposite of the sleek public persona Ferber had established by the time the book was published. It promises that there is far more to Ferber than her reading public had ever imagined, and that the book might well take you to those heretofore unknown places. The rest of Ferber's autobiographical photos are also unlike her usual publicity shots. They are candid, vulnerable, even silly, until the very last one, a somber photo inserted into the last chapter wherein Ferber importunes fellow Americans to take action against the Holocaust in Europe. Rather than choosing images to "illustrate" their texts, as was expected and traditional within autobiographies, Stein's and Wells's veiled autobiographies utilize images that lead the reader away from a knowable, visible self. Also resisting the public gaze, Margaret Deland's *If This Be I* includes only one photograph. While Deland was seventy-eight when the book was published, she is six years old in the picture.

Although some writers resisted participating in the visual discourse associated with celebrity culture, rising public curiosity about the private lives of professional women in general had become a driver in both American literature and film in the 1920s and 1930s. In response to public curiosity about "these modern women," the *Nation* ran a series from 1926 through 1927 featuring autobiographical articles by famous women, including Mary Austin, with careers ranging from politics to writing fiction. The magazine's editors wanted to "discover the origin of their modern point-of-view toward men, marriage, children, and jobs. Do spirited ancestors explain their rebellion? Or is it due to thwarted ambition or distaste for domestic drudgery?"[99] As terms like "rebellion," "thwarted," and "distaste" suggest, these modern working women were often confronted with loaded questions about their personal and professional choices. By the end of the 1920s, popular magazines were regularly publishing and promoting fictional and nonfictional accounts of accomplished career women, and writers like Fannie Hurst and Christopher Morley depicted the evolution of the working woman in novels like *Back Street* (1931), *Imitation of Life* (1933), and *Kitty Foyle* (1939), all of which were adapted into films, as did movie scripts like 1933's *Baby Face* and 1936's *Career Woman.* By the mid-1930s, the "career woman" had "achieved her own conventionality" as a central character in American storytelling.[100]

Within the larger cultural discourse about "career women," the semiprivate, semipublic lives of writers became a popular 1930s subgenre. Magazine articles about the financial dealings of writers, publishers, and literary agents proliferated in response to public interest in that aspect of the field—and not only in literary journals. As Wilson notes, magazines written to all classes and all audiences promoted the new interest in writing.[101] Movie scripts about female writers and reporters drew big star power in films like *Theodora Goes Wild* (1936), wherein a quiet, small-town spinster—portrayed by Irene Dunne—secretly authors a scandalous bestseller, while Jean Arthur played the lead opposite William Powell in *The Ex-Mrs. Bradford* (1936), a comic whodunnit in which a divorced mystery writer gets her husband back. *Back in Circulation* (1937), a film about a journalist who uses her work to bring a former chorus girl to trial for murder, examines the power female writers could wield in society, as does *His Girl Friday* (1940), in which a reporter played by Rosalind Russell scoops her all-male newsroom colleagues and saves a wrongfully condemned man's life. The public's awareness of different templates for female authorship is especially highlighted in Bette Davis's performance in *Old Acquaintance,* wherein Davis plays a highbrow female novelist. The movie traces the lifelong tension between Davis's character and an old rival who writes popular romances. While *Old Acquaintance* was released in 1943, the film would not have been produced without the public's understanding of discourse about the differences between the "artist" and the "celebrity" templates for female authorship, which had developed throughout the 1930s. I have come to believe that Depression-era literary autobiographies both drew from and contributed to the establishment of these templates for authorship in the American imagination. In particular, Mary Roberts Rinehart's 1931 *My Story* shaped the "professional" template as a means to resist her own dismissal as a "popular" celebrity; this newer template for women writers gave other writers like Edna Ferber and Harriet Monroe more appropriate options for characterizing the nature of their own endeavors.

While it emerges most overtly as a guiding force in Rinehart's autobiography, the professional template for authorship makes its influence felt in many of these texts. Because of the economic conditions of the Depression and the resulting changes in publishing, writing was considered more and more a professional business for women instead of a genteel hobby. Charlotte Perkins Gilman openly heralded these changes as an opportunity for greater artistic freedom, with "fresh fields of fiction" for the emancipated woman.[102] Wharton's autobiography speaks of how writing to deadline made her "master [her] tools"—acknowledging writing as a profession, despite how genteel and domestic her actual routine of writing in bed in the mornings and then entertaining or visiting in the afternoons may have been.[103] (Wharton reveals nothing of these domestic rituals in *A Backward Glance*.) Powerful 1930s publishers like Doubleday believed that "once a writer gained a wide public, his work 'becomes a business and must be treated as such,'" and the autobiographies of Mary Roberts Rinehart and Edna Ferber reveal Doubleday's motto in action.[104]

Reviews of 1930s literary autobiographies reveal that these women were expected to engage questions about writing as a business in their memoirs. Some reviews of Ferber's *A Peculiar Treasure* focused on the notion of success, recommending the text for aspiring writers to learn from. For Ferber's fans, this was a natural expectation, as she first found fame through publishing a series of magazine stories about a successful woman in business. It is interesting to observe which of these writers talk openly about earning money in their autobiographies, such as Ferber, Monroe, Gilman, and Rinehart, and which of them do not, such as Wharton, Stein, Deland, and King. This divide generally falls along the lines of whether the autobiographer wishes to emphasize an artistic or activist identity over a professional one, and also how much they wish to affiliate or identify with their female readers. Biographies about these women demonstrate how shrewd and assertive many of them could be as businesswomen, but sometimes their autobiographies mask their concerns with financial success or sublimate those concerns beneath artistic triumph or rejection. These strategies may have been intended to lift these authors above the curiosity the mass audience felt toward all working women, to distance them from the ambitious women who may have composed part of their reading audience, or to insulate them from the implication that they should be content with popular or financial success, rather than fighting for artistic status.

POPULAR AND CRITICAL RECEPTION

Although they had all been accustomed to deadlines and editorial pressure for decades before they started writing their autobiographies, most of these women found the unique pressures of composing autobiography for a curious reading public comparatively unpleasant. Wharton referred to her autobiography as a "confounded thing" while she was writing it.[105] Austin wrote to a friend that she "dreaded" her autobiographical task.[106] Acknowledging the tension between the demand for and discomfort within these women's autobiographies is crucial to understanding them, for they jointly imply that these women knew all the reasons why their potential audiences would be interested in reading their life stories and felt uneasy about the impression their books would make. Their uneasiness had due cause: when Wharton's editor forwarded her the news that the editor at *Ladies' Home Journal* wanted to cut her reminiscences by almost one half, to excise the "dull parts," she acerbically replied that she had "always wondered how [her autobiography] could interest such a public as the American illustrated magazines are addressed to."[107] Mary Roberts Rinehart's text was compromised as well: she had to cut the sections that the editorship felt might not appeal to *Good Housekeeping*'s mass audience.[108]

The quandary of presenting one's life to an audience who is primed for misunderstanding was a common frustration for these women. How can one define oneself in opposition to the values of the very audience who determines the success of one's book? Mary Austin's 1912 semi-autobiographical novel, *A Woman of Genius,* prefigures the situation she and the other autobiographers in this study would later face. In the novel's introduction, she assesses the problem of audience for an "accomplished woman" who is writing her autobiography: "I thought then of writing the life of an accomplished woman, and not so much of the accomplishment as of the woman." The heroine of Austin's novel, a fictionalized version of herself as an actress, begins her autobiography: "It is strange that I can never think of writing any account of my life without thinking of Pauline Mills and wondering what she would think of it. Pauline is rather given to reading the autobiographies of distinguished people . . . and finding in them new persuasions of the fundamental rightness of her scheme of things." The heroine, Olivia Lattermore, goes on to explain that Pauline, who represents the social norms of femininity in the novel, is prone to willfully misunderstanding the lives of other women. Therefore, Olivia is "highly suspicious of the social estimate of women, by the general social conspiracy against her telling the truth about herself."[109] This description implies a fear that the real truth about an unconventional woman must remain incomprehensible to the average reader.

Austin's insight foreshadows the dual audience for women's literary autobiography during the Depression: the massive popular readership and the more highbrow audience that directed the mechanisms of modernism. These autobiographers depended on both audiences. One controlled their financial success, and the other their critical reputations. How could they address them both? This question forms a central dilemma in the composition and reception of these books. How could these authors create texts that would appeal both to the reading masses and to critics who viewed themselves as an antidote to the reading masses? These literary autobiographies are constantly anticipating and confronting this dilemma, among others, and to understand them in their context, we must ask these critical questions:

1. How did contemporary audiences—both the mass readership and the literary elite—react to these texts when they were published?
2. How do the autobiographies reveal the ways in which these women tried to define themselves in relationship to both the high-modernist template of the artist as antidomestic, antisentimental, isolated, and elite?
3. How do these autobiographies use the available templates for authorship to either work with or against the type of public image these authors already enjoyed or deplored throughout their careers?
4. How much do these autobiographers embrace or reject the notions of female solidarity, feminist activism, writing for financial motives, or being a role model for aspiring authors?

To answer these crucial questions, each chapter in this project reconstructs the composition and reception of these autobiographies through reviews, drafts, letters, and biographical research. The reactions of editors, readers, and critics to each text disclose how successfully these autobiographers navigated touchy topics such as genius, feminism, celebrity, sexuality, and money.

Examining the rhetorical and narrative choices these autobiographers made reveals how skillfully each author uses or combines the artist, activist, professional, or celebrity templates to frame her life-story. Borrowing from the templates allowed these writers simultaneously to satisfy and subvert the expectations of their multiple critical and commercial audiences and reveal shifting dynamics in the public's understanding of modern authorship. The dynamics within these literary autobiographies illustrate that these women were not just writing their lives—they were *rewriting* them in the context of many other popular and critical narratives about them. To this end, each chapter traces a pair of authors' reconstructions of their careers along the lines of one of the four templates and analyzes the various types of resistance to unwanted interpretations that their choice of textually constructed self-image employs. In chapter 1, I delineate how Edith Wharton's *A Backward Glance* and Grace King's *Memories of a Southern Woman of Letters* assert strong artistic identities through textual erasures of people and events that might contradict their coherent trajectory of apprenticeship to mastery. Chapter 2 examines how Gertrude Atherton and Margaret Anderson, who had always enjoyed their celebrity notoriety, denounce all personal and professional boundaries in *Adventures of a Novelist* and *My Thirty Years' War.* Chapter 3 traces the ways in which Charlotte Perkins Gilman's *The Living of Charlotte Perkins Gilman* and Margaret Deland's *If This Be I* downplay questions of art in favor of activism. Chapter 4 demonstrates how Mary Austin and Harriet Monroe dispersed the tension between the conflicting elements of their narratives through creating multiple autobiographical voices and emphasizing their identities as regional visionaries. Chapter 5 argues that middlebrow writers Mary Roberts Rinehart's and Edna Ferber's stunning popularity may have stemmed from their insistence on a female professionalism that does not reject domesticity, allowing them to assert an "American Everywoman" image in *My Story* and *A Peculiar Treasure.* Finally, chapter 6 analyzes the success of the veiled autobiographies of Gertrude Stein and Carolyn Wells. These authors crafted a series of strategic diversions in *The Autobiography of Alice B. Toklas* and *The Rest of My Life,* employing humor to amuse their audiences into submission with what they reveal or conceal, and creating a uniquely populist appeal for their personal brands of genius.

In order to facilitate the pairing of books that utilize the same templates and techniques, the autobiographies are not treated in chronological order. Instead, the chapters progress from analyzing texts that conform most closely to a preexisting template or autobiographical tradition first, and move toward examining those autobiographies that either reject a preexisting template or attempt to create a new one. Ordering the pairings in this way also allows me to better demonstrate not only the influence these authors had on one another's careers but the implicit conversation (or, in a couple of cases, the overt debate) that was taking place both within and between these autobiographies. Finally, this nonchronological method invites us to perceive how important the 1930s were in breaking down barriers for the next generation of female literary autobiographers, as the chapters also progress from treating the least to the most innovative texts.

The choices these autobiographers made, and the templates they adopted, adapted, or dismantled, tell us something about the sources of this generation's confidence and consternation as women writers. The difficult task of acknowledging both their past achievements and their ongoing frustrations in their autobiographies illuminates the self-censorship and rhetorical gamesmanship that have frustrated readers of these texts for nearly a century. Perhaps those difficulties explain why these authors' "official" literary autobiographies are not the only ways in which these women sought to tell their life-stories. Many of them also left other unpublished biographical or autobiographical material behind, fictionalized their careers in other stories, or published literary criticism of their own. Studying these texts in juxtaposition with their unpublished and semi-autobiographical material and with the works of biographers and historians, we can see that in the tumultuous climate of the 1930s, these autobiographers risked writing self-mutilating narratives with fears of their own effectiveness as portraiture. To read these autobiographies together in their shared cultural context offers us a greater understanding of the ways in which these authors' private senses of identity reflected or conflicted with their public images in the marketplace.

Chapter 1

The Artist's Soul or the Woman's Life

Renunciation in Edith Wharton's *A Backward Glance* and Grace King's *Memories of a Southern Woman of Letters*

IN HER 1932 autobiography, *Memories of a Southern Woman of Letters,* Grace King vividly recalls the moment—some seventy years earlier—when she decided to become a writer. As a child of only ten years, she was walking along the levee on her family's plantation in New Iberia, Louisiana, where they had gone into hiding from the ravages of the Civil War. She noticed the sun shining "like a conflagration behind the cypress forest on the opposite bank" and the "black looking water of the bayou [that] flowed in a swift current between."[1] Incipient in this imagery of boundaries and hidden depths are the major elements of King's career: her written work always essayed to reconcile the surface of society with its depths, particularly the tensions between nineteenth-century ideologies of gender, the lived reality of women's experience, and her own private opinions and ambitions.

Edith Wharton's autobiography, *A Backward Glance* (1933), also tells the story of Wharton's origins as a writer, declaring that she started creating stories before she learned to read them. Early in the published autobiography, Wharton describes how she used to "make up" stories as a child by holding a book and imagining the tales that might fill its pages. The "call," she explains, "came regularly and imperiously; and though . . . it caught me at inconvenient moments, I would struggle against it conscientiously," but "the struggle was always a losing one." For Wharton, as for King, there was a chasm between the two worlds she inhabited: Old New York with its myriad social codes and expectations was a far cry from the free and fervent world of her imagination. In the autobiography, Wharton asserts that she "always had to be alone to 'make up,'" and would shoo her mother, father, and nurse from the room. When the little girl instructed her mother to entertain a friend who had come over to play so that little Edith could go make up stories, *A Backward Glance* affirms that "there was not one [playmate] I would not have renounced forever rather than have my 'making up' interfered with."[2] As did the dividing current in King's symbolic imagery, the scenes Wharton describes prefigure the gap these autobiographies evoke between the disparate aspects of their lives as women and as writers. Both *Memories of a Southern Woman of Letters* and *A Backward Glance* divide Wharton's and King's individual identities as artists from their experiences as women, privileging the former and suppressing much of the truth about the latter.

Grace Elizabeth King (1852–1932) was the oldest girl and third child of William Woodson King, a respected and successful lawyer in New Orleans, Louisiana. The family lived quite comfortably until the occupation of the city by the federal government during the Civil War forced them to flee the city and go into hiding. The trauma and uncertainty of war made for King's most powerful and telling early memories, but the painful social, economic, and cultural struggles she and her family endured during Reconstruction were the roots of much of her fiction. King often observed that the real losers in war—any war—were the women and children, sagely observing, "There are no fortunes of war for women and children—it is all misfortune."[3] Much of King's work—fiction and nonfiction—reveals an "insistent . . .

emphasis on female marginality [that] claims for the muted, invisible women of the South a space of their own."[4] Readers and critics have long been baffled about how to read and respond to the shifting, often contradictory tones in King's work, and her biographer, Robert Bush, compares her irony to that of her good friend and mentor Mark Twain.[5] Her most well-known fiction includes *Balcony Stories, Monsieur Motte,* and *The Pleasant Ways of St. Medard,* but she also wrote history, historical fiction, and textbooks. Grace King's social training and literary interests ran parallel to Edith Wharton's in a number of ways. Like Wharton, King was raised in a tradition of rigid cultural codes surrounding class and gender, and was also deeply interested in the differences between European and American culture, French culture in particular. King deeply admired the influential French intellectual Marie Therese de Solms, known in literary circles simply as Madame Blanc, and her work often traced the French origins of Creole society. In her final decade, King reigned as the grande dame of New Orleans letters. Her work was regularly featured in American literature textbooks and studies of the 1920s, including Fred Lewis Pattee's *A History of American Literature since 1870* (1922) and *The Development of the American Short Story* (1923).[6] In 1924, having collaborated with her two sisters for decades, King founded an all-female salon, exclusively designed to bring intellectual women together, eight years before her death at age eighty.

Both of these women's autobiographies illustrate the impact of the elaborate, ritualistic cultures in which they were raised and tell the tales of their campaigns to control their own lives despite these influences. Comparing their published life-writings to their private drafts, journals, and letters reveals that Wharton and King used renunciation as a rhetorical strategy in *A Backward Glance* and *Memories of a Southern Woman of Letters,* defining themselves by emphasizing what they had walked away from, editing out the private emotions, acerbic opinions, and ironic outlooks in which their unpublished life-writings abound.

Most of this reticence was likely due to their era and upbringing. Since both of them came of age during the 1870s, Wharton and King were heavily influenced by nineteenth-century ideals of feminine modesty and gentility. Their regional roots played another role in this, as both Old New York and the Old South enforced rigid behavioral codes for ladies. However, *A Backward Glance* and *Memories of a Southern Woman of Letters* reject the feminine "domestic" autobiographical tradition, aggressively sublimating their private lives as women to their public ideals as artists. This decision too likely had its roots in some shared experiences, for both women wished to be known as "serious" artists, and both endured some painful and difficult family relationships. Their autobiographies excise the truth about most of those relationships—for Wharton, with her mother and husband, and for King, with her mother, sisters, and alcoholic brother—from their life-stories. Both autobiographers also disassociate themselves from the trappings of traditional ornamental femininity yet paradoxically cling to traditional feminine modesty, often letting other voices speak for them rather than asserting themselves on their own behalf. So much remains under the surface in these texts that one can only sense the tensions Wharton and King faced through their frequent tonal shifts, which critics and readers have found frustrating or bewildering.

An intensely private person, Edith Wharton struggled with choosing both a direction and a tone for her autobiography. Her unpublished partial autobiographical draft, entitled *Life and I,* demonstrates that she wavered in trying to decide what the tenor of the book would be. Her frustrated composition process may have something to do with the fact that, all told, Wharton's book appeared in three very different venues—an early chapter of *A Backward Glance* was published as an essay in *The Atlantic* before *Ladies' Home Journal* ran a much-truncated version as a serial in late 1933. Then in 1934, Scribner's released the complete text as a lovely, expensive volume. Since Wharton knew that her book would be read in both popular and literary circles, confronting such different audiences may have caused some of the frustration she felt during its composition. Although the chapter that had been published in *The Atlantic* as "Confessions of a Novelist" was warmly received, Wharton did not anticipate the same reaction from *Journal* readers. Magazines like the *Journal,* she felt, were interested in her famous name but not in her art. In fact, Wharton asked her friends not to read the *Ladies' Home Journal*'s installments. She requested that they wait for the book version: it "made [her] sick" to think of her friends reading her autobiography in "choppy fragments."[7] Wharton's concern with the format suggests that her autobiography was carefully constructed to leave an overall impression. But the full version of *A Backward Glance* still seems fragmentary. Most Wharton scholars acknowledge that the autobiography gives us a persona that is out of balance with the facts we know from other sources. Based on *A Backward Glance,* biographers have often portrayed her mother and husband as emotional and physical obstacles to Wharton's writing career. However, Laura Rattray's *Edith Wharton in Context,* analyzing forty years of recently rediscovered correspondence between Wharton and her tutor Anna Bahlmann, reveals how very reconstructed Wharton's depiction of her youth and relationships with her mother and husband are in her autobiography. The letters reveal that the repressed, quiet girl; the discouraged budding writer; and the cold or strained relationships we find in *A Backward Glance* may have been retroactive projections from an older Wharton who had been critiquing the "frivolous society" of Old New York and all its denizens in her fiction for years, rather than accurate representations of the active, exuberant girl who loved sports and reading; whose family and friends reveled in her wit and cleverness; and whose husband indulged her love for travel and was awed by her intimidating intellect.[8]

Contemporary reviewers held divided opinions on *A Backward Glance;* they were either impressed by Wharton's autobiographical composure or suspected that they were being held at arm's length. Amy

Loveman called *A Backward Glance* "the recollections of a singularly happy life" with a few "sidelights on her art."[9] E. M. Forster incisively observed that Wharton's "career (or such of it as she has chosen to describe) has few moments of high tension; the dominant impression is comfort."[10] Percy Hutchison noted that the book "seems to lack dramatic episodes."[11] Another reviewer observed that Wharton "was a serious enough writer to look critically at the foibles of her set [but she] never looked any farther inward than that."[12] Others shared this sense of frustration. E. K. Brown wrote in *American Literature,* "The book is disappointing as an account of her creative activity. Only one chapter is devoted to this; and this chapter opens with an apology for its presence, digresses at length from its true theme, and loses itself in speculation."[13] Then as now, many readers in literary circles wanted a more intimate view of the relationship between Wharton's life and her art.

As a sustained work of art, King's *Memories of a Southern Woman of Letters* feels as frustrating and elusive as Wharton's autobiography. One reviewer praised the first third of King's book—set while the family was in hiding during the Civil War—for its "drama and color," lamenting that after that point the book loses its "story teller's attitude" and becomes flat and "stereotyped."[14] The only really complimentary review of *Memories of a Southern Woman of Letters* terms King a "delightful raconteur" but qualifies the description by specifying "as a traveler."[15] As Katherine Capshaw Smith asks, "Why does the Southern Woman of Letters seem to avoid the South?"[16] Several of King's contemporary reviewers noticed this as well: E. P. Noyes of *Books* noted that although most of King's life was lived in New Orleans, her trips to Europe and accounts of her "friendships with artists, statesmen, and authors of note"—almost all of them northerners—dominate the volume.[17] Smith theorizes that King's text "strains to suppress and minimize ugly moments of regional, economic, and racial tension." It is true that King spends a great deal of time in *Memories* describing her three trips to

Europe, which only accounted for about five years of her adult life. However, King may have used travel in her autobiography in the same way she had in her life, "to escape the emotional distress, economic deprivation, racial tension, and literary and historical ignorance that characterized her home."[18] As the reviewers pointed out, King's tone is different when she describes life in the South than when she is away from home. As discussed later in this chapter, Wharton's text evidences similar tonal shifts, most likely because both writers were brought up to be well-mannered ladies who would never display pain or discomfort in public. The most terse, flat passages in these two autobiographies either signify where they are suppressing their most conflicted memories or where they are editing their lives to conform to the template of the "serious" artist.

Like many of Wharton's readers, King's biographer, Robert Bush, found her autobiography disappointing. Bush dismisses the book as "sketchy and vapid," commenting that King "seems to have thought that her autobiographical legacy should be a polite account of all her public experiences."[19] Comparing it unfavorably to Ellen Glasgow's more intimate autobiography *The Woman Within* (1954), Bush does not consider that Glasgow was not writing for the 1930s market, nor does he note that Glasgow never intended her memoirs to be published while she was living. King and Wharton, writing when and where they did, had two very limited (and oppositional) modes of autobiography from which to choose: the "public man" model or the feminine genteel tradition. King's title indicates that she was trying to adapt the former model to her experience as a woman, but as neither model could allow her to accurately represent her life, King weaves layers of both traditions throughout her confounding text, sometimes switching from one to the other in midsentence. Wharton's *A Backward Glance* reveals the same tensions. Readers, in their time and ours, must carefully sort through pages upon pages of veiled hints and apparent contradictions to piece together the narratives. Because of these difficulties, biographers and critics have often characterized these two autobiographies as failures on the part of their authors. Ironically, when we encounter confusing texts by other authors of the same era (particularly highbrow, male authors), narrative difficulty and disjointed perspectives are viewed positively as innovations. This chapter reads Wharton's and King's works as important case studies in the tradition of women's literary autobiography, as complex—but highly compromised—solutions to the agonizing puzzle of writing their lives under the generic, historical, and literary pressures of their time.

The difficulties and frustrations inherent in both Wharton's and King's texts illustrate the difficult dynamics of writing autobiography within multiple traditions to disparate audiences. Fortunately, both women also left more forthright, personal texts behind, so we can compare their published memoirs with their private memories and impressions. King's correspondence with her family and friends reveals the private opinions and personal dynamics that *Memories* conceals, while Wharton's draft autobiography suggests that she toyed with the notion of writing a more intimate one, only to abandon it. Instead, both women tell the public story of a successful artist—the position that granted them the opportunity to publish an autobiography—even though that particular autobiographical tradition had never welcomed women. However, using the artistic template brought up another set of obstacles. Telling a story of the artist as woman in a time when "artistic" and "feminine" concerns were seen as antithetical could give critics cause to dismiss their work as "women's fiction," while emphasizing their success in a man's world could bring them accusations of egotism. Erasing all the obstacles they faced in pursuing their careers might make it appear that their literary status was simply a reflection of class privilege, rather than talent and struggle. In reality, the elite social circles into which both were born were not just privileges but also prisons. In *A Backward Glance* and *Memories of a Southern Woman of Letters,* the "feminine" priorities foisted on them as young "ladies"—beauty, clothing, marriage, wealth, and leisure—felt more like what Simone de Beauvoir called "feminitude," a term referring to all the oppressive or confining ways in which the "feminine" has been culturally constructed. These two surviving members of the elite social and literary worlds of the Old South and Old New York wrote autobiographies that exposed the problematic boundaries and labels which had been imposed on them by their families and their class status. These labels stung, which explains how stridently their texts renounce the traditions and expectations of these dying subcultures—particularly the ways the Old South and Old New York (reflected in their depictions of their mothers) constrained the course of women's lives.

To combat the condescending labels they resented and to redefine their lives on their own terms, these two autobiographies appropriate diverse traditions, discourses, and narrative strategies, addressing each of their topics within a different trope and with a different tone. The Edith Wharton of *A Backward Glance* shifts between assertive and self-effacing personas. This strategic interplay creates several autobiographical "I"s—an insignificant I inscribed by the feminine norms of Old New York and an authoritative I that redefines significance itself—allowing Wharton to shift between asserting or effacing herself at any given point in the text. These dual personas were probably authentic to Wharton's multiple social roles; we know that they were to Grace King's as well. In a letter, the man King once hoped to marry noted that there were two versions of Grace King. One was "brave" and "unembarrassed," but the other Grace was "timid" and "earnest."[20] Shifts between these personas happen frequently and without notice in King's text—sometimes in midsentence. Weaving together a series of shifts and renunciations, *A Backward Glance* and *Memories of a Southern Woman of Letters* never lose sight of the one identity they absolutely affirm: Edith Wharton the artist and Grace King the southern *woman* (rather than a southern "lady," for being a lady was a crucially important renunciation for King) of letters.

In *A Backward Glance,* Wharton employs tonal shifts to distinguish her artist's soul from the perfunctory demands of her privileged upbringing. She found "ecstasy" and "rapture" in the "secret" world of her imagination, also described as a land of "enchantment," "richness and mystery," a "sea of dreams." Speaking of the time spent in her father's library, where she "dragg[ed] out book after book in a secret ecstasy of communion," Wharton explains that "the child knows instinctively when it will be understood, and from the first I kept my adventures with books to myself."[21] Even as a little girl who precociously understood her relative powerlessness in the confines of the Joneses' household, Wharton asserted the solitary persona of the artist and located herself within her father's library.

Grace King's autobiography also locates her origins as a writer within libraries: that of her father and of a close family friend. Unlike most southern gentlemen of his era, William Woodson King, a lawyer, educated his daughters alongside his sons at home in a course of serious reading and academic subjects, unlike most other young ladies of their class. William King was not content with merely seeing his girls "finished" for society, as was the priority of his wife, Sarah Ann Miller "Mimi" King. These years of homeschooling resulted in a "genuine love of learning" for the King girls, Grace in particular.[22] Not only was King's father an avid and scholarly reader but Grace's enthusiasm for books, languages, and local history was also likely encouraged by Louisiana historian Charles Gayarre, a friend of the family who granted her access to his exclusive and impressive collection of historical materials as her career developed. In addition to studying history, languages, and classics, King kept up an enthusiastic reading list, including all the newest fiction and social theory, before she began to write. As did Wharton, King read Herbert Spencer, the popular Social Darwinist, in the 1870s. She also devoured the works of Tolstoy and Dostoevsky in the 1880s, studied the biography of George Eliot, and followed the careers of both Henry James and Edith Wharton with interest.

While King briefly refers to her admiration of Wharton's work in her autobiography, Wharton does not acknowledge any other American women writers in hers. Perhaps Wharton had been singled out as an exception among women writers often enough that to affiliate with other women may have felt like a step down.

King's first published work was a strident piece of literary criticism entitled "Heroines of Novels." First published anonymously in a local newspaper but later acknowledged as her work, King's essay analyzed and commented on four national literatures—American, British, French, and German—in terms of their portrayal of women. In the essay, King finds French novels to be the best for their realism, and female novelists to be more accurate in their portrayal of their own gender than male authors, bringing Charles Dickens, William Makepeace Thackeray, and Henry James under her critical scrutiny. Although King felt extremely fearful about reading the paper at a literary society meeting and expressed her anxiety about speaking in public in her private letters, the essay itself exhibits a boldness, definitiveness, and assurance of superior judgment that sounds like the "brave" and "unembarrassed" side of her dual persona.[23] As does the young Edith Wharton in *A Backward Glance,* Grace King the writer appears to have possessed a confident self-assurance from the beginning.

Louis Auchincloss, in his original introduction to *A Backward Glance,* pronounced that "[Wharton's] life was a revolution" against her society's conceptions of a lady.[24] However, Wharton's unpublished draft autobiography, "Life and I," does not produce the same impression. The difference between the two versions highlights the pattern of Wharton's editorial decision-making, for the segments of *A Backward Glance* that discuss Wharton's youth seem dedicated to renouncing the ornamental femininity she associated with her mother and the society of Old New York. In contrast with "Life and I" and other accounts, Wharton's official written life overdramatizes her rejection of femininity and fashion. In *A Backward Glance,* Wharton's first memory is walking down the street with her father, wearing a "white satin gathered bonnet patterned with pink and green raised velvet plaid, with a brim over thick ruffles of silky blond lace," awakening "to the importance of dress, and of herself as a subject for adornment." The scene ends in a kiss from a young cousin, thus Wharton "was wakened to conscious life by the two tremendous forces of love and vanity."[25] In this first scene, the differences between "Life and I" and *A Backward Glance* demonstrate that Wharton distanced herself from the femininity of these early sections in the published autobiography much more than she had originally planned. In "Life and I" she refers to her desire "to look pretty" as part of "*my* feminine instinct of pleasing."[26] But in *A Backward Glance,* the little girl who "woke to the importance of dress, and of herself as a subject of adornment," is mostly referred to in the third person. Wharton's description of herself as "a soft, anonymous morsel of humanity—this little girl, who bore my name," is revealing that, as scholar Judith Fryer states, "[Wharton] quite literally sees someone else, 'she,' not 'I' . . . the feminine 'me' that the little girl presents is Wharton as she might have become." Fryer declares that the "sense of otherness" in the passage is deliberate, and looks at the self of that passage as "indelibly marked by what Simone de Beauvoir called *feminitude*—a culturally determined status of difference and oppression."[27] In decoding Wharton's and King's autobiographies, it might be helpful to understand their feminitude as a specific subcategory of their femininity, just as being a "lady" could be considered a potential subcategory for being a woman. As a teenager, Wharton was "publicly shamed" when a gossip column reported that her first engagement had ended because she was too "ambitious"—a crime that amounted to unmarriageability in a young lady in Old New York.[28] The intimate, feminine voice of "Life and I" denies Wharton's ambition, declaring, "I did not want to dominate—I wanted to be adored!"[29] However, in *A Backward Glance,* Wharton treats the desires to be adorned and adored ironically, rejecting social, ornamental roles in favor of a solitary, artistic self.

For instance, though she thoroughly enjoyed participating in fashion and design throughout her life, Wharton disassociates herself from clothes in *A Backward Glance.* Wharton's mother, Lucretia Jones, known as the "best dressed woman in New York," clearly passed her impeccable taste on to her daughter. However, Wharton separates herself from clothing in her official autobiography. She writes that, on the occasion of her debut, she was "*put into* a low-necked bodice of pale green brocade, above a white muslin skirt ruffled with rows and rows of Valenciennes" to spend an evening of "speechless misery."[30] The passage suggests that compulsory feminine adornment is a form of subjugation—a mark of feminitude, for under those "rows and rows" of lace, Wharton is rendered silent and miserable. *A Backward Glance*'s representation of her debut seems self-consciously rhetorical when read in light of her earlier characterization of the evening in "Life and I," which finds her "with [her] shoulders bare and [her] head *coiffee*," in a "pink blur of emotion." She declares, "Oh, how I loved it all—my pretty frocks, the flowers, the music, the sense that everybody 'liked me' and wanted to talk to me and dance with me."[31]

However, Wharton repeatedly opposes ornamental femininity to artistic sensibility in *A Backward Glance.* When she relates her first two encounters with Henry James, she mocks her attempts to catch his attention through fetching attire. At the age of twenty-five, she "could think of only one way of deserving" to meet James: "to put on my newest *doucet* dress, and try to look my prettiest!" She further explains that believing her "youth, and [her] pretty frock" were all she had to "commend" her to James was a naive assumption based on how she "had been brought up" in a society where looks and clothes were the only acceptable feminine ways to get attention. But the autobiography notes that her new dress "neither gave me the courage to speak, nor attracted the attention of the great man." Again, pretty clothes are aligned with feminine silence and passivity. Dressed up, Wharton waits, mute, for James to approach her. She tries again later in "a beautiful new hat!" but, of course, James does not even recall having met her on these occasions. Only when she had "found myself, and was no longer afraid to talk to Henry James of the things we both cared about," does their friendship begin. In these passages, Wharton assures her readers that it is not her charm or style that inspired his interest but her writing. Throughout *A Backward Glance,* Wharton's renunciation of the trappings of feminitude is underscored by vignettes like this one and other carefully chosen anecdotes that demonstrates how ill-suited a fashionable lady was within circles of artists and intellectuals. In one such anecdote, Wharton tells of a "fashionable beauty" at an elegant English house party who was perplexed at the proposition that she was to meet Henry James. The lady offered to read both *The Wings of the Dove* and *The Golden Bowl* in one day, but before lunch the next day, she "thumped them down on the table, and turned her lovely smile on [Wharton]. 'Well, of all the *tosh!*' she said gaily."[32] In this tableau, it is clearly the lovely but superficial lady, not Edith Wharton, who is out of place. The beauty's feminitude has rendered her incapable of reading James's work—she is an example of the narrow life that Wharton has escaped.

Growing up in a southern culture just as entrenched in the notion that beauty, fashion, and social grace were a lady's only desirable characteristics, King clearly gave these things a great deal of thought as well. In her journal, she muses, "It is the ugly women who set the fashions and the pretty women who follow them. The beautiful women do neither."[33] When she mentions women's fashion in the autobiography, King, like Wharton, associates it with rigid, confining traditions and opposes it to female intellectualism, noting that Madame Blanc wore a simple "black skirt and grey jacket, with large, loose, soiled kid gloves." In contrast, the woman of fashion as evoked in *Memories* is as narrow, uninspired, and self-absorbed as the woman of fashion in Wharton's autobiography. Describing a dinner King attended given by a grand-niece of Napoleon, King notes not just the silk, lace, and rubies of the lady's costume but the "tiny *fin-de-siècle* fan . . . tied with reddish-brown ribbon, the loops passed over her wrists." In case the reader fails to catch the inflection of the looped wrists, King goes on to write that the lady's steps were "short, mincing . . . as though in the habit of curtseying at every step." In *Memories,* King draws the line between ladies like these and female intellectuals, such as herself, noting that Madame Blanc "talked with the aplomb of a man" and observing that "nowhere except in France, I am sure, could such an old woman have a showing."[34]

King's fiction also focuses on clothing as a tool for the subjection and objectification of women. Closely reading her work as a whole, Anna Shannon Elfenbein finds that King examined the costly complicity of ladies' fashion in the sexual entrapment of southern women throughout her career.[35] King repeatedly associated feminine clothing with helplessness, discomfort, and lack of privacy—marks of southern feminitude. For instance, the spotless white satin boots that the heroine's feet are painfully forced into in King's first short story, "Mousier Motte," are too tight to put on without assistance, so the girl cannot get dressed alone. The boots and the clothes that King—and many of her female characters—generally cannot wait to remove and toss into a heap like piles of lacy satin refuse symbolize something bigger: the double position of southern ladies, outwardly pampered and inwardly imprisoned. The narrator in *The Pleasant Ways of St. Medard,* King's most well-known novel, points out that society matrons without any other means of support were hired to "teach [young girls] how to dress" so that "their capital of beauty . . . could be profitably increased."[36] King's deep suspicion of the fashion industry and its complicity with the subjection of women comes through quite clearly in the book. Knowing that *Pleasant Ways* was not "a story such as people love to read," King resisted editorial and familial urgings to change it by giving it a romantic focus and a happy ending.[37] However, King would never compromise its satiric observations to make the book more salable.

The Pleasant Ways of St. Medard was rejected multiple times in ten years by George Brett at Macmillan, the very publisher who had commissioned it, before it was finally released in 1916.

Despite the stand she took about keeping the ironically titled *Pleasant Ways* too unpleasant for her publisher, King's published voice, in both her autobiography and her fiction, is still much more muted than the private voice we hear in her journals. The ideology of the southern lady was a powerful force in King's youth, one that silenced her preferences and subordinated her talents and ambitions to its dictates. Because "ladies didn't labor," King's mother insisted on upholding the gentility, leisure, and pride of a southern Lady even after the family fortune was lost in the Civil War.[38] So when Grace became engaged at age nineteen to a young man named Garret Walker, who would eventually succeed in the railroad business, Mimi King felt he had not enough money to keep Grace in the grand family tradition and insisted the couple wait two years before getting married. According to King's biographers, Mimi then used those two years to coerce her daughter into breaking the engagement. Grace must have regretted and resented her mother's interference, for she saved all of Walker's love letters—now housed in the Louisiana State University library archives—and not only never married but never seriously dated again, to her mother's great dismay. While Wharton's mother may have helped to lead her daughter into making a mismatched marriage to avoid the social shame of having raised a spinster, King's mother prevented her daughter's marriage and forced her into an angry spinsterhood, all to uphold the feminine traditions to which they clung. It is no wonder that both Wharton's and King's autobiographies renounce the feminitude that warped their choices as young women.

The ornamental and frivolous women that young Edith Jones and Grace King were expected to become serve as emblems of the petty concerns and desires Wharton and King renounced as mature artists. Even with initial success as an author, Wharton's autobiography explains, she was not socially in demand in New York, for its natives "were afraid [she] was too intelligent to be fashionable." The few lengthier descriptions of Old New York revolve around clothes, such as "floating silks or muslins . . . wide leghorn hats and heavy veils," which, as Wharton notes, were "very uncomfortable for the wearers [of those veils], who could hardly see or breathe." By pointing out, once again, the confinement and discomfort involved in performing ornamental femininity, Wharton shows how stunted an identity that revolves around such concerns can be. Her text records that the first question any Old New Yorker would ask about a "newcomer" would be, "Is she pretty?" Aware that she was not considered beautiful, Wharton claims that, in a society where there was "an almost pagan worship of physical beauty," she "never dreamed that [she] was in any way their superior."[39]

Although her editorial decisions prevented her from telling the whole truth about her life, Wharton used *A Backward Glance* to declare her independence from Old New York's assessment of her as a poor ornamental object. The solitary persona she creates in this text aspires to higher callings than that. However, the exquisitely groomed portrait Wharton chose for her frontispiece, and the lavish, impeccably designed gowns she wears in all her other publicity photographs, further contradict Wharton's overt renunciation of this aspect of her identity. Sadly, conforming to the artistic template seems to have forced Wharton into the uncomfortable position of downplaying aspects of herself that gave her genuine pleasure. Her love of lace and hats and furs may have reminded her of a world in which she was made to feel inferior. Her beautiful clothes may have felt indelibly marked with the feminitude that had accompanied them in her early life. Or her interest in fashion may simply have seemed too frivolous to fit into the self-portrait of a woman writer who had always struggled to free herself from the label of "society novelist."

Wharton seems to have initially succeeded in publicly crafting a solitary, antifeminine, authorial image through her published life-writings. In the 1940s, Wharton's first biographer, Percy Lubbock, termed her trajectory as that of a "self-made man."[40] David Kirby's biography makes a similar claim about Grace King. He theorizes that King's work is often about women who transcend the boundaries of nineteenth-century femininity—including herself as depicted in her *Memories*—to become what King called "female men of action."[41] King's biographers all note that there weren't many southern female role models for King as she sought to find a scholarly career for herself. When she began to write, there was only one southern woman writer she really respected, Mary Noailles Murfree, who wrote under a male pseudonym (Charles Eggbert Craddock) like many Victorian women. Helen Taylor's feminist analysis of King's life focuses on the "repressive, reactionary influence of the genteel literary tradition," in contrast to the "liberalizing and liberating effect which the lives, works, and friendships of other woman writers were to have on her own."[42] King understood the sexual inflections—and ironies—involved in being known as a genius and noted in her journal, "There is no position so hard for a man of genius to maintain but dignity at being adored by women."[43] Even once King was established as a writer, Taylor notes the influence of gendered traditions on King's voice. Taylor analyzes the disparate voices King used in her letters to male and female correspondents, which Taylor labels as "self-deprecatory and flirtatious" with men and "honest" and "ambitio[us]" with women.[44] However, while King's letters reveal the power of southern feminitude, King's autobiography rejects it once and for all.

Both Wharton's and King's rejections of feminitude in their autobiographies are based on their claim to the identity of "artist." Wharton justifies this rejection throughout *A Backward Glance,* often through her choice of anecdote. In one of the stories she includes, a young doctor instructs his assistant to mix some chemicals for him, only to find the boy dead from the fumes. Investigating the death, the doctor discovers that the boy's heart had turned into a beautiful jewel. He brings it to his mistress, whose only reply is to insist that he get her another one, for she "wear[s] no ornaments but earrings." The cold and shallow mistress, a Philistine incapable of appreciating beauty for anything but a possession and insensitive to the suffering of others, represents the attitude of Old New York society to young Edith Jones's ambitions. The question Wharton asks in her memoir—whether or not the "indifference of everyone around [her]" had really "hindered" her as a writer—suggests that she ultimately fared better than both the doctor and the boy in the story.[45]

King's autobiography also contends that she transcended the gendered boundaries of the Old South. As an unmarried, grown daughter living at home, King's ambitions were subordinated to her gender. Again and again, King's *Memories* demonstrate how the social codes for a southern lady stood in direct conflict with her artistic calling. For instance, to pursue a literary career, King was compelled to transgress against southern codes of conduct for young ladies by writing an unsolicited letter to a man. Her motive, as she explains, was purely artistic: "The article touched me so vividly that I could not keep from writing to the author." When the author in question, Hamilton Mabie, came to call in response, King "was still so much embarrassed and shocked at my temerity in writing to a young man whom I did not know that I could not talk at my ease." This scene in *Memories of a Southern Woman of Letters* is analogous to Wharton's first awkward meetings with Henry James in *A Backward Glance.* In both autobiographies it becomes clear that breaking away from the social rules governing conventional feminine behavior was key to approaching famous writers like James and Mabie as fellow artists. Wharton and King ultimately had to choose between being conventional young ladies or aspiring artists, and their autobiographies attest to the inherent correctness of their decisions. Wharton's friendship with James is widely known as a bond between artists today, and as King notes in *Memories,* Mabie's "letters during twenty years never failed to give me encouragement" as she pursued her career.[46]

King had to confront many other barriers that being a traditional southern lady posed to her literary career, and she delineates some of them in her autobiography. Although King's mother did not oppose her daughter's writing and often used her social connections to network on her daughter's behalf, Mimi King still believed that, as a southern lady, Grace's responsibilities to the family came before everything else. Because of this, King's brothers assumed authority over her daily activities, and King often found herself quarreling with her mother, brothers, and sisters about domestic roles and responsibilities. After particularly significant disagreements when Mimi King rebuked Grace for not deferring her needs to those of her brothers, Grace would go out and ride the New Orleans streetcars for hours, too angry and hurt to return home but having nowhere else to go. Desperately seeking both emotional and financial independence in her early thirties, when King received the check for her first story, she wrote to her sister Nina that it was "the first really well satisfied moment of my life."[47] Although she first published it anonymously in deference to feminine modesty, once "Monsieur Motte" was well-received, King took public ownership of her work, which amounted to another step away from being a "lady" and toward being the "woman of letters" she later termed herself. Having announced her authorship, King then allowed her photo to be published for advertising purposes, which *Memories* explains was another taboo for a southern lady. Because of these decisions, King was included in a prestigious list of southern writers in 1887, and subsequently wrote, "My business activities increased and filled my life, which seemed already overflowing with social and family duties."[48] King's *Memories* implies that it took several transgressions against the definition of "lady" to bring King to the point where her writing could occupy a space equal to the gendered demands that the Old South and her family placed on her time.

Just as Wharton opposed the expectations of Old New York to her intellectual pursuits, King repeatedly drew the line between the traditions of her old southern family and her work as an artist. When recording the deaths of her mother and brothers in the autobiography, King notes that when she was deluged by family memories, she would become temporarily unable to read the books with which she surrounded herself. In one anecdote, King has to return home from a work-related trip because one of her uncles had died of gout. Back home, she describes his ornate glassware, procured by a "standing order from Tiffanys," remarking, "How small and insignificant now appeared all my jaunting among literary folk! What, after all, was literary success in comparison with good family ties?" Here, King's exclamatory use of "insignificant" rings false, as the tone and punctuation do not match the style of the chapter in which they are placed. Similarly odd tonal shifts recur throughout King's text, in passages like, "I was slightly overwhelmed by the honor of the invitation [from Macmillan, to contribute a book on New Orleans to his 'great cities' series] and felt that only by the blessing of Providence could I make a presentable appearance in the august company of the authors the series proposed."[49] It is interesting to note that King uses the language of a debutante to describe this intimidating literary endeavor—hoping to make a "presentable appearance." This is not the only instance where the code of feminitude in which King was raised slips into her *Memories:* when she was listed alongside famous names like George Washington Cable, Joel Chandler Harris, and Lafcadio Hearn in a *Harper's Monthly* article, King viewed it as "equivalent to the presentation of a debutante at court."[50] While King may have renounced southern feminitude, she could not wholly expunge it from her vocabulary. Or perhaps in applying debutante language to her inclusion in a community of authors, King is intentionally substituting literary significance for social success, as Wharton does in *A Backward Glance* when she implicitly compares herself to the "fashionable beauty" at that house party.

However, when King refers to herself as a "woman of letters" and not a "lady" in her autobiography, she is not merely renouncing the importance of social success. She is also directly confronting her mother's dictum about ladies not laboring. In her autobiography and elsewhere, King reveals an emphasis that amounts to a fascination with women who work. Taking a steamboat journey with her mentor and fellow writer Madame Blanc, King observes that "best of all, perhaps, to the overworked literary woman, were the days of rest" when they sat on the deck and watched the river go by.[51] One of King's *Balcony Stories,* "An Old Lady's Restoration," offers some insight into this question as well. In it, a formerly wealthy southern lady has descended into nearly abject poverty after the Civil War. However, when her family fortune is miraculously restored, the society friends who had ostracized her when she was poor come to visit, expecting her to indulge them by sharing her newly affordable luxuries. But because she has now learned what it is to work for money, the old lady has refined her understanding of what is necessary and what is luxurious and will not leave her new working-class community. The society ladies who visit her do not understand; they declare her insane and suggest she should be interned in a sanitarium. Perhaps King considered herself akin to the old lady in the story: perhaps she had seen too much and worked too hard to claim the title of lady either. Notably, King used the money from selling her first story to make the exact same purchase the old lady makes in the story. They both bought clean, cotton linens, ordinary household items that they had taken for granted until poverty placed them out of reach. Perhaps King's frustrations with her mother's insistence on King's pursuit of a rich suitor ultimately made King decide she would rather work for money than wait to marry it. *Memories* makes it clear that King preferred being an independent working woman to being a proper southern lady.

Wharton too ties her independence directly to her writing in *A Backward Glance,* going so far as to assert, "I had as yet no personality of my own. . . . I was not to acquire one till my first volume of short stories was published." Recalling the publication of two or three short stories in *Scribner's,* one of the more prestigious and best-known monthly magazines on the East Coast at that time, Wharton's seemingly incredulous repetitions of the word "I" in the pages following this revelation are significant and ingenuous: "*I* had written short stories that were worthy of preservation! Was it the same insignificant *I* that I had always known? My friends could not be more astonished and incredulous than I was." Yet her incredulity and insignificance are belied in the very next paragraph as she denounces a critic who condescended to criticize her stories for not beginning with dialogue. Wharton declared that even her insignificant I "knew that this was ridiculous. I had never consciously formulated the principles of my craft, but during my years of experimenting I had pondered on them deeply. . . . Every short story, I now saw, like every other work of art, contains within itself the germ of its own particular form and dimensions, and *ab ovo* is the artist's only rule." Although she calls herself an "insignificant I," the passage reveals a Wharton who is empowered by the very difference that made her feel insignificant in Old New York. Brushing off the "indifference" of her New York relations to her writing, Wharton reached a point in which she "no longer cared, for my recognition as a writer had transformed my life."[52] Wharton's autobiographical I has achieved independence and now has the authority to reject or accept those who do not acknowledge her point of view, just as King's old lady feels free to reject the worldview of her former friends. In both these autobiographies, *author*ity is conceived of as the opposite of feminitude.

While Wharton shifts from one I to another in *A Backward Glance* to denote her status as an author, King often shifts from "we" to "I" in *Memories* for the same purpose. This may be because, by the end of King's career, it was publicly known that her sisters' research supported Grace's writing. The last formal portrait of King as an artist, done six years before her death, reflects this: Grace sits in the foreground, upright and facing the viewer, holding a book in one hand, while Nan and Nina King read among piles and piles of books in the background, making the portrait into a triangle with Grace at the apex. However, in the autobiography, while King often uses the pronoun "we" in the text (always referring to herself and her sisters), the moments where her customary use of "we" suddenly is pared down to an individualized "I" demand attention and parallel Wharton's shift from a modest, insignificant I to an assertive, confident one.

These transitions are most frequent when King is emphasizing her artistic identity. For example, on her first trip to Europe with her sisters, King states, "We went at once to a little hotel much patronized by New Orleanians" but then leaves her sisters, while she goes to live in fellow writer Madame Blanc's apartments in a villa because "I was held by a longstanding promise" to stay with Blanc. During their stay in Oxford, King writes, "*We* lived such a peaceful and pleasant life. In the morning, we all retired to our rooms with our books; *I* with my work." When King is awarded an honorary doctorate from Tulane, she notes, "My sisters and I took the short ride over the city" to the university, where King alone "was conducted to the place reserved for *me* on the stage." However, she further observes, "One of my sisters has preserved the words of conference."[53] King either does not recall or does not feel it necessary to mention which sister did so.

Not only were her sisters essential to King's achievements, but her mother was as well. Grace King's most famous collection, *Balcony Stories,* is built on the New Orleans tradition of ladies sitting on their balconies whispering and gossiping to each other in the evenings when their husbands are out and their children are asleep nearby. They are primarily reimagined from stories that King was told by her mother and grandmother when she was very young. In her autobiography, King explains, "My mother had an appreciation of the romantic and picturesque in life that I have never seen equaled," so "the *Balcony Stories* had been gathering in my mind until I felt I must put them on paper to get relief from them. They wrote themselves." It appears that Mimi King was a powerful and talented storyteller, but King downplays this in her autobiography, feminizing and trivializing her mother's influence by referring to her as a "charming raconteuse" who "furnished spirited material for a writer." Like the portrait of Lucretia Jones in *A Backward Glance,* the brief impressions *Memories* gives us of Mimi King are heavily edited and somewhat misshapen. King's mother's influence is revealed in other writings that King left behind, such as the foreword to *Balcony Stories,* but King acknowledges it in only a sidelong manner in *Memories* by presenting her mother a copy of *New Orleans: The Place and the People,* a commissioned work in which King combined scholarly regional history with insightful explanations of local customs and cultural heritage, as a Christmas gift in 1895. As King acknowledges, it was Mimi King's unlimited knowledge of all the public and private doings of New Orleans society that made this book possible. However, that moment is quickly overshadowed in *Memories* by the fact that the Doubledays were inspired to travel to New Orleans and call on King because of the strength of her work. According to this chapter in her autobiography, the only role King's mother played in the visits of literary people was deciding for whom she would prepare her famous "salmi of turtle."[54]

King's narrative gaps, evasions, and trivializations in her depiction of Mimi King are similar in character to Wharton's treatment of her mother. *A Backward Glance* implies that Wharton had to shed her mother's influence in order to become a writer. Often, the mere voice Wharton uses to describe her mother condemns her. Wharton's references to her mother are usually characterized by a prosaic terseness, making Lucretia Jones seem like a rude intruder in *A Backward Glance.* Reminiscing about New York life early in the book, Edith Wharton interjects, "I may add that once, several years after my marriage, a new coachman, who did not know my mother's carriage by sight, accidentally drove me past it on the fashionable ocean drive at Newport, and that I had to hasten the next morning to apologize to my mother, whose only comment was, when I explained that the coachman could not have known the offence he was committing: 'You might have told him.'" The coldness implied in Wharton's mother's tone here is similar to the coldness that Wharton often adopts when speaking of her mother in her autobiography. In one key instance, the different tones Wharton uses in *A Backward Glance*—expansive and lyrical versus flat and dry—are set in dramatic juxtaposition with one another. When Wharton describes the cooking in her mother's household, we read that Wharton's mother, "if left to herself, would probably not have been much interested in the pleasures of the table . . . but to know about good cooking was a part of every young wife's equipment." Emphasizing her mother's prosaic approach to her duties, Wharton sets this minimalist description against the next sentences that portray cooking—when her mother is not involved—with the vividness of a painting. She launches into a much more expansive and lyrical description of their famous cooks, who "stand out, brilliantly turbaned and ear-ringed, from a Snyders-like background of game, fish, and vegetables transformed into a succession of succulent repasts by their indefatigable blue-nailed hands."[55] Compared to the family's cooks, and later to close friends like Henry James, Wharton's mother is treated coldly in the prose. With her petty attention to the etiquette of coach-driving and her perfunctory but uninspired knowledge of cooking, Lucretia Jones's worldview is defined by social rules and roles, epitomizing the circumscribed life that Wharton renounces in her official autobiography. The cursory attention Wharton's mother receives in the prose renders her nearly as insignificant as Old New York society made her daughter feel.

Wharton's renunciation of her mother's social legacy prefigures the disassociation of her marriage from her artistic identity in *A Backward Glance*. Edith Wharton's husband, Teddy Wharton, also receives curt treatment in the autobiography. Only one happy memory of their twenty-seven-year marriage is included: the cruise they took to the

Aegean. The trip, her idea, was "the greatest step forward in my making," she declares, but she enlarges much more on their traveling companion, James Van Alen, than the times she and her husband had together. For the most part, the memoir illustrates that being Teddy Wharton's wife was a barrier to her artistic pursuits. For instance, after a triumphant literary trip to London, Wharton observes, "I should have enjoyed intensely following up this first glimpse of success; but my husband was bored in London, where he would have been amused only among the sporting set, while I wanted to know the writers." Once, "lucky enough to be made welcome in the editorial groups of the *Revue de Paris* and the *Revue des Deux Mondes,*" Wharton remarks, "oddly enough, it was an old American friend of my husband's who enlarged my range in this direction." When she does meet writers through Teddy's connections, he embarrasses her. "During one of [Henry James's] visits . . . my husband imprudently blurted out an allusion to 'Edith's new story,'" she remarks. Throughout the last half of the memoirs, Wharton's husband mostly figures in asides referring to the varying moves necessitated by his illness or instability. Without making any direct statement, Wharton implies that Teddy's companionship was not personally fulfilling and did not nurture her as an artist. Delineating places where they considered living together, she writes, "in none could I hope to find the kind of human communion I cared for." What "would have made me happy," she explains, was "a house and garden of my own." Hinting that "I should have preferred London," she characterizes their move to Paris: "It was easy to go south for the sunshine when the weather grew too damp for my husband." Wharton here reverts to feminine autobiographical tradition, showing a well-mannered delicacy in her handling of the situation. She characterizes the marriage negatively without directly attacking her husband. Instead, she wistfully mentions the happiness, the communion, and the self-determination that she could not find with him. The dissolution of the Whartons' marriage in *A Backward Glance* is much less discussed than the ends of Gertrude Atherton's, Charlotte Perkins Gilman's, or Mary Austin's marriages in their respective autobiographies. Wharton neglects to mention their divorce, for which she filed, except through a shift in pronoun, skimming over it in speaking of the Paris flat: "*We* hired a Paris flat and there *I* remained till 1920."[56]

King also excises difficult familial relationships that were detrimental to her career from *Memories.* During the time in which King was publicly establishing her own new identity as a literary success, her life at home was growing increasingly difficult due to her brother Will's alcoholism. Not only did his condition cause great emotional pain to the entire family, but it created financial strain, as his drinking prevented him from supporting his wife and children. King deeply and actively resented Mimi King's creed that "a Southern lady must always forgive and accept the selfishness of men."[57] While you would be hard pressed to catch more than a hint of this in *Memories,* it consumed many of King's private reflections in her journals. Mimi enabled Will's drinking in what Grace considered an outrageous fashion, and her journal speculates that this enabling "would drain us of our last cent. She [Mimi] would crush the life out of us" by "taking his part and putting his needs before everyone else's." In another journal entry entitled "Subjects for a Southern Novel," King castigates the "reckless extravagance" of southern men; more specifically, she calls out "Brothers—who let their sisters toil at home in wearysome unremitted drudgery . . . these brothers drinking themselves drunk on champagne."[58] When Will died (possibly by suicide, as he was found in a locked room with the gas jet on), King had to spend a significant portion of her literary earnings making up for her brother's financial and personal failures. She became the guardian of Will's son and provided for his upbringing and education.[59] Just as Wharton skims over Teddy's instabilities and perfidies in *A Backward Glance,* King minimizes the strain of Will's alcoholism and Mimi's enabling, as well as Grace's sister Nina's neurosis in her autobiography. Although *Memories* usually refers to the sisters Nan and Nina together, King's journals and letters make it clear that Grace also struggled with her sister Nina's embrace of Mimi King's ideals. Grace compared Nina to an "English governess . . . [who] has a despairing hope that I may still turn out to be a prim, well-behaved little lady someday."[60] But *Memories* merely notes that, on their final trip to Europe, Grace paid to place Nina in a sanitarium, sliding delicately away from decades of strain in their relationship just as delicately as Wharton slips away from Teddy in her brief mention of the Paris flat.

Just as the Grace King who appears in *Memories* divests herself of the family relationships that suppressed her freedom to work, Wharton's *A Backward Glance* implies that both Wharton's husband and her mother misunderstood her creative drive. Even when Edith cannot deny that these two people helped her develop as a writer, her autobiography robs them of agency. Telling of these early relationships in which she was subject to their rules (in the case of her mother) and needs (in the case of her husband), Wharton exercises her new artistic authority by turning the tables on them or rendering them ineffectual. Whenever Lucretia Jones or Teddy Wharton furthered her progress toward becoming a writer, she paints their influences as either incidental or accidental. When her mother gives Edith the volumes of Keats and Shelley that made the "gates of the realm [swing] wide," Wharton explains that the gift was the result of her mother's "despairing" request to a Mr. North at Scribner's to tell her "what she could give the child for her birthday." And while Wharton explains that "by denying me the opportunity of wasting my time over ephemeral rubbish my mother threw me back on the great classics, and thereby helped to give my mind a temper which my too easy studies could not have produced," she qualifies this acknowledgment with the following explanation:

> My mother, perplexed by the discovery that she had produced an omnivorous reader, and not knowing how to direct my reading, had perhaps expected the governess to do it for her. Being an indolent woman, she

> finally turned the difficulty by reviving a rule of her own schoolroom days, and decreeing that I should never read a novel without her permission. . . . In order to save further trouble she almost always refused to let me read it—a fact hardly to be wondered at, since her own mother had forbidden her to read any of Scott's novels, except "Waverly," till after she was married.

Passages like these dramatize what Wharton might have been had she fallen into line with the women of her family. The homogeneity of Wharton's female ancestry is emphasized in *A Backward Glance:* of her mother and aunts, she writes, "like all young ladies of their day," they learned languages, fine work, and drawing, and "suffered" the same "sick headaches."[61] Wharton's assertions of independence and isolation from her mother and other women are part of a strategy to present herself as an individual and an artist. As with King's treatment of her mother and brother in *Memories,* Wharton's brief depictions of her mother and husband assign them to the realm of insignificance; in *A Backward Glance,* they are mere objects to her subject. Perhaps Wharton and King are also wreaking a bit of revenge on these family members for the control they temporarily exerted over the writers' lives.

This vengeance, however, was mitigated by two things. According to biographer Shari Benstock, one of them was a commandment issued to little Edith Newbold Jones by her mother: always be polite. But the other one was located directly in Wharton's own disapproval of another new trend in women's autobiography, represented in Margaret Anderson's and Gertrude Atherton's 1930 and 1931 texts, which are probably the unnamed books that disgusted Wharton, those which "set down in detail every defect and absurdity in others, and every resentment in the writer." In fact, though her mother and husband are condemned by implication, Wharton's complaints about them are quite restrained in comparison to the way other autobiographers of the decade handled the same topics. "Life and I" gives an indication of one hurt Wharton omitted to mention: that her mother refused to explain to her what would happen on her wedding night, and that the consequences of her sexual ignorance were devastating. However, Wharton leaves this painful episode out of *A Backward Glance.* As if to illustrate the concept of a "book [of old hurts] I seldom open," Wharton remains silent where she might have more roundly condemned Lucretia Jones and Teddy Wharton.[62] She merely renounces their importance by treating them minimally and excluding their photos from the memoir.

Although the artistic identity that Wharton and King construct in *A Backward Glance* and *Memories of a Southern Woman of Letters* silences some of their personal memories, it does allow them to focus on the friendships they formed with other artists. After publishing *The Greater Inclination,* Wharton recalls, "I was overmastered by the longing to meet people who shared my interests. . . . What I wanted above all was to get to know other writers, to be welcomed among people who lived for the things I had always secretly lived for." In defining herself in relationship to a new, continental, more cultured community, Wharton claims her right to belong. This pattern of self-representation is shown early in her description of her writing career: she begins a paragraph with, "Among the friendships then made I should like to record with particular gratitude," and concludes it with, "I feel that I have never properly expressed my appreciation of their helpfulness. Their intelligent collaboration gave *Italian Villas* its chief value, and I like to recall the joy I had in making the book by naming the friends who helped me." These gracious lists of friends and acquaintances abound in the latter half of *A Backward Glance.* About her visits in London, she comments, "I should be ungrateful not to add to their names" or "I should be sorry to leave out the names of any to whom I am thus indebted." Talking of her visits to the famous Parisian salon hostess Countess Rosa de Fitz-James's drawing room, she considers the "lists of names" and contemplates which academicians are "entitled to be named first." As the text progresses, Wharton's earlier identities as daughter and wife in *A Backward Glance* are renounced in favor of her more "significant" identity as an artist. In the drawing rooms of London or the salons of Paris, her identity as a writer opens doors for her. She dismisses Henry James's claim that he gave her the idea to "do New York!" which resulted in her first overwhelmingly successful novel, *The House of Mirth.* Instead, she writes, "Fate had planted me in New York, and my instinct as a storyteller counselled me to use the material nearest to hand, and most familiarly my own."[63] As passages such as these suggest, Wharton seeks to dispel the notion that she was James's disciple. Instead, she presents an equal interchange of ideas between friends.

As it did in her early descriptions of "making up," Wharton's prose becomes warmer and more lyrical in the passages praising her friends, again providing a stylistic contrast to the voice she uses when she writes of her mother, husband, or Old New York. With these friends her creative imagination is nurtured and she infuses the prose with images similar to those she used to describe the world of making up. She is in a grown-up "land of enchantment" this time, a "land of letters," as scholar Susan Goodman puts it.[64] In passages where Wharton is discussing her friends instead of herself, she is more expansive than in other parts of the autobiography, reveling in her memories. One can read the change in tone as she and Countess Fitz-James motor through Spain, or as she and Geoffrey Scott explore Tuscany and Umbria. Scott was both a poet and an architectural historian, so their shared interests in beauty and design made them ideal touring companions. (Not only did Wharton design or renovate several magnificent homes for herself but she also wrote and published *The Decoration of Houses* with another friend, architect Ogden Codman, in 1914.) Wharton can "find no words delicate and imponderable enough to describe the Psyche-like tremor of those folded but never quiet wings" of Minnie Bourget, a close friend of Wharton's who was the wife of the influential French novelist and cultural critic Paul Bourget, and thus one more example of how becoming a successful author opened the doors for Wharton to find the true friends and kindred spirits she had not found in the glittering but superficial social circles of Old New York. According to *A Backward Glance,* Minnie Bourget's death made Wharton feel as if "a part of me is dead also." Wharton basks in the "irradiation" of Henry James's genius and describes conversation with him as having "a cobweb bridge flung from his mind" to his listeners.[65] The treatment of her friends—in sharp contrast to that of her mother and husband—pays tribute to who they were.

Yet, in this flurry of tributes, Edith Wharton's "I" nearly disappears. In a maneuver that allows her to avoid appearing immodest, Wharton's persona fades into the background again once she establishes her significance as an author. These sections more closely resemble the way that women have traditionally constructed their autobiographical selves in relationship to one or several "others." In these passages, Wharton's very personality is defined by intellectual community. "What is one's personality," she asks, "detached from that of the friends with whom fate has linked one?" For instance, Wharton describes her sense of humor only indirectly, through her friendship with James, remarking on the "real marriage of true minds is for any two people to possess a sense of humour or irony pitched in exactly the same key." In passages about her friends, she uses "us" more often than "I," deriving her identity from her acceptance by her friends. In the chapter on Henry James, she speaks of "what I have called the inner group. In this group an almost immediate sympathy had established itself between the various members, so that our common stock of allusions, cross references, pleasantries was always increasing, and new waves of interest in the same book or picture, or any sort of dramatic event in life or letters would simultaneously flood through our minds."[66] There is a possibility that Wharton is using this technique strategically, rhetorically.

Like many female autobiographers before her, she can efface herself and avoid discussion of her private life by focusing instead on others. Although she modestly fades into the background in these sections, describing instead her friends, her inclusion in these circles is still an unmistakable sign that she has "arrived."

King's book utilizes the same strategy. A number of chapters in her autobiography are odes to public figures, scholars, and writers like local Pastor Doctor Palmer (chapter 2); prominent New England writer, abolition activist, and feminist Julia Ward Howe (chapter 3); and Charles Dudley Warner, the editor of *Harper's* (chapter 5), in whose work or wisdom she presumably found inspiration and support. Indeed, it was King's friendship with Warner that opened the most doors for her as a writer. When he invited her to visit his home in Hartford, Connecticut, her stay there confirmed her ambitions and introduced her to some of the most powerful and important American literary figures of that time, including Mark Twain, Sarah Orne Jewett, Mary Wilkins Freeman, Ruth McEnery Stuart, and even the redoubtable William Dean Howells. When she meets the editor of *Harper's,* Henry Alden, King calls it "one of the great events of my life." Like Wharton, King downplays both money and fame in her *Memories,* expressing her belief that the true "reward for a literary life" was "the friendships one acquired." King heavily emphasizes the scholarly nature of her work by highlighting her friendships with male professors, forged when she was invited to give lectures for the Louisiana Historical Society, as much as with fellow writers throughout the second half of her autobiography.[67]

However, like Wharton's, King's autobiography makes it clear that she is no acolyte but an equal and confident voice among these companions. In *Memories,* King also highlights the stories that she wrote in order to correct the flaws she finds in others' work. One of her earliest stories was inspired by a "taunt" from an editor who supported the stories of George Washington Cable, whose writing King abhorred.

Unable to sleep, King decides to "show Mr. Gilder that we in New Orleans . . . are not entirely dependent upon Mr. George Cable's pen!" She writes a tale to do just that but then mails it anonymously, "certain it would be refused immediately." Other chapters read like lists of tributes to writers and scholars whom King has known, for, as she notes at the beginning of chapter 14, "the reward for a literary life came not from money or fame but from the friendships that one acquired."[68] Just as Wharton would do, King leaves little room in her autobiography for either her private life or her private thoughts. In fact, the last one hundred pages of King's text reads like a list of obituaries.

Yet, though the relational, self-effacing nature of these passages seems to align with feminine autobiographical traditions, the friendships Wharton and King emphasize tend to bolster the "self-made man" or "female man of action" personas. In building an intellectual persona, King also regularly associates herself with professors in *Memories* but decidedly distances herself from popular female novelists like Ouida and Vernon Lee, slighting them in her descriptions of their brief encounters in Italy.[69] At other times in the text, King abruptly transitions from a lengthy focus on someone else to suddenly take center stage in the narration. For instance, at the end of a four-page description of the burial of an old friend, botany professor Reginald Somers-Cocks, she appends what may seem like a non sequitur to conclude the chapter, informing the reader that she was made a fellow in the Royal Society of England that same year. The sentence feels like an awkward sleight of hand: look at the wonderful accomplishments of our wonderful deceased friend, and by the way, here's one of mine.

While both Madame Blanc and Charles Warner were decidedly more influential in launching and supporting King's career than Mark Twain, her *Memories* emphasizes her friendship with him more heavily. King and Twain admired each other's intellect. *Memories* indicates that she believed he had a place among the greats in American literature before the rest of the literary world did, and that he believed greatly in her talent, not only encouraging her in their correspondence but introducing her to other influential literary figures. King was a regular guest in Clemens's family circle, both in the United States and in Italy, and Mark Twain's daughters considered her an honorary sibling. King became especially close to Twain's wife, Olivia, with whom she corresponded for years, but King's autobiography focuses more on Twain himself, including reprints of letters he wrote to her. *Memories* quotes Twain's family only to support her opinion of Twain. Just as Wharton opposes her friendship with James to the values of Old New York, so King opposes her friendship with Twain to the customs of the Old South. On a return visit with Twain, she "found myself talking to him in the frank, free way of an old friend, without any reservation or reticence."[70] Just as Wharton's relationship with James in *A Backward Glance* indicates that she had "found [her]self" as a writer, so does King's "frank, free" conversation with Twain.[71]

Wharton edited her relationships in *A Backward Glance* to create a similarly distorted effect, blending herself into a habitual group composed mostly of men. As Susan Goodman observes, "In *A Backward Glance* Wharton left posterity with an incomplete image of herself surrounded by a series of appreciative men. . . . Where are the women whose friendships also sustained Wharton? Where are Sally Norton, Daisy Chanler, Mary Cadwalader Jones, Beatrix Farrand, and Elisina Tyler?" Wharton corresponded as much with Norton as with any of her male correspondents for more than twenty years. These women formed her closest friendships, but there seems to be no room in the autobiographical persona that Wharton constructs in *A Backward Glance* to discuss them. Goodman speculates that Wharton may have been drawn to the "power and authority" the men represented, and it is quite likely the same was true of King.[72] However, it may also be because the shared experiences that bind female friendships were not the experiences these women felt were appropriate for literary autobiography. For one thing, these relationships may have been too intimate to invoke, to describe. An offhand comment in King's *Memories* sheds credence to this possibility. She writes of a time in her life when "I wrote along contentedly . . . seeing no one and talking to no one but my sister Nannie, who was merely my other self."[73] While this may read as dismissive of Nannie now, it was probably not intended to be. It may simply be that because this intimate sisterhood was King's everyday support system, talking about it would have played down the challenges, barriers, and individual achievements that were prerequisite plot elements for literary autobiography. Under similar pressures to highlight and preserve their serious reputations, King and Wharton edited their lives as if they were cutting them from the same pattern.

Just as Wharton seems to verbally renounce many of her most sustained female friendships by leaving them out of her autobiography, King renounces the South much more overtly in *Memories.* Scholar Katherine Capshaw Smith observes that in *Memories,* "King rarely depicts herself as living in New Orleans, in Louisiana, in the South, or even in the United States."[74] Although King spent less than five years of her life in Europe, her descriptions of those three trips make up nearly two-thirds of the book. In King's case, focusing on those trips may have served multiple purposes. First, she could not write much about her life at home without violating her pride and her family's privacy. However, she also may have minimized and excised New Orleans from her *Memories* because she considered it as insignificant in light of her career as she had been made to feel as an unmarried daughter living at home. Like Wharton's, King's tone also transforms itself based on the topic, and King's tone is often sardonic when she speaks of New Orleans. Calling on a friend upon her return from her second trip to Europe, King remarks, "Did we talk about Europe and what I had seen and done over there? Not at all. We talked about New Orleans—its news, political, social, and religious. That was what interested her more than anything Europe held." Over and over, King reveals her conflicted feelings about the South through shifts in tone.

For instance, after having had to talk of home one night at dinner in Antwerp, they turn from the trivial "gay chat of the table" to "again lighting the taper of our enthusiasm before the altar of Rembrandts and Rubens." Like Old New York in *A Backward Glance,* the frivolous, shallow South depicted in *Memories* is no place for artists and intellectuals. *Memories* explains that even when northern papers gave her books "splendid notices . . . the Southern papers hardly noticed it."[75] As Wharton's tone distances herself from the Philistines of Old New York, King dissociates herself from the lack of intellectualism in the South where her books were not popular, she explains, because books in general were not popular. As she acerbically commented to a friend, "Books are of no account in the South, I am sorry to say. The Macmillans do not count upon New Orleans at all in the sale of my books."[76] It also galled her that New Orleans promptly forgot her mentor, Charles Gayarre, noting his death "created hardly a ripple of interest in the city in which he had lived and which he had loved." Perhaps King worried that if Gayarre's passing only made a "ripple" in the current of New Orleans's consciousness, her own death might go completely unnoticed there. Thus, *Memories* may also present King's bid for her work to be established and valued nationally in case the South neglected her. King's autobiography quotes a review of *The Pleasant Ways of St. Medard* that speculates, "Will not its exquisite shades of feeling, delicate in vibrating sadness, give the novel a permanent place in American classics?" Further, King ends her *Memories* with the inscription of a silver cup she had recently received: "Scholar, Historian, Essayist, Writer of Fiction," emphasizing the range of her intellectual contributions.[77]

Wharton's autobiography also tries to divorce her work from narrow, regional interpretations, especially from the label of "society novelist." *A Backward Glance* directly answers criticism about *Ethan Frome* and *The House of Mirth,* stating, "There could be no greater critical ineptitude than to judge a novel according to *what it ought to have been about,*" and mocking the "absurdity" of the charge that she put real people into her novels. She rails against the "puerile form of criticism" exercised by American readers who "snatched at" her books merely out of curiosity about which of the "heroes and heroines of the society column are to be found in it." Like King, Wharton defines her motives and work broadly: "The greatest service a writer can render to letters is to follow his own conscience," she writes. "I thought I owed it to less lucky colleagues to fight for the independence they might not always be in a position to assert." As an independent artist, she links literary criticism with the market—both are necessary evils, it seems, but neither is of real importance: "If one has sought the publicity of print, and sold one's wares in the open market, one has sold to the purchasers the right to think what they choose about one's books; and the novelist's best safeguard is to put out of his mind the quality of praise or blame bestowed on him by reviewers and readers, and to write only for that dispassionate and ironic critics who dwells within the breast."[78] Although, in reality, Wharton cared a great deal about her critical notices, *A Backward Glance* adds criticism to the growing list of petty concerns she renounces as beneath the true artist.

Through their rhetorical renunciations, Wharton and King created fluctuating autobiographical personas, insignificant and significant, solitary and communal, that adroitly shift throughout *A Backward Glance* and *Memories of a Southern Woman of Letters.* In writing the story of their lives as artists, these two women privileged male autobiographical tradition, censoring the ironic, passionate voices we find in their more intimate drafts, journals, and correspondence, and omitting much of their personal lives, relationships, and struggles. The gaps between the truth of these women's lives and the gender ideologies of the regions in which they grew up is effectively mirrored by the gaps in their autobiographies. But while it has often been viewed negatively in the study of women's lives, silence can also signify power. In these two autobiographies, Wharton's and King's multiple silences signify their artistic control over the shapes of their lives and their renunciations of the ideologies and the people who might once have held them back. Their self-censorship was purposeful, for through it they transcended the dying cultures—Old New York and the Old South—that once made them feel insignificant and enslaved to the legacies of feminitude. Ultimately, *A Backward Glance* and *Memories of a Southern Woman of Letters* give us compelling and innovative portraits of the schism between Wharton's and King's two identities. As famous writers they had gained mastery, confidence and freedom, and as female literary autobiographers in the 1930s they faced a new, intimidating, uncomfortable task. Writing into this gap engendered texts that strain between multiple autobiographical traditions, tones, and personas, none of which could possibly have contained the whole truths about their lives.

Chapter 2

Daring Denunciations

Celebrity Drama in Gertrude Atherton's *Adventures of a Novelist* and Margaret Anderson's *My Thirty Years' War*

BY THE end of 1932, Gertrude Atherton's autobiography, *Adventures of a Novelist* (1931), had gone into a third edition. Since *Adventures* read more like a celebrity memoir than an artist's bildung, a division of Doubleday called Blue Ribbon Books had issued a one-dollar reprint of the book, believing it would make appealing reading for a mass audience. As did her contemporaries Grace King and Edith Wharton, Atherton wrote her memoirs near the end of her career; however, Atherton's book has little in common with other writers of her generation. In fact, *Adventures* bears a striking resemblance in tone to the memoirs of a much younger woman, Margaret Anderson, best known for her work as editor of the literary journal *Little Review.* Because of the growing demand for literary memoirs, Anderson published *My Thirty Years' War,* the first of her three autobiographies, in 1930, when she was in her early forties. If Wharton's and King's autobiographies are largely exercises in renunciation, exhibiting deft rhetorical maneuvers around sensitive or painful parts of their pasts, Atherton's and Anderson's are constructed along opposite lines, as exercises in daring and denunciation. The boldness of Atherton's and Anderson's memoirs stands in such sharp contrast to Wharton's and King's autobiographical reserve that it is difficult to comprehend how these texts were published within three years of each other in the same genre. Only the oppositional values of the artistic and celebrity templates for authorship can illuminate the dramatic differences between them.

Falling within both the "artistic" cultural template and the "genteel" autobiographical tradition, Wharton's and King's texts disdained to entertain readers, causing their reviewers to complain about the lack of "storytelling" and "dramatic incident" in *A Backward Glance* and *Memories of a Southern Woman of Letters.* Atherton's and Anderson's texts, by contrast, align themselves more with the "celebrity" template for authorship; they prioritize the creation and depiction of drama in their autobiographies. Atherton's flamboyant autobiographical persona more closely resembles that of a Hollywood celebrity than that of a "lady novelist," while the skirmishes in Anderson's "war" also sound like incidents one might see onscreen. With episodes such as Atherton's runaway elopement with her mother's fiancé, or Anderson selling her silk negligees to buy a train ticket to Chicago, these two autobiographies do not suffer from the "lack of dramatic incident" that was attributed to Wharton's and King's texts. Because of their constant evocation of both verbal and narrative drama, Atherton's and Anderson's autobiographies feel rather capricious. They jump from incident to scandalous incident, sometimes without preamble, context, or transition, occasionally dwindling into amusing but heartless character sketches of the authors' famous acquaintances. Their flamboyant and fast-paced autobiographies have a filmic feel. The personas their life-writings invoke embody Grace King's observation about publicity-seeking writers who apparently "wish to be an *art* rather than artists."[1] In fact, Anderson's autobiography openly ascribes to this approach: delineating her editorial method for the *Little Review,* she wrote that she "always accepted or rejected manuscripts on one basis: art as the person, An artist is an exceptional person."[2]

Both *Adventures of a Novelist* and *My Thirty Years' War* seem determined to demonstrate their authors' exceptionalism, regardless of the cost to dignity or decorum. Given Wharton's remarks in the preface to *A Backward Glance,* which she was writing when Atherton's and Anderson's texts were published, it is likely that Wharton's text is more constrained in both content and tone than it might otherwise have been because it was partially designed to repudiate these two dramatic, arrogant autobiographies. While Wharton chose not to openly acknowledge Atherton's existence in her autobiography or elsewhere, Atherton considered herself to be Wharton's greatest rival among American literary women and was equally as famous as Wharton—or perhaps more so—in her lifetime. However, unlike Wharton's, Atherton's literary reputation fluctuated wildly throughout her fifty-year career. Although she was arguably the most read woman writer of her generation, Atherton was rarely referred to as a preeminent woman of letters like Edith Wharton, Willa Cather, Mary Austin, or Grace King.[3] The English considered her the equivalent of an American Marie Corelli, a popular British romance novelist whom high modernists sometimes used as a foil to distinguish mass fiction from "literature." At several points in her career, Atherton decided to aspire to "serious literary fiction," starting with *The Doomswoman* in 1893.[4] However, *Doomswoman* did not sell well, despite great reviews. Atherton's autobiography briefly notes this quandary: she declares herself "flattered" to place a novel in *Lippincott's,* only to quickly observe that the magazine wasn't "particularly generous" to its contributors.[5]

While she does not acknowledge this in her *Adventures,* Atherton would often use the money from writing potboilers and articles for Hearst publications to buy her time to write books that were of higher literary quality. In 1919, Atherton went to Hollywood to find a way to "reinvent herself."[6] Her time there paid off, resulting in new publicity, including an interview wherein she compared herself to a "prima donna," and in new paychecks: by the end of her life, seven of Atherton's novels were made into films.[7] *Adventures* reveals that Atherton was aware there were distinctions between getting attention and earning respect, but she appears to have been primarily concerned with keeping her image fresh and maintaining financial independence. In the early 1920s, Atherton underwent the Steinach treatment, which was intended to make aging women feel young again by subjecting their ovaries to mild radiation treatments; her bestselling 1923 novel, *Black Oxen,* based partially on her own experience with the treatment—to which she proudly confessed in the press—became a popular film depicting a woman's mysterious physical and sexual regeneration in middle age.[8] When her historical novel of ancient Greece, *The Immortal Marriage* (1927)—a book as assiduously researched as some of Grace King's historical work—was assigned by college professors, Atherton felt briefly "legitimized" as a "learned woman of letters." However, her efforts to continue in the same scholarly vein failed when the stock market crashed.[9]

Ultimately, she was viewed as a legitimate artist only in limited circles. For example, she founded a PEN chapter in San Francisco, California, her hometown, in the 1920s, but the New York PEN rejected her application.[10] Despite the dramatic fluctuations of her reputation, Atherton's autobiography spends a good deal of time quoting from favorable reviews of her work. These include a blurb that described her as "America's most intellectual novelist," fellow writer Harold Frederic's comment that she had "a clearer vocation to write novels than any woman I know of," Dr. Robertson Nicoll's placement of her as the "leading woman novelist," and William Sharp's praise for her "true realism."[11] In 1934, after her autobiography revived some name recognition for her, Atherton finally and triumphantly had a collection of stories entitled *The Foghorn* published by the highly respected firm of Houghton Mifflin, which had turned down her first novel forty years earlier.[12]

Atherton's persona in *Adventures of a Novelist* seems to have flummoxed reviewers more thoroughly than any other 1930s autobiography. Mary Ellen Chase of *Commonweal* called *Adventures* "a baffling book," going to explain her reasons: "It is irritating in its egoism and cock-sureness, repelling through its bad taste, barren through its total lack of anything remotely spiritual; it is filled with prejudices, which make one skeptical as to the judgments of its author. . . . It reveals a personality energetic, fearless, adventuresome, but cold and basically selfish."[13] Chase was not alone in her reaction. Arthur Waugh's review scolds Atherton for her "offences against good taste," declaring, "There are some tales that good manners refrain from telling."[14] The reviewer in the *New Yorker* pronounced, "She has enjoyed much popular success and—quite sensibly—asks for nothing more."[15] The very title of Dorothy Van Doren's review critiques Atherton's pretentiousness: while Atherton claimed she was the reincarnation of Aspasia, an influential and glamorous woman from Ancient Greece, Van Doren entitled her review "Not Quite Aspasia."[16] Others termed the book "unusually frank," "very outspoken," "relentless," and "caustic."[17] One tactfully noted, "It is unfortunate for Mrs. Atherton that so many books of reminiscence . . . have recently appeared. . . . Those written with a richer understanding of the cultural life of the day, afford us a measure of just how much of that life Mrs. Atherton missed."[18] Isabel Patterson defended Atherton, writing, "She does not spare herself, so that her ruthless criticism of others may be forgiven," but Arthur Colton felt that "Mrs. Atherton's rather hit or miss combativeness leads one to take exceptions."[19] Perhaps Atherton's reviews illustrate what modern literary scholar Lois Palken Rudnick has observed: "Readers demand of female biographical subjects a 'niceness' that has never been expected of men."[20]

The "cock-sure" persona that Chase's review identifies was almost unheard of in women's literary autobiography until Atherton's and Anderson's memoirs were published. This new phenomenon generated considerable comment, even when it came from a much younger writer like Margaret Anderson. In her review of *My Thirty Years' War*, Fanny Butcher referred to Anderson as "the most egocentric [mind] that literature or its labors has produced during this generation."[21] Another reviewer called Anderson "one of those clever exhibitionists who claims to be fighting for the freedom of the artist and who is actually exploiting only her own ego."[22] Anderson, however, reveled in being known as an exhibitionist, considering exhibitionism to be a clever strategy of self-promotion. In *My Thirty Years' War,* she explains, "Exhibitionism merely means choosing one phase of your personality for conscious and intelligent exploitation."[23] Anderson's unabashed embrace of exhibitionism helps provide context for some of Grace King's privately expressed concerns about the exhibitionism of certain unnamed authors. Other writers, such as Harriet Monroe, tried to be diplomatic. In Monroe's review of *My Thirty Years' War* in the November 1930 issue of *Poetry,* she merely notes that "one misses in [Anderson's] career a certain human feeling and depth of human thinking." Some reviewers simply called Anderson's book "arrogant" or "irritating," pointing out Anderson's "errors of perspective and taste."[24] However, certain reviews—particularly those written by younger, female reviewers—appeared to take this egotism in stride. Despite Anderson's exhibitionism—or rather because of it—Butcher found *My Thirty Years' War* "alluring" and labeled it "the most amusing book of the spring," while Babette Deutsch called it "lively," "continuously interesting," and "much what you would expect a self-portrait of this extraordinary woman to be."[25] Other readers were willing to tolerate the arrogance and rudeness within *My Thirty Years' War* because it rang true to Anderson's character. For instance, Louise Kronenberger postulates that "as a writer [Anderson] is (one guesses) the same as she is a person."[26] Likewise, Sherwood Anderson called the book "a flash-back of [Anderson] herself."[27]

The tone of Anderson's *My Thirty Years' War* is just as self-assured as that of Atherton's autobiography. Purportedly "a record of . . . refusals," Anderson's book begins, "You're always being suppressed if you're inspired and always pushed into a corner if you're exceptional.

I won't be cornered and I won't be suppressed."[28] Since Anderson was best known for her work as editor of the *Little Review,* she published *My Thirty Years' War* the year after the magazine ceased publication, while the scandal of her arrest for publishing banned sections of James Joyce's *Ulysses* was still relatively fresh in public memory.[29] Her primary motivation for writing the book was financial, a way to capitalize on both the market for autobiography and her personal notoriety.

Anderson grew up in the American Midwest, in Indiana and Ohio, moving to Chicago when she was still a teenager, then to New York, and finally to Europe in her continual quest for an exciting life. Scholar Ian Hamilton characterizes her as "an eager, arrogant, and rather beautiful girl from the backwoods," as well as an accomplished, enthusiastic pianist who would come to believe that music could be a form of imagist art, just as new movements in visual art, such as cubism, were considered to be stylistically influenced by the imagist movement in poetry. Hugh Ford notes that those who knew her as a child claimed she was always "wild" and "impetuous" and found Midwestern life claustrophobic.[30] Having dropped out of the Western College for Women after three years, Anderson moved to Chicago with her sister Lois, interviewing celebrities and writing occasional book reviews until the exorbitant bills the girls charged at the city's department stores forced their parents to bring them back home. Margaret wangled a second chance at city life by securing a job in a bookshop that led to work as a reviewer and assistant editor, first with the *Dial* and then for the *Continent.* Frustrated in having to conform to public taste, Anderson eventually decided to publish her own magazine and used her existing contacts in artistic circles to talk up her idea, networking at parties in the belief that she would eventually convince someone to fund her dream. Her confidence in her powers of attraction and persuasion were well placed. The first issue of the *Little Review* was published in March 1914, and for a while the magazine was partially funded by a monthly pledge of support from Chicago journalist DeWitt Wing and about $450 in initial advertising contracts. A rather amorphous publication, the *Little Review* found a temporary focus when Anderson attended a lecture by Emma Goldman and made it an instrument of anarchism in May 1914. Later that year, Anderson met Amy Lowell and started to include imagism in the magazine, reprinting part of Ezra Pound's *Des Imagists.*

Pleased at the notoriety that both the anarchism and imagism caused, Anderson kept the magazine going on each track through 1915, but due to a visit from the police after she printed an editorial inciting readers to violence and arson, there was no January 1916 issue. Under financial pressure, Anderson left Chicago to pursue a cheaper lifestyle, camping with her divorced sister Lois, Lois's children, and a maid on Lake Bluff. According to Hamilton, "the encampment . . . attracted just the publicity she needed," and by April 1916, Anderson had two thousand subscribers for the *Little Review.* More importantly, she had met Jane Heap, who would reignite Anderson's flagging enthusiasm for the project, become her live-in partner for four years, and serve as her coeditor for the *Little Review* for four additional years until 1924.[31] In September 1916, Anderson and Heap took a long sojourn to California and published a notorious issue with thirteen blank pages bemoaning the dearth of meaningful art. Anderson had abandoned anarchism by then, and they only published three more issues before April 1917. By May 1917, Ezra Pound had become the *Little Review*'s foreign editor, and though his recommendations were often in conflict with Jane Heap's ideals, his vision and the original work he brought to the magazine—including his own, T. S. Eliot's, William Carlos Williams's, William Butler Yeats's, and James Joyce's—dominated its most impactful era. After Anderson and Heap moved to New York, Pound's influence and the publication of about half of James Joyce's *Ulysses* from March 1918 through most of 1920 brought national notoriety but canceled subscriptions. *My Thirty Years' War* records that "the subscription list dwindled during the whole of the L.R.'s best period." With the *Ulysses* issues burned at the post office on four occasions, Anderson and Heap were eventually brought to trial, fingerprinted, and fined one hundred dollars for purveying obscenity to the public in 1921. The last three active years of the *Little Review* (1924–1927) were exclusively edited by Jane Heap, as Anderson left to travel to Europe as accompanist and companion to her new crush, singer Georgette LeBlanc. Between 1927 and 1929, only two issues of the *Little Review* were published, at which point Heap finally agreed with Anderson that "there had been enough of this."[32]

My Thirty Years' War is largely Anderson's colorful account of the behind-the-scenes drama involved in starting up, editing, and discontinuing the *Little Review.* However, Anderson's "war" is not depicted as a sustained battle of ideals in the autobiography, which often portrays Anderson's own rapid shifts in interests and ideals rather flippantly. As Anderson tells it in *My Thirty Years' War,* she became an anarchist in one afternoon, through attending a lecture of Emma Goldman's. According to Anderson, she had just enough time between the end of Goldman's lecture to transform the magazine into an anarchist instrument "before the presses closed." However, she abandoned the ideology within a couple of years, as "in the natural course of events I had naturally turned from anarchism." Although the tone is combative throughout the book, *My Thirty Years' War* offers neither a clear sense of what Anderson was fighting for nor a coherent artistic or political vision. In fact, Anderson characterizes these things as weaknesses, mocking an aspiring writer who had once come to her for advice, saying the writer had an "earnestness that would prevent anyone from achieving anything."[33] By the end of her life, Anderson came to understand herself best as a dilettante, because, as she explained in the dedication to her final autobiography, "As a dilettante, I am free to be as light or as serious as I please. . . . What attitude could be more exhilarating, more amusing, more confusing, or more rewarding?"[34] It is certainly true that in *My Thirty Years' War,* being exhilarating and amusing seem to take precedence over all other considerations.

Atherton's and Anderson's autobiographies are notable markers in the history of autobiography because they present a level of "egotism"—a pop psychology term that both these women, and their critics, frequently employed—not previously found in women's literary autobiography. As a woman who urged the advertisers of her books to pronounce her the greatest American female novelist, Atherton eschews the concepts of both feminine modesty and artistic apprenticeship in her *Adventures.*[35] Egotism is far preferable, she explains, to "start[ing] out in life with an inferiority complex." Atherton justifies her own egotism with an anecdote about another artist, James Whistler, saying, "Of course he was an egotist, but, as there never was a more interesting one, what matter?" In building a case for her exceptionalism, Atherton reprints an entire letter from Harold Frederic, who believed she had talent but also felt that her work lacked polish, in *Adventures.* In it, Frederic warns her to "take the pace a little more slowly and listen with a more solicitous reflective ear" to her prose. However, Atherton explains why she did not heed his advice: "Style is a matter of temperament, and unless one is cool and placid and suave by nature . . . one cannot preserve a uniform style." She further defends her erratic style by characterizing it as a quality that sets her apart from other writers, remarking that "it is easy enough to write well, [but] individuality is inborn."[36] Like Atherton, Anderson seems to have equated genius with idiosyncrasy: if Anderson found a person interesting, then she would print their work whether it had any or merit or not. Defying sound advice from both Ezra Pound and Harriet Monroe, the *Little Review* printed a good deal of embarrassing, nonsensical, automatic writing from Baroness Elsa von Freytag von Loringhoven, a fellow exhibitionist who made herself clothing with bits of refuse from the streets or kitchen appliances that she had shoplifted, because Anderson felt she was unique. Again and again, a comparison of these two texts shows that both Atherton and Anderson believed that an interesting or idiosyncratic person (or persona) *is* a type of art, and therefore needs neither training nor critique.

In *My Thirty Years' War,* Anderson depicts no apprenticeship of reading and presents no narrative of developing her craft; instead, she boasts about reviewing fifty books for the *Chicago Evening Post* in one weekend without sacrificing her social life. Her record, she claims, was writing reviews for one hundred books in a single afternoon, without having read a single one of them. According to *My Thirty Years' War,* "The meaning of genius is that it doesn't have to work to attain what people without it must labor for—and not attain." Throughout the text, Anderson makes casual remarks about her own brilliance, lamenting having to "carefully pull the slower brains into my momentum." Even when she is rebuffed for her egotism by someone whom she is trying to cajole into doing her a favor, her confidence that she is intrinsically exceptional remains undiminished. When someone says to her "I don't know what you think you are, really," Anderson buoyantly replies, "Yes, you do. I think I'm interesting. That's why you wanted me to visit you."[37]

Perhaps that is the inner logic to this pair of autobiographies: Atherton and Anderson do not mind being thought self-centered, arrogant, inconsistent, or inarticulate, as long as no one finds them dull. At one point, while she was living in New York, Anderson took to cold-calling stockbrokers in their Wall Street offices, soliciting subscriptions to the *Little Review* by pointing out their civic responsibility to support the arts. This practice was a less-organized version of Harriet Monroe's diligent canvassing to start up *Poetry* magazine in Chicago several years earlier, but Anderson gives Monroe no acknowledgment for thinking it up in *My Thirty Years' War.* The technique worked, but Anderson didn't follow up with it, reflecting, "If I had had the stamina to continue an effort that was distasteful to me, I might have developed a business out of these hold-up methods." But to Anderson, persistence is boring and therefore anathema. Anderson's autobiography declares that she was proud to be "considered heartless, flippant, ruthless, devastating" because her dramatic, rapid shifts in behavior always kept things interesting.[38] To lose the spotlight was anathema to Atherton as well. Like the chilling realization Grace King had had when her friends Madame Blanc and Charles Gayarre were so quickly forgotten, Atherton saw what could happen to older writers, pointing out in her autobiography that Henry James "lost his large public during his second phase and was little read now save by intellectuals, who never supported anybody"—perhaps as an implicit defense of her own dramatic efforts to keep her public at any price.[39] Atherton would not risk losing the spotlight if she could help it and could not comprehend why any other author would risk it. Like minor Hollywood celebrities of their day, these two women appear to have engaged in a series of publicity stunts. Their version of Pound's "Make It New" appears to have been to continually shift their ideological foundations and/or geographical locations and to write or print shocking material to keep their names fresh and interesting in the press. Read in this light, we can see these two autobiographies as both a catalogue of their authors' previous publicity stunts and as new publicity stunts in their own right.

Because of their rapid pace of living and projected self-assurance, a pattern of dramatic conflict repeats itself frequently in these two autobiographies. Atherton claims, "Half the spice of the career would be gone if there were no hostile element to fight."[40] Anderson seems to have molded her own adventures along similar lines, declaring that she "made [her]self into a fighter" and made weekly lists "in ink—of fights that had to be won during the week or never."[41] Both women appear to be constantly looking for a fight. Atherton notes, "I made several enemies among the 'lady novelists' of England. One . . . owned a literary weekly in which she took care I should be constantly slammed. She even turned her back on me pointedly one night when she was receiving with the hostess at a literary party, and tried to blackball me."[42] Both women reveled in making waves—and enemies—in their respective literary scenes. At the end of her first full year of publishing the *Little Review,* Anderson claimed that she was most proud of having "been denounced as 'uncritical, indiscriminate, juvenile, exuberant, chaotic, [and] amateurish,'" among other things.[43] The truth or untruth of these accusations did not matter (though Anderson acknowledged them as generally true in her last autobiography)—it was shocking people enough to fight her that mattered most.

Since both of these autobiographers cast themselves as "fighters," they are ruthless to anyone or anything that stands in their way. According to her *Adventures,* Atherton's grandmother tried to dress her nicely, only to have her roll in the mud; enjoined her to be good for company, only to face a temper tantrum; and reportedly had to tie her to a chair when teaching her to sew.[44] As Dorothy Van Doren observed, Atherton seems to "pride herself on her brattishness."[45] However, because sentiment was considered passé by the 1930s, Atherton's antisentimental, antidomestic image won her some limited approval. One reader praised Atherton for ignoring the female "genteel tradition" into which she was born, singling out the autobiography as unique because "perhaps no woman, nor man either, ever drew a portrait so free of self-justifying sentimentality."[46] This was an accurate enough description, for even in a scene describing her elopement with George Atherton, Atherton is unapologetic about the fact that he was engaged to her mother at the time. *Adventures* exhibits little feeling for anyone at all, Atherton's mother, Gertrude Franklin, included: Franklin is a vapid and capricious background figure who "*sometimes* came into [her] room to say goodnight before leaving" for a party. The dominant impression Atherton provides of her mother, a southern lady who had come to California when her husband's fortunes failed in the Civil War, is of a passive and useless woman who insisted on being "treated like a queen," one who "would have expected to be waited on . . . [with] the wolf at the door." Most likely raised with the same insidious southern notion that "ladies didn't labor" that had encumbered Grace King's ambitions, passive Gertrude Franklin becomes a foil for her daughter's inexhaustible self-assertion in *Adventures.* Reiterating that her mother "never thought in [her] life," Atherton's autobiography also dissociates her mother from intellect, ambition, and activity as did Wharton and King in their texts.[47]

Although she was willing to hurt and humiliate her mother by eloping with George Atherton, Gertrude Atherton does not exhibit much affection for her husband either. Atherton's *Adventures* continues in this antisentimental vein in her depiction of her marriage. Perhaps the most startling breach of etiquette in *Adventures* is Atherton's expressed wish for her husband's death and her admission that one of her early novels dramatized her fantasy that her husband would die: "George was my heroine's temporary husband, doomed to extermination by poison." Her unfeeling descriptions of her husband and family may be part of the autobiography's calculated rejection of domesticity or of Atherton's desire to create shock-value. Her husband did die young, though not by poison, and Atherton relates his demise as an amusing anecdote in *Adventures.* This is partially understandable, since George Atherton died at sea and his body was preserved for burial inside a barrel of rum; however, as Atherton tells it, she was more upset that the sailors wished her to reimburse them for the spoiled liquor than she was about the loss of her husband. Even in writing about the death of her young son, Atherton eschews sentimentality, briefly noting that diphtheria "made short work" of him but that life that year was otherwise "monotonous."[48]

In these scenes and many others, *Adventures of a Novelist* depicts Gertrude Atherton in a continual state of rebellion against traditional female roles. The Athertons, she explains, were descendants of the old Spanish aristocracy, so her in-laws believed that a woman's place was in the home and that "ladies in Spain do not write." Like Teddy Wharton in *A Backward Glance,* Atherton's husband is depicted as an obstacle to Gertrude's writing career. But Wharton's tactful reticence about the real burdens her marriage placed on her was not Atherton's style. Instead, Atherton asserts, "The worst trial I had yet been called upon to endure was having a husband continually on my hands," explaining that she threatened to leave him if he did not get a place in San Francisco for her to live in and have a "salon." Moments like this may account for the "heartlessness" readers found in her book, especially as Atherton reveals that she traded the custody of her surviving child—a daughter named Muriel—to her in-laws in exchange for enough money to go to New York and pursue a career. Never apologetic, Atherton dismisses motherhood along with marriage in *Adventures,* claiming, "The maternal instinct had been left out of me." To her, motherhood was simply "a highly specialized form of martyrdom." In one of the few passages about her daughter, Atherton notes, "I had little to do with her bringing up, which no doubt was fortunate for her." The only compliment Atherton pays her daughter in *Adventures* is that Muriel was "a marvelous housekeeper" who made the dinners that followed Atherton's literary afternoons in New York some decades later.[49] This relegation of other women to domestic support roles in service of the careers of their exceptional mothers, daughters, or sisters, forms a pattern that echoes Grace King's relegation of her mother to chef and hostess in support of her own career in *Memories.* However, Atherton's rejection of domesticity in *Adventures* is also an extension of the anti-genteel, antisentimental public image she cultivated throughout her career. Part of Atherton's image was writing each novel in a different location, and she reviews some of these locations in *Adventures,* describing French convents, a Yonkers boardinghouse, the homes of British nobility, and the apartment she kept in Munich for almost ten years. When a chapter on her appeared in the 1903 volume *Women Authors of Our Day in Their Homes,* Atherton's interview proudly begins, "I have no home."[50] This was a consistent part of Atherton's public persona. Nearly thirty years later, *Adventures* asserts that "it was my intention to write every book in a new place, combining travel with work."[51]

Margaret Anderson's tone regarding home and family in *My Thirty Years' War* is much the same. Coming across as every bit the *enfant terrible* as Atherton, Anderson's autobiography is outspoken in her refusal of traditional roles, painstakingly delineating that she is *not* "someone's daughter, niece, aunt, wife, mistress, or mother" at the outset of the text. The book claims that Anderson sent a twenty-page letter to her father "exposing the criminality of our family life and offering a program upon which he could act in every domestic crisis" when she was in her teens. Anderson, like Wharton, King, and Atherton, also positions her own ambitions in direct opposition to her mother's ambitions for her in *My Thirty Years' War.* According to Anderson, her mother "liked being a victim of nerves" and "made a scene" when her daughter devoted herself to reading or playing piano instead of being "social." Anderson enjoyed drama, but only of her own making, and she and her mother seemed to have had opposite interests, for "Mother had always said that my enthusiasm on any subject sickened her." Like Atherton, Anderson left home when she was still in her teens. Twenty-seven years after Atherton's defiant "I have no home" proclamation, Anderson made a similar declaration in *My Thirty Years' War:* "I have no place in the world—no fixed position." Like Atherton before her, Anderson was known for her peripatetic lifestyle, but her movements garnered even more publicity. Recalling her notorious public encampment in a tent on Chicago's North Shore, Anderson comments, "My mother's hopes of breaking my spirit had never been more completely at a discount." While this and other passages of sardonic commentary in *My Thirty Years' War* are often humorous, not all of them are funny. Her cold sarcasm when she recalls Jane Heap's suicide threats is distressing: "My freedom from scenes gave Jane no freedom for power. . . . Her favorite device was the suicide theme. I have nothing against suicide. But indulged in merely as a contemplation and a menace I have always found it slightly repellent."[52]

Some reviewers of these two autobiographies recoiled at statements like the one above. But it is still worth asking why Atherton's and

Anderson's autobiographies treat any attempt to curtail their freedom, to control or confine them in any way or by any means, up to and including suicide, with such emphatic, almost brutal refusals. Many incidents in *Adventures* reveal that Atherton's writing career was as much about attaining personal freedom as it was about creative drive. For example, Atherton explains that it was her financial dependence on her husband that first prompted her to write. Reminding her readers of the world into which she had been born nearly eighty years earlier, she declares, "No doubt if the world had emerged from the stifling Victorian era, I should have 'gone out and found a job.' But I had never heard of women supporting themselves save by teaching or 'taking in boarders.'" Atherton's decision to pursue writing seems also to have been at least partially inspired by dreams of freedom and fame. Upon hearing of Atherton's wish to write, an older friend tells her, "Many writers have not traveled. . . . They make themselves famous by using the materials at hand." Atherton responds, "I want to live in New York, Paris, London. I want to see the beautiful things in Europe and meet all sorts and kinds of people as different from these as possible. I know they would inspire me to write, and I am stagnating."[53]

Restlessness forms another strong motif in both memoirs. From the earliest pages in her text, Atherton links the ability to write with the freedom to travel. Her true "craving," she explains, is "mental adventure." *Adventures of a Novelist* insists that Atherton had "the instinct of an explorer," for her "every book has been an adventure, a new plunge, with few exceptions, into uncharted seas."[54] Indeed, both Atherton's and Anderson's autobiographies read like insatiable quests for new experiences. Anderson compared editing her magazine to making "a polar expedition" in the tenth anniversary issue, and her biography makes it clear that she lived as peripatetic a life as Atherton did. Some reviewers noticed this and speculated that the *Little Review* was merely a device to satisfy Anderson's craving for "adventure."[55] Friend and patron Eunice Tietjens claimed that the irresistible, "absurd"

Anderson "was herself the adventure."[56] Anderson claims the same double motivation for her work in *My Thirty Years' War* as Atherton does in *Adventures.* According to Anderson, she took on the literary editorship of the *Continent* because it gave her the opportunity to travel to a big city and meet people. She highlights that her decision gave her "a chance to know New York" and "to interview all the publishers about their forthcoming books." Anderson's insatiable craving for newness is likely the reason that it was her idea—one very much opposed by Jane Heap—to stop publishing the *Little Review. My Thirty Years' War* explains Anderson's reasons: "For a long time I had wanted freedom from household drudgery, from publishing drudgery. I wanted to escape both."[57] Their authors' continual desire to escape becomes a common thread in the dramatic plots of both these autobiographies.

Atherton's *Adventures* defends her insatiable desire for freedom and self-determination by including other women's stories as cautionary tales of the consequences of emotional and intellectual confinement. In one of Atherton's rare positive descriptions of another woman, she reflects on her admiration and sympathy for Lady Colin Campbell. She refers to Campbell as a woman "with every gift that nature could shower on her" who had been "blindly sacrificed" by a "stupid mother" to an "inferior" husband. Another story of thwarted female potential occurs when Atherton journeys to Haworth to pay homage to the Brontës. She writes briefly of the daughter of her landlord there: "She was a nervous highly strung girl, no doubt full of dreams and aspirations that could never be realized. . . . She died insane a few years later."[58] The link between frustration of ambition and death is as real to Atherton here as it was to the Brontës and to anyone who has ever read Charlotte Perkins Gilman's "The Yellow Wall-Paper." Atherton's *Adventures* flaunts her refusal to be one of the thwarted women she finds in her travels.

Women's right to seek personal freedom far outweighs the importance of decorum in Atherton's *Adventures,* as she illustrates through another anecdote. When a princess tries to flatter Atherton by praising six of her books—none of which were actually by Atherton—she is not angry. Instead of pointing out the woman's error, she declares, "The poor woman was practicing her *salon* manner on me, and far be it from me to discourage her. It was a worthy object and I wished her success; I too had once been excruciatingly bored, and I too had lit out the moment I was free to get what I wanted."[59] Just as Atherton pursued writing for adventure and fame, *My Thirty Years' War* characterizes Anderson's use of the *Little Review* in her concurrent quests for freedom and notoriety. Anderson's geographical moves are made in the interest of expanding both her experience and the *Little Review*'s publicity. Although Jane Heap strongly opposed it, Anderson insisted on moving from Chicago to New York because she believed "our position would be more commanding" in New York. After that, Anderson hoped to move on to Europe, as "we hadn't yet met all the interesting people in the world."[60]

My Thirty Years' War and *Adventures of a Novelist* both protest against female confinement or domestic drudgery, but protest is the closest either text comes to feminism. These autobiographies lack solidarity, sympathy, or activism on behalf of other women. Although Atherton and Anderson each toy with an "activist" image from time to time when it serves them, these two autobiographers seem much more interested in exhibiting their own exceptionalism than in really changing conditions for women. Despite their appropriation of New Woman ideology regarding their own freedom and independence from patriarchal structures or gendered codes of conduct, neither Atherton nor Anderson's autobiographies are truly feminist—neither seems particularly concerned with women's rights or female solidarity. In *Adventures,* Atherton disparages a group of women writers who invited her to join their Greenwich Village circle, denigrating their personal hygiene and appearance, rather than expressing gratitude for their gesture of sisterhood. Atherton declares in her autobiography that she rejected Charlotte Perkins Gilman's request for aid in the women's cause in 1891, since she was able "to take care of myself and owed nothing to any organization." Even when she takes credit for her "pioneer book [*Patience Sparhawk*] that would play its part in loosening the shackles of women both in life and literature," Atherton claims, "I was an unconscious instrument, consumed with no holy fire in the cause of woman."[61] Her biographer implies that it was more a desire to stay on trend with the times than to make a political gesture that led Atherton to join the suffrage campaign in 1910.[62] Still, *Adventures* insults the suffragists Atherton met because she found them personally unappealing: she describes them as "the embodiment of cold intellect . . . [with] about as much charm as an embryo in a bottle." Even though she had participated in it, Atherton is flippant about the battle for women's suffrage: when her suffrage novel, *Julia France and Her Times,* was not well received, she notes that "English feminists were indignant because the heroine . . . [married] an American instead of going to prison and being fed through the nose."[63] Although Atherton and Anderson fiercely document their battles for their own freedom in *Adventures* and *My Thirty Years' War,* these texts are neither truly feminist nor truly activist. The difference between these two books and women's autobiographies that promote freedom, equality, and/or progress for women in general becomes quite clear in chapter 3, which focuses on Charlotte Perkins Gilman's and Margaret Deland's activist texts.

Instead of focusing on activism, Atherton's and Anderson's life-writings proudly record their dexterous use of the mechanisms of celebrity, including publicity and networking. Anderson remarks that by her early twenties, "I was now planning my career from the viewpoint of a general."[64] Shrewdly deciding to mail a copy of the *Little Review* to Ezra Pound after his contretemps with Harriet Monroe over her critique of T. S. Eliot's *Prufrock,* Anderson managed to acquire Pound as her foreign editor at the right psychological moment. Under Pound's editorial expertise, the *Little Review* went from "flailing eccentricity" to benefit from a steady pipeline of "work far superior to anything that she herself had been able to dig up."[65] Even though she and Heap resented Pound's presumptive editorial control, Anderson relished the notoriety the work he sent gave them—especially then-scandalous pieces like Wyndham Lewis's "Cantleman's Spring Mate" and other works that included taboo sexual content for which she could then make a sardonic defense in her *Little Review* editorials.

Besides breaking early twentieth-century sexual taboos to ensure their work's notoriety, both writers also associated their professional success with their personal sexuality in their autobiographies. Like many celebrities, Atherton's and Anderson's looks and style were an important part of their brands. Well into her eighties, Atherton insisted on wearing off-the-shoulder gowns in her publicity shots and frontispieces. Unlike Wharton, whose autobiography distances her image as an artist from her interest in fashion, Atherton recalls the "satisfaction . . . of knowing [she] was the best-dressed woman on the platform" when she spoke at a rally for Woodrow Wilson. Atherton seems so concerned with maintaining her reputation for sex appeal in her autobiography that she provides glimpses into her boudoir, discussing getting facials, penciling her eyebrows, and undergoing anti-aging treatments. She recalls scenes from her personal life, including mocking Ambrose Bierce for kissing her next to a pigsty. *Adventures* emphasizes that Atherton used her sex appeal as a means to gather new material for her books, although the text is careful to imply that she did not actually have sex with any of the men to whom she refers. Her purported response to one proposal of marriage illustrates her creative method: "I intend to be a novelist and I've only been making a study of you. You are not interesting in yourself, but through you I have learned something of the world. . . . But even from the writer's point of view you don't interest me any longer." According to *Adventures,* this was a scene Atherton often reprised in her career: her relationship with a "new man" gave her "mental stimulation" to write the next novel, and when the book was done, "he was tactfully or abruptly discarded."[66] Here Atherton is perhaps adopting a persona more often found in younger male writers. Theodore Dreiser, who published his autobiography the year before Atherton did, was also reputed to have discarded throngs of female muses, making this method—if it is indeed described accurately in *Adventures*—one more instance of a traditionally male privilege that Atherton usurps for herself. She molded her celebrity image as a self-proclaimed "intellectual siren" all her life: when she was eighty-seven, one newspaper interviewer described her as having "that strange intangible known as sex appeal."[67] While Atherton's ceaseless vigilance regarding her "image" seems to have yielded her some power over what was written about her, a few journalists, like Isabel Paterson, eventually refused to interview Atherton because she was "too controlling" of her publicity.[68]

Anderson also carefully builds the narrative of how her sex appeal contributed to her success in *My Thirty Years' War.* She quips, "It would be unbecoming of me not to know that I was extravagantly pretty in those days—extravagantly and disgustingly pretty." She claims to have given this advice to an aspiring writer: "Use a little lip rouge. Beauty may bring you experiences to write about," a recommendation that dovetails perfectly with the creative methods Atherton describes in her autobiography. Anderson also seems pleased to defy cultural stereotypes about dowdy female intellectuals, mentioning that Emma Goldman initially snubbed her because she "looked too chic" to be the editor of the *Little Review.* Anderson, who had a flair for clothes, prides herself on "those tributes without which I could not live: You look so beautifully well-groomed!"[69] Over and over, Anderson pays tribute to her own charms in *My Thirty Years' War,* highlighting her willingness to use them to get what she wants, from groceries, money, or clothes to a piano or a place to live. Scholar Hugh Ford notes, "Only those impervious to her feminine qualities, which she learned to use to the fullest—could resist her."[70] After recalling one notable failure in which a woman she had charmed into giving her the use of a Highland Park beach house for free withdrew the offer after reading about her in the paper, Anderson chuckles that "it had been a great shock to her to discover that anyone who appeared so charming could be so depraved." *My Thirty Years' War* quotes Otto Kahn instructing her to save the *Little Review*'s failing finances in this way: "Let people see the color of your eyes and your hair and the way you wear your clothes."[71]

Like Atherton, Anderson used her glamorous image both to get herself into interesting situations and to keep herself out of serious trouble. During her phase as a disciple of Goldman's philosophical anarchism, Anderson wrote an editorial suggesting that someone should "shoot the governor of Utah" for not pardoning a condemned anarchist. When the police opened an investigation of her activity, a social acquaintance got her off the hook by successfully characterizing Anderson as a "flighty society girl who meant nothing she said."[72] In other episodes depicted in *My Thirty Years' War,* Anderson uses her *sang-froid* and good looks to gain entree into Wall Street offices and to manipulate policemen when she is being fingerprinted after her arrest for printing *Ulysses.* According to Janet Flanner, a mutual friend of both Gertrude Stein and Margaret Anderson, when Anderson could not command the center of attention, such as when she was in the presence of Gertrude Stein, she would "strike out at everyone with taunts, punctuated by spiraling laughter." Labeled a "hysteric" by Stein the first time they met, Anderson's wild flippancy in *My Thirty Years' War* resembles that of a madcap film heroine.[73] Honestly, Claudette Colbert or Barbara Stanwyck could have played the lead in a film version of either of these autobiographies. Reading some of the scenes, one wonders if Atherton hoped for a film adaptation of *Adventures,* as had happened for a number of her other books.

In fact, Atherton and Anderson both went for shock value repeatedly in their texts, treating many of their fellow celebrities ruthlessly or dismissively in the process. Hardly anyone escapes unscathed. For instance, Atherton writes, "I think it a pity that [William Dean] Howells ever lived," and describes Bret Harte as walking "as if his patent leather shoes were too small for him." Even having proclaimed herself a "Henry James fool" early in her career, and having pronounced *The Wings of the Dove* "one of the greatest novels in the history of fiction," Atherton mocks James's conversational style in *Adventures,* which Wharton likens to a "fine cobweb" in *A Backward Glance.* Atherton writes, "I wish I could remember his reply. But it was so involved, there were so many colons and semi-colons, so many commas and dashes, with never a period, that by the time he had finished I was too bewildered to do anything but stare at him." Although the English literati welcomed her when she was shunned in the United States, Atherton does not spare them either, saying they were "a little given to posing." Her treatment of other celebrities whom she met only very briefly is yet more rude: she claims that Oscar Wilde reminded her of a "bloated monster of the deep" because of his "lascivious coarse repulsive mouth." Even those who furthered her career do not escape Atherton's personal remarks. For example, she calls John Lane, the only publisher who would look at her first major novel, *Patience Sparhawk and Her Times,* a "fat white frog" whom she suspected of withholding some of her profits.[74]

Anderson too spares no one in *My Thirty Years' War,* not even those who were instrumental supporters of the *Little Review.* For example, although J. S. Watson of the *Dial* "kept the [*Little Review*] alive" by sending hundred dollar bills to Anderson and Heap at regular intervals, Anderson seems proud of having attacked the *Dial* as "a de-alcoholized version of the *Little Review*" throughout Watson's generous patronage. Friendship, respect, or gratitude do not stay Anderson's acerbic commentary any more than they do Atherton's. Although Gertrude Stein had extended her famous hospitality to her, Anderson mocks Stein's style, saying it evokes neither "understanding" nor "interest" for her, and that Stein's use of repetition "I don't deny that it gives weight, but to me it is the weight of boredom."[75] Even John Quinn, whose generosity with both time and money were vital to the *Little Review* in its most important decade, receives no acknowledgment in *My Thirty Years' War,* only Anderson's standard sarcasm. When one knows the facts about Quinn's labors on the *Little Review*'s behalf, this omission seems an offense against decency. No love seems to have been lost between them, however, as Quinn privately wrote that when Anderson and her friends arrived in court for the *Ulysses* trial, it looked "as though a fashionable whorehouse had been pinched."[76] Finally, even though Harriet Monroe tried to help Anderson with her project, inviting her to *Poetry* events, offering her leads for funding for her financially floundering *Little Review,* and introducing her to Amy Lowell, Anderson disrespectfully dismisses Monroe's *Poetry* in *My Thirty Years' War.*[77] While Monroe, the longtime yeoman editor of *Poetry,* always tried to take the high road in her dealings with Anderson—at least until Monroe was forced to correct some of Anderson's misstatements in her own autobiography—Anderson never seemed to shake her belief that her brashness was what made her interesting.

Perhaps because both autobiographies reveal a disposition to amuse readers rather than to inform them, Anderson and Atherton seem to rely on entertaining barbs rather than substantive discussion of other artists in their texts. As was customary in literary autobiographies, Atherton and Anderson list other authors of their acquaintance. These lists are often used as part of an autobiographer's strategy to avoid discussing their personal lives or to illustrate their own importance by proxy. But other autobiographers of this decade do not simultaneously utilize the lists to affirm their belonging in literary circles and then proceed to dismantle the dignity of their fellow artists, such as by observing, as Atherton does, that Thomas Hardy bored her by talking exclusively of the American system of streetcars when she met him. Atherton even includes lists of people she never met in *Adventures,* so she can repeat snippets of gossip or craft clever comebacks. She notes that she missed her chance to meet George Meredith, "repl[ying] haughtily [to an invitation] that [she] had never gone out of [her] way to meet a man in [her] life and would not pay George Meredith or anyone else that compliment."[78]

In this double usage of the lists, name-dropping lends these two autobiographers significance. At the same time, Atherton and Anderson rarely show any respect for the people behind the names. When they speak of their fellow celebrities, their autobiographies exude an aura of false intimacy, the tone one might find in a gossip column or scandal sheet. No one who is famous is safe from Anderson's mocking eye. Although she had pestered Jane Heap to move to New York for so long, Anderson unhesitatingly expresses her disappointment in New York society, where she ranks the first literary soiree she attended as "a second-rate evening." Anderson must have known that Ezra Pound's photo and his impassioned, blunt, profane letters—which she freely reprints in her text—were heavily effective in promoting the sales of *My Thirty Years' War.* But she writes that Pound gave her "the sensation of watching a large baby" and declares that she is "very fond of Ezra. Only it will be more interesting to know him when he has grown up." Rather than seriously engaging with other artists, Anderson seems to revel in snappy, insider commentary about them, as seen in her description of concert pianist Georgette LeBlanc: "At those times when she was supposed to be devouring men she could be found at home devouring cold carrots." Anderson dissects James Joyce's demeanor in *My Thirty Years' War,* conveying the impression of an overly sensitive man who did not talk until he had had enough wine. Like Atherton, Anderson specializes in creating clever insults that she perhaps thought would be more entertaining to readers than expressing sincere admiration for other writers of her time. While she praises his novel *Carrie,* Anderson also remarks that "Dreiser had no more wit than a cow" and "was never any good until some exchange of sex-magnetism put him at his ease." Likewise, while expressing admiration for *A Farewell to Arms* as "the best novel that has come out of America for a long time," she mocks Ernest Hemingway's perpetual love affairs, amusedly recalling his unrequited passion for a woman "who refused to succumb." F. Scott Fitzgerald fares even worse. Anderson depicts him "blushing because he was receiving checks from *Harper's Bazaar*, while good writers like Djuna Barnes had to give their stories to the *Little Review* for nothing."[79] That particular sentence couldn't have been too pleasant for either Fitzgerald or Barnes to contemplate.

These autobiographers' ill-mannered descriptions of famous acquaintances were called out for malice in multiple reviews. One critic pointedly questioned whether Atherton's one brief meeting with Thomas Hardy gave her any right to write about him at all. As for Anderson, perhaps her early experience as an extremely speedy book reviewer prevailed in *My Thirty Years' War:* her short, piercing, observations, on the border between clever and insolent, permeate the volume but also make it quite choppy, leaving only her insouciant tone to unify the book at all. In possibly her worst lapse of decency, Anderson dismisses the importance of the Harlem Renaissance, lamenting that "America today seems to be looking toward the negro as toward a new force," and comparing the "negro craze" to "the alcohol craze. Alcohol isn't a stimulant, it's a release. It is releasing to identify oneself with an easy insouciant amused race. It is not a push up and on."[80] In her attempts to be witty, Anderson sometimes achieves a repellent, inhuman detachment.

At other times, these two autobiographers' contrariness dwindles into diatribe. Atherton writes, "The world, and the United States in particular, is full of narrow-minded, ignorant, moronic, bigoted, cowardly, self-righteous, anemic, pig-headed, stupid, puritanical, hypocritical, prejudiced, fanatical, cocoa-blooded atavists, who soothe their inferiority complex by barking their hatred of anything new." While many American autobiographers—including Wharton and

King—would depict their travels in European circles to validate their reputations and provide a "cultured" contrast to America, Atherton's continental experiences are treated flippantly, as when she observes, "I hate ruins." Nor is she much interested in the traditions of the European aristocracy: "I was not much impressed by the first duchess I met," she writes. "Americans must not expect too much of England." She even declares, "The longer I lived in Europe the firmer was my conclusion that the better class of Americans were the only people who had really fine table manners."[81]

Although she was living in Paris when she wrote the book, Anderson, like Atherton, also seems critical of Europe and all its denizens in *My Thirty Years' War,* briefly and decidedly denouncing France for its "brutality," Italy for its corruption, Germany for its "stolidity," Spain for its "cruelty," and Belgium for its "stubbornness." In turn, she explains, the Europeans she met considered her an "ill-mannered . . . vulgar American." Unapologetically, Anderson quips, "I saw no reason why I shouldn't go on fighting everything that was unintelligent" because "I like being disliked by people I designate to dislike me."[82]

Although both Atherton and Anderson seem to have specialized in the art of antagonism, they each strike back against bad press. Anderson's farewell editorial to her magazine states that she "didn't want to hear any more about the artist transforming life" as she is "not interested at the moment in transformation." Having thus summarily dismissed the artists in whom she was so interested before, she turns to dismiss the critics in *My Thirty Years' War,* just as Atherton does in *Adventures,* wryly observing that "judging by the editorial comment it received in the American press, [Heap's editorial perspective] was not widely understood."[83] Atherton too rarely treats criticism of her work as legitimate in her autobiography. In *Adventures,* she labels critics "quaint creatures. There seems to be no standard and the wonder is they have any influence." When she does describe rejection or failure, Atherton blames either the critics or the marketplace but never herself.

Describing the rejection by "every publisher in the United States" of her third novel, *What Dreams May Come,* Atherton characterizes it as merely being written before its time, explaining that "a few years later the market was flooded with 'reincarnation novels.'" Atherton often bemoans what she saw as the "stodginess" of the old guard of literary publishers, explaining her 1922 decision to sign with the scandalous Horace Liveright (who was delighted when one of his books got banned in Boston), saying, "He was the most scintillating of the younger publishers, very enterprising, with original methods of advertising, and might never have heard the word 'rut'; more than could be said for the older group, who had had things their way far too long." Using her autobiography to answer a common critique of her haphazard, hasty writing, Atherton claims she purposely avoided developing a "flowing style" because "too many had it."[84] This public combativeness was an authentic, lifelong stance for Atherton: it began as early as 1907 in an early *New York Times* article entitled "Gertrude Atherton Assails 'The Powers,'" and extended until one of her last interviews, at age eighty-seven, in which she calls herself a "literary non-conformist." Resistance to authority remained a constant in Atherton's defenses of her work. In a 1944 interview, she proudly referred to herself as an "intellectual anarchist."[85] It may well be that Gertrude Atherton's true legacy lies with the all-female punk rock band named for her.

Atherton's "intellectual anarchism" could also be used to describe Margaret Anderson's approach to her work as a reviewer and editor. Never having clearly expressed a stable editorial vision for the *Little Review,* Anderson acknowledges that her shifting editorials over the years came across as "didacticism, dogmatism, fanaticism, aestheticism, exoticism."[86] Putting Anderson's temporary infatuation with political anarchism aside, friend Janet Flanner described Anderson as "lawless by nature," claiming that "polite anarchy" was "her basis of conduct."[87] Perhaps what made Anderson's text the less offensive of the two autobiographies was the age difference between the authors. People expected an element of brashness from one of Anderson's generation but not from one of Atherton's. But it is really Anderson's relationship with Jane Heap that sets these two defiant autobiographies apart for the reader. The Margaret Anderson one encounters in the parts of the text before she meets Jane and the years after she abandons her to produce the *Little Review* on her own is off-putting. Although Anderson acknowledges that her combative personality led to constant arguments between them, her affection and admiration for Heap are winsome, and the parts of the text wherein they are living, working, and traveling together are more readable, more human. Anderson recurringly refers to Heap as a genius and says, "I had seen no more highly organized mental-emotional equipment anywhere. I had chosen her mind as representative of what I called the creative mind. I wanted the *Little Review* to reflect this point of view above any other."[88] But like all of Anderson's enthusiasms, her attachment to Heap is temporary, and the Anderson-Heap relationship becomes strained rather quickly in *My Thirty Years' War* when Anderson wants to move on, first to new places and then to new relationships.

Anderson's inconsistent literary taste is also marked in *My Thirty Years' War.* She acknowledges, "It is certain that the *Little Review* has printed work which will not hold up as art. This is inevitable." The inconsistency is probably largely due to Anderson's tendency to publish work based on how personally interesting she found the author, rather than on the quality of the work itself. In the very first issue of the *Little Review,* Anderson foregrounds her life-as-art approach, somewhat borrowed from Oscar Wilde's aesthetic movement: "Life is a glorious performance." Full of the "perfectly inexpressible enthusiasm" for the impressions we give and receive as we "rush along" through our lives, Anderson may well have seen all the world as her stage long before and long after that first issue. According to *My Thirty Years' War,* she became a longtime fan of prima donna Mary Garden because Garden "furnishe[d] a striking example, in the visual arts, of the artist 'creating in his own image.'"[89] The image of a prima donna, invoked by both these autobiographers, might be the most apt way to understand Anderson's and Atherton's life-writings. Like the diva Mary Garden, their primary works of art may have been their own public images.

Atherton's and Anderson's constant pursuit of both new settings and new modes of self-expression typify the adage that "there's no such thing as bad publicity." For both these women, their literary autobiographies are ultimately not about literature or writing—they are about where those pursuits could take them, and the notoriety they could garner along the way. Since their texts erase any personal vulnerability and take a combative attitude to the rest of the world, there is a fundamental unbelievability—a brittleness to these books. It is inconceivable that their lives could possibly have really been as their books describe. In prioritizing drama and incident, Atherton and Anderson may have inadvertently invented a new feminine picaresque autobiography—a type we see much more often today—traveling roguishly across continents from one adventure to the next, churning out amusing, provocative, or outrageous copy to keep the public's attention along the way. Ultimately, the personas of *Adventures of a Novelist* and *My Thirty Years' War* embody a famous saying of Alfred Orage, which Anderson claims changed her outlook on life: "Act . . . don't be acted upon."[90] One gets an impression of frantic scrambling and scribbling for celebrity and survival in these authors' biographies as much as one does of heedless bulldozing to stake a claim to literary history in their autobiographies. Yet there is still something admirable in their daring, their determination to "act," to make something happen, even if that action turns out to be imperfect, ephemeral, offensive, or an outright failure. The official autobiographies of most other women writers of the decade contrive to at least *appear* to observe the proprieties of modesty, tact, artistic vision, or professional courtesy. But not these two. Never content to conform in any way, Gertrude Atherton and Margaret Anderson broke all the rules.

Chapter 3

Refusing Nostalgia, Denying Desire

Didactic Activism in the Autobiographies of Margaret Deland and Charlotte Perkins Gilman

WHEN CHARLOTTE Perkins Gilman contracted to sell her memoirs to D. Appleton Century in 1934, the press disagreed with her about the book's title. The publisher disliked *The Living of Charlotte Perkins Gilman* (1935), but the wording was important to Gilman, and she prevailed.[1] Gilman insisted that her title differentiated between the "trivial" external appearance of a person's life and the "earnest 'living'" going on inside. As she explains, "The difference is great between one's outside 'life,' the things which happen to one, incidents, pains, and pleasures, and one's 'living.'"[2] The title Margaret Deland gave her first autobiography, *If This Be I, as I Suppose It Be* (1935), also implies an awareness of this difference, as well as a similar determination to detach external events from the inner self that participates in them. To distinguish it from her "life," "Living" is often capitalized in Gilman's autobiography. Similarly, Deland's use of capitalization reveals a tendency to lecture on abstract concepts: her chapters include "War, Patriotism, and Love"; "Honor, Death, and Truth"; "Law, Justice, and Compassion"; "Fear, Gossip, and Savagery"; and "God, Nature, and Vanity."

Both autobiographies use these distancing techniques to guide their readers' judgment. Throughout her text, Gilman clearly wishes to be judged for her conscious, interior "Living" and not for the external facts of her life. Deland also uses bifurcation as a rhetorical technique, but her binary terms are "body" and "self," not "life" and "Living." As Deland explains, "The body is only the house the Self lives in." Throughout *If This Be I,* Deland refers to her younger self in the third person, as "Maggie," detaching the little girl depicted in the text from her present self by asserting, "I know very little of Maggie's thoughts."[3] There are three versions of Deland in *If This Be I:* "Maggie," the child; "Margaret," the grown woman who once was Maggie and who remembers how it felt to be Maggie; and the autobiographical "I," presumably the famous author known to the reading public as "Mrs. Deland," a voice that is expressly separate from both Maggie's and Margaret's in the text. For the reader, Deland's distancing techniques result in a similar effect to Gilman's separation of "life" and "Living." In their desire to transform their individual experiences into abstract lessons for humanity, both Gilman's and Deland's autobiographies read as didactic attempts to subjugate sentimental nostalgia and personal desire to a generalized desire for progress and enlightenment.

Like many previous female activist autobiographers, Gilman appears to have written autobiography in order to transcend prior judgments of her life. *The Living of Charlotte Perkins Gilman* asserts that, regardless of who one seems to be from the "outside," on the "inside" dwells a "conscious humanity, immensely beyond self." In an autobiography that makes heavy use of old diaries, Gilman uses the diaries not to create intimacy but as a means to ideologically contrast the "life" represented by the facts of her past with the "Living" that was really going on in her mind at the time. The first two times Gilman uses the term "Living" in the autobiography, she points out that one would never know the "real" Charlotte Anna Perkins from the descriptions of the "trivial," "meager, poverty-stricken, repressed life" found in her teenage diaries.[4] Because of the gap between the two voices in *Living,* literary scholar Patricia Meyer Spacks describes Gilman's life-writing as all "superego and sickness."[5] The contrast between the two is the contrast Gilman saw in herself. In one of her letters to her second husband, Gilman acknowledges that though she "loom[s] big and brilliant" in the public eye, she still has a "pitiful wish to be picked up and consoled."[6] "Pitiful" may seem an odd way for such an influential woman to describe herself, but by the time she wrote her autobiography, Gilman had struggled with mental illness (particularly depression) for nearly seventy years. Like Deland's "Maggie," "Margaret," and "I," Gilman the public figure and Gilman the private sufferer are distinguished from one another throughout *The Living of Charlotte Perkins Gilman.*

Gilman's depiction of her mental illness in her autobiography was shocking not only to readers; the extent of the suffering she professes in the book surprised even her friends. After the publication of *Living,* Harriet Howe observed that it "reveal[ed] conditions which none of us fully realized. It is difficult to reconcile the gay and gallant courage with which she did all tasks and met all problems, with the serious, even pitiful conditions described in the book."[7] *Living* acknowledges that many of Gilman's acquaintances probably did not understand her emotional struggles, her physical exhaustion, or her occasional memory lapses. Gilman's determination to speak out about her struggle with depression may be why her biographer Ann Lane finds an "emotional truth" in Gilman's *Living,* and why Martha Bensley Bruere, a personal friend of Gilman's, called it an "amazing piece of self-analysis."[8] Gilman devotes an entire chapter in her autobiography to illustrating the debilitating effects of her disease. She includes experiments she has made to determine how long it takes her to become exhausted from reading and anecdotes of what seemed to be rude behavior that was really the fault of her "flaccid vacant brain." She appears to be trying to remedy the fact that "[her] public activities do not show weakness, nor [her] writings" by emphasizing her invisible disability.[9] In this way, Gilman's text enacts a sort of double-activism: she not only recommits to her early reputation as a pioneering feminist but also becomes a pioneer in speaking out about depression.

Living emphasizes the general misunderstanding of Gilman's illness in this striking anecdote: "A sympathetic lady once remarked, 'Yes, it is a sad thing to see a strong mind in a weak body.' Whereas I promptly picked her up and carried her around the room. 'Please understand,' said I, 'that what ails me is a weak mind in a strong body.' But she didn't understand. They never do. Only those near enough to watch the long, blank months of idleness, the endless hours of driveling solitaire, the black empty days and staring nights, know." Passages like this might lead one to think that the real "Living" of Charlotte Perkins Gilman was the mental illness she enlarges on in the autobiography. But this is not the case. Gilman also distinguishes her illness from her "Living" in the text. She writes, "This 'Living' of mine has been done under a heavy handicap." If her lifelong struggle with depression (which she and others referred to as postpartum depression, neurasthenia, or nervous breakdown) is a "handicap" to her "Living," then it is clearly not the "Living" itself. *Living* is, in part, a story of what might have been—Gilman literally totals up the years of work her personal suffering has cost her, calculating how much more she could have done if she had not suffered so.[10] *Living* thus reveals a woman ahead of her time in its rhetorical assertion, "I am not my illness."

Since Gilman distances her "Living" from both her activities and her illness, her definition of "Living" seems to reside in her ideals, her potential, and her intentions. Gilman's internal sense of her vast potential is conveyed through her repeated use of the words "power" and "powerful." These words are repeated over twenty times in the first seventy-five pages of the autobiography. After the chapter entitled "The Breakdown," Gilman begins to use the words "pitiful" or "piteous" over and over again to describe herself and her circumstances. The transition from power to piteousness, however, is not a permanent shift in persona marked by one chapter in *Living.* Gilman's personal desires for happiness, justice, and power keep cropping up in the midst of her self-described weakness; she cannot mute them, though she tries to minimize them. Just as her sense of power in *Living* seems to contradict her protestations of weakness, Gilman's "piteousness" intrudes on her moments of triumph and pleasure, serving as an explanation of why she did not accomplish still more in her lifetime. In its double focus on achievement and suffering, Gilman's *Living* actively seeks understanding for the material and emotional conditions of her life while asserting her determined transcendence over the painful conditions she enumerates. "My 'self' I was sorry for," Gilman writes. "When the suffering was extreme I would look at myself as if it were a little creature in my hand and stroke it softly, saying, 'You poor little thing! You do have a hard time, don't you?'"[11] Depicting the reciprocal relationship between power and piteousness, strength and self-denial, the autobiography evolves into a text that enables Gilman to command both praise and pity.

Deland's text functions through a similarly doubled and detached perspective of herself. Paging through old photographs to spur memories for her autobiography, she writes, "Looking at Maggie's small complacent face, I thought, 'You queer little thing! I don't know you.'" Indeed, like Gilman's "poor little" self, Deland's little Maggie is more pitiable than charming or attractive. *If This Be I* declares that Maggie, the autobiographical subject, and Margaret Deland the author/autobiographer, would not have liked each other. Like Gilman, Deland can barely recognize her younger self in the autobiography, writing, "It is almost unbelievable to me that the anxious woman, who to-day can hardly face the miseries and sins and imbecilities of the front page of the morning paper, can be the unfeeling Pennsylvania imp of 1863!"[12]

Although there is no record of the two authors ever meeting one another, Deland and Gilman were true contemporaries: born only three years apart, they both launched their literary careers with controversially progressive fiction between 1888 and 1890. While today Gilman (1860–1935) is remembered for works like "The Yellow Wall-Paper" and *Herland,* Margaret Deland (1857–1945) was more prolific, more influential, and more widely known in their time. Orphaned by age four, Margaret Wade Campbell was raised by her aunt and uncle in Allegheny, Pennsylvania. She sought financial independence for herself at age nineteen, moving to New York to study and then teach drawing. Once she married Lorin Deland, they moved to Boston, where Deland began her writing career as a greeting-card poet to bring in extra income. While she later stated that writing or publishing novels had "hardly occurred to me," Deland's first novel, *John Ward, Preacher,* an intense, dramatized dismantling of the doctrine of predestination and the question of hell, was so controversial and so popular that it made much more money than anyone anticipated. The Delands went from trying to stretch the household budget to purchasing a vacation cottage in Kennebunkport, Maine, very quickly.[13] The money and fame allowed her to become one of Boston's social leaders as well.

As a novelist, Deland's work often shocked nineteenth-century readers. She used some of her work to take on the most deeply felt controversies of her time, skillfully sketching characters representing different choices or values in her work. She wrote about single mothers (she and Lorin regularly sheltered unmarried mothers and their babies in their home), female leaders of business and industry, and extramarital sexual relationships. Her work often alienated advocates on both sides of any issue with her uncompromising use of detail and insistence on a nuanced approach to controversy. For instance, Deland believed that women should be men's equal in the workforce, but she did not fully support women's suffrage. Her most well-known novels, *The Awakening of Helena Richie* and *The Iron Woman,* combine the kind of nineteenth-century sentimental diction you find in her volume of poetry, *The Old Garden and Other Verses* (1886), with what was then considered outspoken social critique of gender roles and social conventions. Because of her longstanding reputation, Deland received several honorary degrees between 1917 and 1920, and was elected to the National Institute of Arts and Letters along with Edith Wharton in 1926. Between 1903 and 1925, she also wrote several volumes of very popular, less controversial stories set in the fictional town of Old Chester, which was probably named for the original Chester County, Pennsylvania, where she grew up.

While Deland's post-1925 fiction lacks the energy and boldness of her earlier work, *If This Be I* (1935) seems to recapture some of Deland's earlier, more forceful voice. Following on the success of *If This Be I,* Deland published an autobiographical sequel, *Golden Yesterdays,* in 1941. *Golden Yesterdays* is primarily a sentimental tribute to her husband and is thus more akin to nineteenth-century women's autobiographical tradition than *If This Be I.* Although there are a few acerbic comments early in *Golden Yesterdays* on the patriarchal structure of her Pennsylvania childhood, it is mostly a story of "two lives, like two brooks flowing into one," a "fluent" memoir that is really a "Love Story."[14] It may be that Deland wanted to counterbalance the bold "Self" she had published in 1935, but it is equally likely that she wanted to write a tribute to Lorin, a loving and supportive life-partner whom she deeply missed as she aged. After her death in 1945, a *Time* magazine obituary called Deland a "soft-spoken gentlewoman" whose fiction "shocked her generation."[15]

While Deland published two successful autobiographies within a decade, Charlotte Perkins Gilman struggled to get her autobiography into print. Having tried to publish a partial draft of *Living* in 1927, she was rejected by most publishers. The only one who would even consider it called for such major revisions that Gilman temporarily abandoned the manuscript. But as the market grew for women's literary autobiography, the situation changed. It must have been a painful realization for a woman who was always looking to the future to have her autobiography marketed as a nod to nostalgia, but Gilman wanted the opportunity to tell her own story. In 1934, diagnosed with cancer and knowing her time was short, Gilman importuned her friend and fellow writer Zona Gale to finish writing her life, as she was struggling with the manuscript, especially the section about her marriage to and divorce from Walter Stetson.[16] But Gale could not be persuaded, and Gilman must have felt that what she had to say was important enough to risk the criticism her earlier draft had occasioned. She decided to go on with the revisions and received an advance for the new version. When her doctor told her that her death from cancer was imminent, Gilman chose photographs to include, selected a cover design, and wrote the last chapter, which included a suicide note to the world. She then chloroformed herself about six weeks before the book was published.

Publicly reinterpreting her life was immensely important to Gilman because the gap between her public image and private self-image was vast. Gilman was known worldwide throughout the Progressive era, and her influence could be seen across the United States in the form of businesses or cooperatives providing cooked food, housework, and child care, the kind of specialized, socially engineered home-life Gilman had advocated throughout her career.[17] She had ties to other activist movements and organizations, including the "Bellamy nationalism, social gospel, social purity, trade unionism, temperance, women's suffrage, and Populist movements."[18] She was well connected in literary circles too, claiming among her acquaintance H. G. Wells, George Bernard Shaw, William Dean Howells, Theodore Dreiser, Ina Coolbrith, Zona Gale, Gertrude Atherton, and Mary Austin.[19] Writing and revising her autobiography was probably such a struggle because there were so many contradictory elements to her "Living" that Gilman wanted to address or include. Many factors in Gilman's life may have contributed to a fragmented sense of herself: the extremely high expectations set for her as a child; her longstanding battle with depression; her struggle to find venues for her writing; her relationships with her first husband and her daughter, Katherine; the gossip and scandal she endured because of those relationships and her feminist activism; and her second, happier marriage to Houghton Gilman. Quite ambitiously, as was always Gilman's way, *Living* tries to reveal coherent interrelationships between them all.

Charlotte Perkins Gilman grew up in awe of her ancestors, for her father was the grandson of Dr. Lyman Beecher, whose children, as Gilman proudly announces in *Living,* "were all world servers."[20] To be connected to the Beechers was awe-inspiring for the young girl. Harriet Beecher Stowe, author of *Uncle Tom's Cabin,* was one of Gilman great-aunts, and Stowe's sisters Catharine and Isabella Beecher also had wide spheres of influence through their writing. The men were mostly preachers, so Gilman's father, Frederick Beecher Perkins, a writer and librarian, had been a disappointment both to the Beechers and to his wife and children. Charlotte Gilman's august ancestral legacy came with the crushing pressure of high expectations, both visionary and literary.

Although Gilman had many interests when she was young, she ultimately decided to pursue both sides of the Beecher family business: to become an author and to serve humanity. Unfortunately, when she really emerged as a writer, Charlotte Perkins Gilman was in the midst of a divorce from her first husband, artist Charles Walter Stetson, and her burgeoning career and divorce were tied together in the press, resulting in unpleasant notoriety. When Gilman sent Katherine to live with her ex-husband and his new wife several years later, the gossip recurred. These circumstances, combined with Gilman's strident public criticism of marriage, motherhood, and the home as they were configured in her time, made her a threatening figure in a society that sentimentalized all three. As a result, Gilman probably suffered more cruel attacks in the press and in the court of public opinion than any other woman writer of her generation. Her autobiography serves as an answer to these attacks. Throughout *Living,* she gives examples of what people thought of her: Mysterious "creeping slanders" based on nothing in particular followed her in San Francisco. Her "name became a football" for the newspapers after her divorce from Stetson. A mean-spirited *San Francisco Examiner* article—"Should Literary Women Marry?"—was only one of the articles that criticized her.[21] Gilman's contemporaries confirmed her opinion that she was often misrepresented in the press and in gossip. Critic Alexander Black wrote, "It once seemed that shuttling crippled quotations of Mrs. Gilman was an established indoor sport."[22] Gilman often found that the circumstances of her personal life as represented in the popular press limited her credibility in her crusade to reconfigure gender relations. For instance, she was told that it was thought "unbecoming" for a woman who had abandoned her child to give lectures about motherhood.[23] The stigma never went away. When Gilman visited her adult daughter in the early 1920s, the local paper identified her as "the woman who thirty years ago gave away her husband."[24] In 1930, an article about her life summarized the ordinary person's perception of Gilman as a "queer," "dangerous" person.[25]

For Gilman, to reassert control over her self-image by writing her life was to run the risk of being misread—again. But it was also an opportunity she could not resist at a time when her influence had declined. Although the National League of Women voters named her the foremost woman thinker in the world in 1930, her literary reputation was almost nonexistent by that time.[26] In 1923, Alexander Black commented that "so much of her preaching that once was regarded as revolutionary is now a matter of polite consideration."[27] Sadly, contemporary readers knew so little about Gilman that most reviews of *Living* begin with an explanation of her importance. "Thirty years ago," a typical review of *Living* declares, "Charlotte Perkins Gilman was a beacon light to girls and women struggling to find a place for themselves in a changing world. . . . She made it all incredibly urgent and thrilling, with a splendid zest, brilliance, and wit and the inspiring force of her own example. And then she faded from sight and the next generation was unaware of her."[28]

By the mid-1930s, Margaret Deland had also been dismissed as a relic from an era gone by, although she was still periodically publishing new novels. She was acclaimed for writing serious "problem novels" between 1890 and 1916 and had merited mention in two sections of a 1917 textbook entitled *A History of American Literature since 1870*.[29] However, by 1930, her name had all but disappeared from textbooks and literary criticism, just as Gilman's had. The reviews of *If This Be I* were generally complimentary, often patronizingly so. Alice Parsons of the *New York Herald Tribune Books* titled her review "Some Gentle Memories of Early Girlhood" and terms it a "delightful narrative," although many of the memories Deland details—of wounded Civil War soldiers packed into cattle cars, recurring nightmares, and tormenting insects—are neither "gentle" nor "delightful."[30] Deland's biographer Diana C. Reep notes that most interviews with Deland were done in the "genteel" fashion, with "reporters repeating her favorite stories, but not apparently seeking significant information about her life or her writing techniques."[31] Sadly, Deland's autobiography, like Gilman's, seemed to have been reviewed according to preconceived expectations of its author or as a tribute to an elderly, formerly famous personage rather than for the book's own qualities or merits. While some reviewers called Deland's work "honest," "vigorous," and "never sentimental," terms that are more accurate descriptions, the overall impression they offer is of an amusing, affectionate piece of nostalgia, which *If This Be I* certainly is not.[32]

As well as being antisentimental, Deland's memoirs refuse nostalgia through her treatment of antebellum and Civil War America. In fact, Deland often compares the past unfavorably with the present, with comments like, "in Maggie's time, grown people didn't know enough to look at the sky that way. Maggie never saw Grandmother Wade lying on her back, staring up into the blue depth. . . . Today's gay grandmothers know better."[33] Deland's lack of sentimental nostalgia is ironic, given that nostalgia was a major marketing point for Depression-era autobiography, but even more so given the enduring popularity of her stories set in Old Chester. Starting with *Old Chester Tales* in 1903, Deland used the town as a setting for many short stories and several novels for over a quarter-century. Her fans loved the fictional town as "a place of traditions, a bit of antiquity."[34] In 1941, book critic George Hellman pointedly noted that "many today still take pleasure in her non-controversial writings, of which *Old Chester Tales* is probably the most engaging."[35]

However, *If This Be I* questions the traditions and ideals that Deland's faithful readers loved about Old Chester, including sacred cows such as patriotism. For instance, Deland explains that Maggie was praised for being enthusiastic about war, for when she said "'H'rah, H'rah,' she was approved of, and told she was a dear little patriotic girl." The text uses six-year-old Maggie's innocent ignorance of the world to expose the brutalities of war. Although her Grandfather Wade hosted a stop on the Underground Railroad, Maggie did not understand this at all, so Deland insists that to Maggie, war, "a word which was often on the lips of grown up people," was only associated with "lovely bloodthirsty games," and that "Mrs. Deland" only found out much later that "war is mankind's most pathetically futile form of courage." The Civil War dominated Maggie's formative years and figures prominently in Deland's autobiography. Watching the grownup women around her host sewing parties and bring baked goods to the wounded soldiers in the Union Hospital in Pittsburgh, Deland writes, "I infer that, to Maggie, Compassion was a name for pleasant things, like cake, and the best china." Deland explains that "[Maggie] sometimes used the word [Compassion] like a parrot, but it was a long time before she experienced it." Since compassion meant cake and china to Maggie, Deland points out that Maggie saw no connection between the word and a hungry child whom she indignantly locked in the garden shed for stealing apples from her uncle's tree. At the end of the section, Deland explains, "I know she had turned into Margaret before she understood that Compassion is Pity in action." But while she was still Maggie, "compassion meant making a play—like the Caterpillar Hospital."[36] Maggie's "play" hospital for caterpillars was not terribly compassionate: the child would hunt for bugs, paint them with mustard (mustard plasters were a common medical remedy at the time), bind them in bandages, and immobilize them. After confining the squirming and struggling insects to their beds, she then built coffins for them. When the caterpillars escape, the reader is grateful, but Maggie is outraged at the insects' ingratitude for her "compassion."

What must Deland have thought when memories such as these were called "gentle" and her tales of smug little Maggie a "delightful narrative?" Like Gilman, Deland may have felt thwarted or overlooked by the 1930s. Perhaps because she was no longer considered relevant, she created an activist autobiography that seems out of step with her reputation as an old-fashioned popular novelist. For Deland's first autobiography is distinctly antisentimental. In her passage considering the nature of love, she writes, "Naturally, as the lovely reiterated word became a part of her vocabulary, Maggie, noticing that when she used it she was approved of—used it whenever she could." *If This Be I* frequently detaches words from their sentimental nineteenth-century context. In addition to the words "compassion" and "patriotism," Maggie found "the two [words] which she used with the greatest frequency, had the least meaning. 'Love' was one; 'God was the other. . . . Both words were just sounds, with no more sense than one of Major's barks."[37] For a little girl to be loving, compassionate, and reverent were standard expectations at the time, but Maggie's enactments of these qualities were often not what her genteel "Mama" (as she called the aunt who raised her after her parents died) expected.

Deland may have viewed *If This Be I* as a chance to dismantle any nostalgic illusions the reading public harbored about the past. In the book, Maggie has spunk and ingenuity but no power to defend herself when she violates Victorian expectations. One day, the whole family goes down to the train station to support the local troops as they leave town for the battlefield. Maggie is eager to prove the patriotism for which she has so often been affirmed. But she has forgotten to bring her handkerchief to wave at the train. Trying to be a good little girl, Maggie takes off her underwear and waves them at the train full of soldiers, bringing the wrath of her relatives down on her. She is surprised and bewildered when she is punished for disgracing the family.[38] In this anecdote, Maggie learns too late that feminine modesty outweighs patriotic fervor in her mama's eyes. Through scenes like these, Deland's text reveals and castigates the powerlessness of Victorian girlhood.

Both these progressive texts condemn the past by intentionally revealing the psychological scars of a nineteenth-century upbringing rather than evoking the nostalgia that 1930s readers may have expected. In *If This Be I,* Deland transforms Maggie's limited understanding into a subtextual indictment of Victorian structures and strictures, like "children must be seen and not heard; they must not speak unless they were spoken to," or "Age, because it was Age, was entitled to respect—a most unsound doctrine." Once, Maggie is scolded for looking through a keyhole when she is sent on an errand to see if a guest was ready for dinner. Told she is "dishonorable" and that her mother is "ashamed," Maggie cries over "the queerness of Mama's telling her to 'find out,' and then scolding her because she did find out." In fact, Maggie receives a number of these inexplicable punishments, like having her ears boxed by her grandmother for repeating stories she had heard about a family that her grandmother and friends had been discussing on the porch the same day. Thereafter, she associated "gossip" with "a burning sense of injustice."[39] Intelligent as she was, little Maggie, the "eye" of the text, was powerless to truly understand, but "Mrs. Deland," the "I" of the text, is not. In *If This Be I,* Deland the author has transcended Maggie's confusion and spoken up in her defense against the things that hurt her.

Gilman's autobiographical persona also tries to transcend the hurt, confusion, and anger she experienced in her youth. As a child, Gilman felt abandoned by both of her parents. The emotionally and financially unstable Frederick Beecher Perkins abandoned his family when Charlotte was young. Even though she, her mother, and her brother were so poor that they had to move nineteen times in eighteen years, Gilman does not elaborate on her father's failures to keep his promises to pay their board at various places in *Living,* as she does in an earlier, unpublished version of the autobiography. She simply states, "My childhood had no father" in the published version. Gilman relates three or four brief encounters with him and then reiterates, "These are the sum of my memories of my father in my childish years."[40] From reading her letters, diaries, and juvenilia, we know Gilman did miss and long for her father's love, but she will not admit it in her public portrait of her life.[41] Instead, she transcends her personal hurt to make a detached, rational calculation of his relative worth to her future work. In the way she reframes her childhood experiences, Gilman's autobiography, like Deland's, reveals her denied childhood desires for both agency and comfort.

Revisited emotional deprivations dominate Gilman's depictions of her mother in *Living.* According to her autobiography, Gilman was "violently well brought up." The focus on deprivation in the descriptions of Gilman's youth can be seen in the titles of the chapters themselves: "The End of Childhood" and "Girlhood—If Any." In the former chapter, she describes her life to the reader: "Outside of schooling, what? Not much. Mother had put on me two more prohibitions, I was to read no novels and to have no intimate friends." In the autobiography, Gilman's mother appears to have discouraged her writing. *Living* tells of Mary Perkins's cold reaction to Charlotte's first attempt at poetry; in a response eerily similar to Edith Wharton's mother's notorious remark about drawing rooms being always tidy, Gilman's mother tells her to "go and put on the teakettle" instead of acknowledging her daughter's creative efforts.[42]

Although she avoids recriminations against her mother, Gilman's depiction of her relationship with her mother in *Living* still evokes pity for the little girl that she was. Gilman begins her description of her mother by saying, "If unswerving love, tireless service, intense and efficient care, and the concentrated devotion of a lifetime that knew no other purpose make a good mother, mine was of the best." One gets the sense Gilman is trying to credit her mother's intentions in her autobiography (just as she wishes the reader to credit her own intentions) while still asserting Mary's failure as a parent. *Living* explains that Gilman's mother, because of her own abandonment by Frederick Perkins, wished to inure her daughter to later disappointments by depriving Charlotte of affection early on. But this explanation seems inadequate in light of the next revelation: Gilman's mother never touched her affectionately unless she was asleep, so little Charlotte would jab herself with pins to stay awake, feigning sleep until her mother came in and hugged her.[43] In spite of Gilman's rational explanation of her mother's strange behavior, she invokes more pity for the deprived child than for the desperate mother who repressed the desire to hug her child day after day.

Deland also describes Maggie's unsatisfied childhood desire for love in *If This Be I.* Having eavesdropped on a conversation about a woman who had died in childbirth (as had her own mother), Maggie decides that her aunt must love her less than she loves her biological daughter and directly accuses her aunt of it. When her aunt tries to reassure Deland that she is equally loved, she interrupts: "No, ma'am," Maggie said calmly, "you don't. You told Jane nobody could love a little baby like its own mother, and you are not m[ine]." At the end of the same chapter, Deland realizes that "wanting to be loved is not loving" and turns her affections elsewhere. Through a "queer, pagan impulse—which she called 'Love,'" Maggie hugs a tree, whispering, "her little lips bruised against the rough bark, 'I love you, tree. I love you." Deland reiterates this image of turning her unsatisfied childhood desire to be loved and to love toward the natural world several times in her text. At the very end of *If This Be I,* the voice of Deland intervenes to resolve the issue: referring to nature as the "Great Mother," she explains that motherless Maggie "put her lips on the earth, and kissed it."[44]

While Maggie turns her unwanted love toward the earth in Deland's autobiography, Gilman transforms her thwarted desires into a childhood world of imagination. Her juvenilia indicates that she wrote many fanciful stories, but in *Living,* Gilman asserts that her imaginative world was founded on justice: "I did not compose, make stories like Frances Hodgson in her childhood, but was already scheming to improve the world." Rather than acknowledging the desires for attention, power, and admiration that her juvenilia reveals, Gilman declares that her "first" wish was, "I wish that everything I wish may be Right!" She began using her magic world to rescue the unhappy children she saw instead of wishing up these things for herself, she asserts, transcending her own desire to create stories by transferring them into service to humanity. But, once she discovered the stories, Gilman's mother forbade her to use her imagination, which "had been my chief happiness for five years." "But obedience was Right," Gilman expostulates, "the thing had to be done, and I did it. Night after night to shut the door on happiness, and hold it shut. Never, when dear, bright, glittering dreams pushed hard, to let them in. Just thirteen."[45] While Gilman verbally privileges being obedient, the repetition she uses in the same passage reveals how agonizing and unjust her mother's command felt.

Maggie's vivid imagination also gets her into trouble in *If This Be I.* Throughout her childhood, Maggie has a recurring nightmare that she is really a Chinese baby dreaming of being Maggie. Deland explains that Maggie's nightmare stemmed from the stories she had been told about heathen foreigners, leading the frightened little girl to believe that being born white in the West was such a great privilege that it must be too good to be true. When she quotes part of a poem from a Victorian children's book called *Songs for the Little Ones* about a Chinese mother throwing her unwanted baby to a crocodile, the reader starts to understand why Maggie is so terrified. Then Deland steps in and says, "but I needn't go on. Some of the Sunday School books of eighty years ago would have made anybody feel unreal!" Maggie suffers this recurring terror in silence until Mrs. Deland's autobiographical privilege allows her to speak her fear, for she explains there was "a certain Maple Grove code, to the effect that it wasn't, so to speak, 'the thing' to use the word 'fear.'"[46] In passages like these, "Mrs. Deland," the older, wiser author and social commentator, mediates between Maggie's raw experience and the reader's reactions to them, refusing a nostalgic or sentimental perspective on an American past that held such deep hypocrisies and prejudices.

Gilman's text also frequently redirects readers' reactions from her personal experience toward a greater social context. *Living* explains that in terms of her real Living, she has placed the "functional relation to society" above all other concerns. She illustrates this idea through an anecdote, telling of a "noted English engineer, whose personal life was open to much criticism, and who was about to die of heart disease." When asked if he was worried about being damned for his behavior, he answered, "When I die, if I come to judgment, I believe that I shall be judged by the bridges I have built." Following this anecdote, she exhorts the reader that human beings are meant "to find our places, our special work in the world, and when found, do it, do it at all costs." In her philosophy, the importance of "world work" transcends all other concerns, including the costs to herself. Her Living is inextricably bound up in her "honest, conscientious nobly-purposed effort" and on "the will power that made it."[47] Assertions like these serve a double purpose: they defend Gilman's "life" and offer a didactic lesson to readers about what "Living" means to her.

Deland's autobiographical technique serves a similarly didactic double purpose. Throughout *If This Be I,* little Maggie struggles conscientiously with big, abstract concepts, although her own efforts do not always have the best results. Deland titles her chapters with abstract concepts Maggie did not understand, like "Honor, Death, and Truth," deconstructing the words through Maggie's experiences with them. Deland recalls little Maggie learning about honor, "which stood for nothing tangible, or audible, or visible—but for an ideal, unknown to some of us who keep within the Law and obey the Ten Commandments—in neither of which does this shining word appear." For instance, Maggie thought she was being honorable in being scrupulously honest about counting the weeds she dug up for a penny each. But when she found a large patch of easy-to-dig weeds, she was not paid for them, for according to Mama, Maggie's ambition to earn money revealed "the taint of trade." This confusing experience is meant to teach Maggie that being honorable is a performance of something "extra," not just being honest.[48]

Gilman's autobiography also performs many transformations of childhood experiences into adult meanings. In one of the most powerful examples, the piteous child who pricked herself with pins to stay awake and was forbidden to use her imagination turns her emotional and physical deprivation into a sense of power. Gilman relates few instances of disobedience to her mother in *Living,* but she uses one to illustrate that her will was stronger than her mother's authority. After disobeying her mother's command to apologize for something she has not done, Gilman says that "one could suffer, one could die if it came to that, but one could not be coerced. I was born." But what was she born into? Gilman immediately decides that as a new "free agent," she "would still obey" her mother until she came of age.[49]

Living spells out how this act of will, transferring a prohibition into a self-determined purpose to become stronger, established a pattern in Gilman's life. Her teen years of self-enforced obedience, she explains, disciplined both her mind and her body. This was the invisible Living of those years—the "game[s] won," games of will power. She spent a year learning to be considerate of others, forcing herself to visit an invalid she did not care for in order to prove she could be thoughtful. She spent hours in the gymnasium so that years later she could still lift and carry that hapless woman who misunderstood the nature of her suffering. She handed down edicts to herself: never to lie, always to rise early and accomplish much each day, keeping painstaking accounts of her success in her diary, down to her bicep measurements.[50] Proud of her adolescent self-discipline, Gilman makes the extraordinary claim, "For eight years I did not do anything I thought wrong, and did, at any cost, what I thought right." Her constant triumphs of self-improvement and discipline gave her a sense of power, of unlimited ability to do anything to which she set her will, and so *Living* reports that Gilman purportedly sat down to solve the problem of evil at age seventeen.[51]

In *If This Be I,* when little Maggie tries to understand good and evil by acting out her childish understanding of the grownups' words, it often has ugly results. In the "Law, Justice, and Compassion" chapter, after a local woman is hung for murdering her husband, Maggie decides to enact "Justice" on the seventeen-year swarm of locusts that are eating the kitchen garden. After all, there is a bounty on their heads of a penny per jarful. But capturing them in a jar is not enough to assuage Maggie's juvenile sense of justice. As Deland remarks, "I can see that Maggie felt that the killing of the crowding enemy . . . was to be accounted unto her as righteousness." Thus, Maggie builds a miniature gallows and hangs as many locusts as she could catch. The child's execution of justice is described thus: "Maggie's memory of it is so vivid, that I see just what she saw; the twelve victims—twisting, struggling, beating their wings, and buzzing, buzzing." Maggie watches "the execution with grave, interested eyes—judicial, unpitying eyes."[52]

Patricia Meyer Spacks's theory of the psychological development of young girls in the nineteenth century may shed some light on Maggie's execution of the locusts: "A female childhood, that, because female, is repressed, fosters angry womanhood. The adult, disguising her anger by her insistent claims of selflessness, fantasizes her 'goodness' into power. By being good she helps all mankind, she wins fame or love. She can be good instead of being gifted, or she can use her gifts in the service of her goodness, thus avoiding the guilt of self-expression."[53] The way that Gilman's autobiography describes both her calling to activism and her first marriage also enacts this psychological dynamic. In Gilman's upbringing, "To be Right was the main thing in life." Being right gave Gilman a sense of control; her autobiography revels in the power her years of self-discipline gave her. When she was twenty-one, after six years of perfectly abiding by the rules and standards she set for herself, she felt a "power, clear glorious power, of ability to do whatever I decided to undertake." That same sense of power informs her sense of purpose, which is one potential interpretation of Living in the book. In "Power and Glory," Gilman explains that her "splendid sense of power" stemmed from her "high though indefinite purpose, the absolute consecration to coming service."[54] While the chapter title echoes the closing of the Lord's Prayer, the last phrase of the sentence sounds like the words of someone taking Holy Orders. In this passage, Gilman's "power" serves as compensation for her circumscribed life, while her emotional deprivation serves as a symbol of her special calling, just as it would for a nun.

Despite her invocation of Holy Orders in this scene, celibacy was not to be a part of Gilman's calling. When Charlotte Perkins met her first husband, Charles Walter Stetson, they were immediately and powerfully attracted to one another, and he quickly proposed marriage. Gilman was conflicted about their relationship. She viewed "the pleasure of association," "sympathy," and "sex-attraction" as obstacles to her "complete devotion to [her] work." Since her association with Stetson was pleasurable, to marry would not be a selfless action—and therefore not in line with her self-consecration—so Gilman seems to have transformed their relationship from a pleasure into a duty. The reason she gives for their engagement in *Living* emphasizes her self-sacrifice, characterizing her marriage as an act of sympathy. When he "met a keen personal disappointment," she writes, "I agreed to marry him." In *Living,* written fifty years later, Gilman proudly relates her self-abnegation in marriage. She even refused to express a preference in home decor, saying she expressed "no taste or desire."[55]

Conversely, Deland's autobiography affirms that perhaps girls do have their own tastes and desires. Maggie expresses hers quite unabashedly. Deland observes, "In those days every young lady was supposed . . . to toil over five-finger exercises until at a Party, she could at least render 'The Maiden's Prayer,'" but Maggie's vehement resistance gets her out of piano lessons. On another occasion, five-year-old Maggie proposes marriage to a handsome soldier she sees on a Pittsburgh streetcar, an offense for which she is peremptorily dragged off the car and into the street. Since Maggie is not yet Mrs. Deland, Deland writes, "I have merely, with the shameless candor of probability, deduced from her own words, her desire to own him." While Gilman characterizes feminine desire as an obstacle to feminine usefulness in *Living,* Deland affirms little Maggie's desire to "own" the soldier as a proto-feminist moment, calling the event an "outburst of feminism, nearly seventy years in advance."[56]

In her insistence that selflessness and service are the best ways to live one's life, Gilman cannot openly admit in her autobiography that repressing all her desires might have made her first marriage unhappy for both her and Stetson. She skims over the question of whether her "increasing depression" might be a symptom of her own discontent in a text that emphasizes selflessness: "I think Walter was happy."[57] His diaries show a man trying to be happy though finding his wife a bit passive. She is perhaps "too subservient," he notes.[58] However Gilman may have rationalized the situation, *Living* still makes it clear that the first really debilitating symptoms of depression began soon after her first marriage. When the depression forced her to face her unhappiness, Gilman explains in *Living,* she blamed herself: "You did it yourself! You did it yourself! You had health and strength and hope and glorious work before you—and you threw it all away. You were called to serve humanity and you cannot serve yourself. No good as a wife, no good as a mother, no good for anything. And you did it yourself!" Her language in this passage asserts that Gilman wants "health and strength and hope"—but only to serve others, not to fulfill herself. Her desire, it seems, is to be "good" for something; happiness is not an avowed concern. This passage seems intended to show that Gilman's uselessness, not her unhappiness, caused her divorce. Explaining her decision to leave her husband in *Living,* Gilman writes, "If I had been of the slightest use to him or to the child, I would have stuck it," but "it seemed plain that if I went crazy it would do my husband no good and be a deadly injury to my child." Unlike Mary Austin, who provides her husband's incompetence as the reason for their divorce in *Earth Horizon,* Gilman praises Stetson as a loving and devoted husband, and castigates herself as a worthless wife.[59] According to *Living,* her own suffering played no part in her decision to leave him.

Within the ideological context that drives Gilman's autobiography, Gilman may have downplayed her personal unhappiness in her first marriage because she deems "pain" to be merely a part of "life," not of real "Living." The extremely selective way that Gilman uses her diaries in her autobiography follows this pattern as well. When she writes about her marriage to Stetson, Gilman includes the entries that demonstrate either her selflessness or her devotion to service but omits those that express her anger at Stetson or her own desire for freedom. In describing her breakdown and the demise of her marriage in her autobiography, Gilman includes this diary entry: "I anticipate a future of failure and suffering. Children sickly and unhappy. Husband miserable because of my distress; and I——! . . . Let me at least learn to be uncomplaining and unselfish. Let me do my work and not fling my pain on others." If Gilman's vision of perfectly selfless wifehood partially contributed to her breakdown, then her vision of motherhood, which she defines simply as "Giving," made her breakdown complete. After her daughter, Katherine, was born, she sank into a severe postpartum depression. In typical fashion, Gilman admits to no resentment or frustration regarding motherhood in *Living,* though she would depict it vividly in both her diaries and her fiction. "The baby?" she writes in the autobiography, "I nursed her for five months. I would hold her close—that lovely child!—and instead of love and happiness, feel only pain. . . . Nothing was more utterly bitter than this, that even motherhood brought no joy."[60]

While new parents are bound to feel exhausted by the constant needs of an infant, Gilman's diary entries for this period (none of which are included in *Living*) reveal clear symptoms of postpartum depression. In one sense, the diaries for this period contain accounts of typical days in the life of a new mother: inadequate sleep, days spent in doing little else but "tending baby."[61] But for Gilman, who had clung to perfectionism as a personal standard for decades, these conditions were overwhelming. For one thing, the needs of an infant were unaccommodating to Gilman's strict, self-imposed physical regimens. The lack of sleep, for instance, was an assault on Gilman's longstanding "five little rules of health." Another of Gilman's longstanding rules, to eat "good food and plenty of it," was violated by her "starving" in order not to upset Katherine's stomach. For a woman whose diary shows her planning her days hour by hour, recording her body measurements, and counting up the number of words she has written, spending her days doing repetitive tasks with frequent interruptions by an infant may have felt unendurable. When *Living* answers the familiar accusation that she had acted selfishly in sending Katherine to live with Stetson and his new wife so that she herself could find work in San Francisco, Gilman uses her own tears, which she declares to be falling as she writes the autobiography, as evidence that "no one suffered from it but myself."[62] Gilman's *Living* does not allow for the possibility that Katherine may have suffered too. To do so would be to admit that Gilman had failed in her resolve not to let her pain impact her loved ones.

Not only does Gilman deny that her daughter may have been hurt by their separation, her autobiography also downplays the sense of relief and freedom she felt after Katherine left. Freedom from domesticity and motherhood seems to have had an energizing effect on Gilman, as it had on Gertrude Atherton. But while Atherton, who had no qualms about being called selfish, celebrates her freedom and her adventures, Gilman subjugates these two things to a sense of her calling. *Living* quotes a poem Gilman wrote to commemorate her solitary journey east; in it, the images of exultation, freedom, and power expressed in the first three lines are redirected outward in the last two:

> As the strong sweet light of the morning,
> As the strong sweet air from the sea,
> As the strong sweet music of the wind among the
>   leaves,
> Comes the voice of my goodwill to a weary world that
>   grieves,
> Crying "Be Glad! Be Free!"[63]

The exhortation of the last line may indeed have been an inward exhortation to herself, but Gilman turns her own desires for happiness and freedom outward, toward a "weary world" instead, just as Maggie turns her desire for love outward toward the world in *If This Be I.*

Insisting on the selflessness of her actions throughout *Living,* Gilman refuses to acknowledge any kind of self-indulgence. In 1900, she married her cousin, Houghton Gilman, and this second marriage was much happier than the first. But her autobiography indicates that it was a struggle for Charlotte to accept happiness, since her philosophy of Living was that "I ought to forego the more intimate personal happiness for complete devotion to my work." Houghton's devotion to her was the one great comfort of Charlotte's life. However, he is nearly absent from her *Living,* though they were married for nearly forty years. It is as if, being a "happy ending" for her, Houghton does not belong in her tale of self-denial. She merely refers to her second marriage as "degradingly comfortable" and contemplates the "insidious drugging effect in spending one's time waiting on one's own tastes and appetites, and those of dear ones," revealing her enduring fear that having selfish desires precludes the glorious exaltation of service. *Living* painstakingly points out that Gilman took a yearly hiatus from the personal comfort and intimacy of her marriage in the form of a three-month lecture tour. When she does discuss her happier life with Houghton in her autobiography, she uses it didactically, by pointing out the charms of a kitchenless home or discussing how many kinds of vegetables they raised in their garden.[64]

On the other hand, Margaret Deland's marriage was, by all accounts, an extremely happy one, which was likely why her sequel autobiography, *Golden Yesterdays,* is as much about Lorin Deland as about herself. Mary Ross of the *New York Tribune Review of Books* rightly called *Golden Yesterdays* "more a story of a marriage than an individual."[65] However, rather than portraying it as "degradingly comfortable," Deland writes of her marriage as a mutual intellectual activism, a merging of two "rebel minds" who work together for a common purpose. She and Lorin supported each other amid the sociopolitical controversies that Margaret Deland's writing caused. However, *Golden Yesterdays* also allows Deland to deny any ambition on her own behalf, just as Gilman does in *Living,* and to deflect her fame as an author into her role as a dutiful wife, just as Gilman deflects her desires into activism in *Living. Golden Yesterdays* is really more about Lorin Deland's careers as a pastor, football coach, advertising executive, and reformer than about Margaret's own steadier career as a writer, and when Deland does discuss her work, she denies any desire for personal achievement, just as Gilman does, claiming that a friend sent her first work (those greeting card poems) to be published, and that her writing became a substitute for the children she could not have. Known to publishers as a hard-nosed negotiator, Deland also claims she was "an excellent woman of business" only because she carefully followed her husband's advice, and that he came up with all her titles. Throughout *Golden Yesterdays,* Deland's writing is subjugated to other things. For instance, before she tells a lengthy story about Teddy Roosevelt, she mentions that their encounter "turns upon a novel of mine."[66] In fact, since she only brings up her literary work casually, as a segue into other topics, *Golden Yesterdays* hardly qualifies as a literary autobiography at all. The book concludes with Lorin Deland's death in 1917, leaving out the last twenty-four years of Deland's career as a novelist. Although Maggie's stories in *If This Be I* obliquely reveal an inquiring mind and creative personality ready to impact the world, *Golden Yesterdays,* published six years later, presents a strange regression in the evolving tradition of American women's literary autobiography. *Golden Yesterdays* reads more like the autobiography of a woman writer from before 1900, not one published in 1941.

Some of the same Victorian ethos of self-denial that contributed to Deland's regressive self-effacement in *Golden Yesterdays* may have also come to bear on the sections of *Living* depicting Gilman's life as an author and lecturer. In these sections, Gilman seems determined to refute any desire for fame, success, or wealth. In the course of her autobiography, Gilman contends that she had many alternate career paths at her command. She could have been a great still-life painter, she explains, or a great actress, or a highly remunerated novelist. Further, she has no doubt that "with the right early training [she] could easily have been an acrobat" or "command[ed] a high salary as a chef" in a New York club. But each of these claims, while asserting Gilman's power to make herself into a person who could command fame, admiration, and money, also substantiate Gilman's ethos of self-denial. In each case, she explains that in those more glamorous, rewarding professions, she could not give herself as fully to humanity, so she did not pursue them. Having all these paths from which to choose, she insists on the "persecut[ion]," "ostraciz[ation]," "misunderstanding," and "opposition" that come with being an "improver."[67]

Unlike the other women writers of Gilman's generation who used their autobiographies to advocate for their literary legacies, Gilman's *Living* argues that she was never trying to be an artist. Rather, she sought to be an activist—although "reformer" is the actual term she employs. In *Pen-Portraits of Literary Women,* professor Helen Gray Cone, one of Gilman's contemporaries, wrote about the tension women writers of their generation experienced between creating art and using literature as activism.[68] Gilman appears to have wholeheartedly embraced the activism option, and her autobiography reads as a defense of that choice. Over and over, she explains that she frustrated more established authors who wished to help further her career by refusing to compromise her activist content, determined never to subordinate it to considerations of style. *Living* explains that William Dean Howells did everything he could to help her publish but finally realized the futility of making Gilman marketable because she refused to listen to him. Gilman also admits that she could have heeded Theodore Dreiser's advice to "consider more what editors want," but it would have violated her principles. Gilman delineates the differences among types of writers: "There are those who write as artists, real ones; they often find it difficult to consider what the editor wants. There are those who write to earn a living, they, if they succeed, *must* please the editor. . . . But if one writes to express important truths, needed yet unpopular, the market is necessarily limited." Clearly, Gilman places herself in the third category. Although the popularity of Deland's most controversial feminist works, *The Awakening of Helena Ritchie,* which focuses on an abusive marriage, an illicit affair, and a single mother's determination to keep and raise her son, and *The Iron Woman,* about an indomitable female mill-owner, prove exceptions to Gilman's claim, Gilman truly could not find a market for most of her fiction. She wrote, edited, and published a magazine, the *Forerunner,* because her manuscripts were piling up "far faster than [she] could sell them." Gilman also formed the Charlton Company with her second husband to publish her books from 1909 to 1916. This venture was similar in purpose to Virginia Woolf's Hogarth Press but on a smaller scale. However, unlike Hogarth, the Charlton Press brought out only Gilman's work: a total of three novels and one nonfiction book, *The Man-Made World,* all of which had appeared in some form in the *Forerunner.* Publishing the *Forerunner* was a purely altruistic effort, Gilman explains; it actually cost her about $1,500 a year instead of earning her anything. Even so, this claim may be a reassertion of her activism and may be masking a desire for critical notice. For instance, Gilman complains about the critical neglect of the *Forerunner* in *Living:* "It has always seemed to me something of a joke on the American critics of this period that not one of them, save a woman who was already a friend, should have recognized this literary *tour de force* by an established author as worth mentioning."[69]

Although she claims not to be an artist in *Living,* Gilman does use her autobiography to develop a theory of activist art. Gilman, who had cut off her imagination as a forbidden luxury as a child, felt that the source of art, like the truth of one's *Living,* was in its intention. The sacred precinct of art, for her, is not the imagination, but the will. "I have never made any pretense about being literary," Gilman writes. "As far as I had any method in mind, it was to express the idea with clearness and vivacity, so that it might be apprehended with ease and pleasure."[70] Frederick Wegener points out that Gilman's response to Edith Wharton's "The Fullness of Life" reveals Gilman's rejection of artistic ambiguity: she decried Wharton's ending because it did not clearly teach a lesson; she wanted literature to be the agent of ideas. "Here is the young woman reader," she wrote. "Why does not the writer give her a true picture of what is going on, both within her and without?"[71] Gilman believed in a "curbed text," the classic story with a moral that confines the reader to a single interpretation, and Gilman's work may not have sold because her ideology had to be so clear that it could not be missed.[72] The truth is that Gilman's fictional characters are often flat, her descriptions hasty, and her plots contrived, while Deland's fictional characters are complex and compelling. Gilman's assumptions fit strictly within the cultural templates for women writers in the early twentieth century: *Living* demonstrates that she believed one could either write for art, for fame, for money, or for ideology. While Wharton falls the furthest on the side of art, Gilman lies at the other extreme, viewing literature as a mere tool for activism. Her most famous story, "The Yellow Wall-Paper," illustrates that Gilman could indeed accomplish both aims in her work. However, writing about the story's critical success, Gilman comments, "I wrote it to preach. If it is literature, that just happened."[73]

Perhaps Gilman considered the pleasures of art and imagination to be self-indulgent. Therefore, she denied her desires for them just as she had denied her other emotional and physical needs. *Living* emphasizes that Gilman's artlessness is a choice, not a flaw, despite her occasional overt protestations that she lacks the talent. "Verse was as easy as prose" for her, she writes, scattering numerous examples of her poetic prowess about the text. In one passage, Gilman relates how Mary Austin told her she could write "if you gave your mind to it." She then proceeds to parody Austin's style before turning back to focus on her activism. "I was not aiming in the least for literary virtuosity, still less at financial success," she claims. However much she demurred, a few passages still reveal that Gilman did have literary aspirations. The thrill she feels upon receiving a compliment from Howells, when she "felt like a real 'author' at last," belies her denials of literary ambition. She also recalls that her first book of poetry, *In This Our World*, which she and her friends brought out by subscription, "was warmly reviewed in certain discerning papers."

And like Gertrude Atherton, Gilman prints flattering letters and refers to good reviews in her autobiography. Gilman notes that she has written twenty-five volumes and hopes for "a 'library edition,' someday, with the best of the *Forerunner* and all my other books, this autobiography trailing along at the end."[74] Although she overtly denies artistic aspirations in *Living,* her hopes for a literary legacy surface in its pages anyway.

Gilman's autobiography also tiptoes around the questions of money and professionalism. She seems torn between asserting her desire for financial independence as a feminist example for other women, and seeming too concerned with money, which, she believes, would compromise her activist persona. In *Living,* Gilman describes her quest to professionalize her work as a lecturer, decrying the genteel tradition of giving female speakers "social attention" instead of payment for their time. She demonstrates that she values her labor and demands to be treated as a professional. She requires, albeit "gently," payment for books a store has sold without sending her a share of the profits.[75] Literary scholar Joanne B. Karpinski argues that Gilman equivocates about her financial situation in her autobiography, pretending she is more self-reliant than she actually is in order to use herself as an example of female self-sufficiency.[76] In reality, Gilman regularly sought loans from friends and sold her belongings when she had to.[77] As one reads the autobiography, one realizes that her financial condition was not entirely due to lack of sales. In *Living,* Gilman refers to the many times she was cheated, such as when she placed a volume of poetry, *In This Our World,* in stores and they sent her no commissions (a not uncommon financial exploitation of poets that Harriet Monroe crusaded to abolish, as chapter 4 demonstrates). Gilman also recalls that either her agent or the *New England Magazine* stiffed her for the forty dollars owed her for "The Yellow Wall-Paper." She accuses another agent of defrauding her of lecture fees, and laments that when *Women and Economics* was translated into several languages, "never a cent did I receive for it—I forget the excuses given."[78]

Although she often worried over money, Gilman makes it clear that she is by no means a businesswoman. Her "business is to preach," not to worry about getting paid. "I lectured and preached, wherever I was asked, for my expenses or for what they could afford to give," she explains. Gilman often spoke for whatever could be gathered in a collection at the end of her lecture, coming closer to being a preacher than any of her female relatives had. She claims that she lived as "propertyless and as desireless as a Buddhist priest." She also explains that she never found a good agent because "such a person, to succeed, must have a strong conviction of the value of my work, *and* business ability. These do not coexist."[79] This statement is perhaps intended to pay tribute to Gilman's integrity of purpose, a personal integrity upon which Wharton also insisted in *A Backward Glance.* But while Wharton is true to her art, Gilman remains true to her ideological vision.

Gilman has her say about the proper relationship between art and money in *Living.* Instead of walking a fine line as do the other writers considered here in their autobiographical discussions of money, Gilman draws the line clearly between those who profit from their work (everyone else) and those who do not (herself). Throughout her career, Gilman had complained about the "popular literature" of her time: "It must be popular because there is so much of it. I am not so certain of its being literature," she wrote. She remarked on the lurid covers designed to sell books, concluding that, in order to make money, popular fiction panders to the "weak spots in humanity." Her definition of literature's taint by the market, then, implied that she was above the market, unlike other women writers, and also reemphasized her view that art has moral obligations.[80] This judgment implicitly informs her descriptions of her career. For instance, *Living* mentions that she turned down "good prices" on principle when a Hearst publication came to ask her to write for them.[81]

However, in stark contrast to her autobiography, Gilman's fiction reveals her longing for the things she declares beneath her in *Living.* In her fiction, she imagines financial success, a receptive audience, revenge against those who hurt her, and the cooperation of the masses. Her stories are full of women who profit hugely from the kind of innovative enterprise that Gilman espoused but never profited from herself. In "Mrs. Mann's Clothes," women open "sensible" dress shops and rake in the money. In "What Diantha Did," women run cooperative enterprises and housekeeping services that are enormously successful. In other stories, like "Three Women" and "The Cottagette," women find a way to balance marriage and career, and the men they love become convinced that they are happier in a home that their wives do not have to run. One could almost view Gilman's fiction as the forbidden world where all her denied desires for money, fame, love, and leisure are played out.

Her fiction also reveals the frustration and anger that Gilman denied were a valid part of her "Living." Only in the clawing and crawling of the heroine of "The Yellow Wall-Paper," the vengeance and justice swiftly dealt to anyone and anything who did not fit in to Gilman's vision of a perfect society in "If I Were a Witch" (1911), and in the multiple murderous acts in *Unpunished* (1929) can we begin to imagine the anger Gilman denies herself throughout the autobiography. The anger, frustration, and violence underlying her later works suggest that, as an autobiographer, she consciously sculpts a persona to transcend both her personal desire for success and her ongoing frustration as an author. *Living* cannot, of course, sustain this persona. As I have argued, anger seeps through between the lines of both Gilman's and Deland's autobiographies. But Gilman is only open about her frustration in the section of *Living* that she wrote just before her death. In the years between writing the first draft of *Living* in 1927 and publishing the revisions in 1935, her sense of her audience may have changed. Her last chapter makes it clear that Gilman felt continually snubbed in those seven years: not only was *Unpunished* rejected but she "offered [her] services" to the League of Women Voters and got a turnout of ten people. Further, a nearby university did not invite her to lecture despite her "world-wide reputation" and her wish to say "so much that was new and strong to say to the coming generation." The last chapter of *Living,* written seven years after the rest of the book, declares, "I did expect better things of women than they have shown." Gilman lambasts many of the social and political trends of post–World War I America. The "optimist reformer," as William Dean Howells had called Gilman in the 1890s, seems to have become something of a pessimist at the last. Her words in that last chapter are blunt and stringent, hardly designed to appeal to the audience of young people that she coveted. Sadly, Gilman's perception of the reading public's attitude toward her was affirmed by the book's poor sales: *Living* sold only 808 copies in six months.[82]

If Gilman had indeed stopped hoping to find favor with the public in the 1930s, at least she was finally free to please herself. In the chapter written in 1934, Gilman seems to have allowed herself to indulge in anger, comfort, and intimacy, briefly abandoning her ethos of selfless, transcendent activism. Her persona in the last chapter is more open than all the rest: not only is it angrier, but it is also more affectionate. Having expressed her annoyance at the younger generation in general, she turns her focus to her contentment with Houghton, Katherine, and her grandchildren. The woman who declares herself wary of "insidious" comfort and prides herself on working twelve-hour days earlier in the autobiography now allows herself some small pleasures, relishing afternoons spent in the shade of an orange tree, its "delicious fragrance drifting over [her], the white petals lightly falling." However, the last words of Gilman's autobiography are unflinchingly consistent with the picture she has drawn throughout the text, affirming her irreproachable self-discipline, self-denial, and the transcendence of her Living: "My life is in Humanity—and that goes on. My contentment is in God—and That goes on. The Social Consciousness, fully accepted, automatically eliminates both selfishness and pride. The one predominant duty is to find one's work and do it, and I have striven mightily at that. The religion, the philosophy set up so early, have seen me through."[83] In completing the text of *Living,* Gilman had given her last lecture, reinscribing her core beliefs over her physical circumstances.

Deland's autobiography too digs beneath the external events of Maggie's life—such as a standard Victorian funeral—to find what Gilman would call Maggie's Living. Forced to look at her dead grandfather in his open casket, Maggie disrupts his funeral when she runs and runs from his "icy face" until she can't run any more. While her exasperated nineteenth-century household saw an incorrigible, sometimes naughty girl, Deland transforms scenes where Maggie's actions are misunderstood back into a didactic, acerbic critique of the Victorian perspective on the abstract concepts for which she titles her chapters. In the chapter on "Honor, Death, and Truth," "Truth" receives this treatment, as "Maggie's understanding of the word, though assisted by a spanking," made her mostly truthful "in regard to facts." However, Deland points out that Maggie's spanking did not teach her about "the wider truthfulness which sometimes transcends facts, the Truth of insincerities, cowardices, expediencies, or the untruth of altruism, when it is selfishness; and of philanthropy, when it is vanity."[84] Over and over in *If This Be I,* Deland uses Maggie's experiences to illustrate her critique of the hypocrisies within Victorian ideology, just as she did in so many of her books.

Both Gilman's and Deland's autobiographies are perplexing reads, but studying them together reveals the frustrations these women shared and the didactic narrative strategies they used to confront their common frustrations. Rather than dismissing these autobiographies for their inconsistencies and importunities, and for their authors' eerie insistence that they have never been properly understood, we can view these autobiographies as their authors likely saw them during the composition process: as their last, best chance to convey their personal ideals and longstanding beliefs. In the final analysis, these two autobiographies are stories with a moral—after all, neither Gilman nor Deland ever wrote a story without one.

Chapter 4

Women of Vision

Pioneering Collaborations in Mary Austin's *Earth Horizon* and Harriet Monroe's *A Poet's Life*

MARY AUSTIN'S *Earth Horizon* and Harriet Monroe's *A Poet's Life* were projects of critical personal importance. Both women toiled over their memoirs for years, conducting exhaustive research, compiling and sorting through piles of documents, correspondence, and previous work. Their labors took a toll: though Austin had eagerly looked forward to the project, she wearied of it and fell behind schedule, working under increasing pressure from her editor to complete the highly anticipated volume and skimming over the last decade in a mere fourteen pages.[1] Monroe, who had been editing *Poetry* magazine since she founded it in 1912, skipped over some difficult years, going straight from 1922 to her 1936 conclusion. Despite the omitted material, Austin's autobiography extends to nearly 400 pages and Monroe's to over 450. These lengthy, dense autobiographies can be read as final manifestos, a last attempt by each of them to pull the many elements of their lives as writers together into one coherent vision. For that is what these two autobiographies are about: visions actualized and visions deferred. Above all, these autobiographies present their authors as literary pioneers, women of vision whose greatness lies in their service to a cause greater than themselves—in Austin's case, the "Earth Horizon," and in Monroe's, poetry itself.

These two autobiographies met with mixed receptions. The reviews of Monroe's *A Poet's Life* were somewhat positive, although it is difficult to say how much of the praise is due to the fact that Monroe died unexpectedly before her autobiography was published. She had started working on *A Poet's Life* in 1932 but died from a cerebral hemorrhage while hiking in the Andes after a 1936 PEN conference in Buenos Aires. Doctors determined that the altitude was simply too much for the seventy-six-year-old from the Great Plains. However, Monroe had written the final chapter on the boat to Argentina (it was found in her luggage), and her friends and coworkers were determined to see the book published. Morton Zabel, then the associate editor of *Poetry,* added two chapters to fill in the fourteen years Monroe had not addressed in the manuscript.[2] Some of the notices for *A Poet's Life* read like obituaries, summarizing Monroe's life and commenting on its significance, rather than analyzing *A Poet's Life*'s success as a book. The highest praise is reserved for Monroe herself, for whom many reviewers expressed a "deep admiration."[3] The *New York Times Book Review* proclaimed, "The courage of Harriet Monroe dominates the book."[4] But the few reviewers who did focus exclusively on its readability called the book "dull" or "tedious."[5] The *Forum* reviewer went so far as to comment that Monroe sounded like "a very serious, though not very inspired, schoolmarm," while E. L. Walton of the *Nation* pointed out that the "impersonal and objective" style is likely attributable to the apparent fact that Monroe was "interested not in her life but in poetry."[6] Many complimented the wealth of meticulous information Monroe provided. Since both Monroe and Margaret Anderson edited little magazines, reviews of *A Poet's Life* provide an interesting contrast with those for Anderson's *My Thirty Years' War.* While Anderson's title sounds as if her book's focus would be on a sustained crusade, it is really an ephemeral expression of personality. And while Monroe's title emphasizes her personal identity, there is little personality in it but a great deal about the battles she fought for her Midwest and her magazine.

As one of her reviewers noted, Monroe's autobiography was indeed the culmination of a lifelong crusade for modern poetry.[7] Defending her editorial vision for *Poetry* magazine had been a struggle since its inception but particularly so since the journal's ten-year anniversary in 1922, and most critics consider the *Poetry* issues between 1922 and Monroe's death to represent a decline in its quality. The 1930s were all about establishing a stable legacy for Monroe, who started the decade working on a third, expanded edition of her collection of critical essays, *Poets and Their Art* (1932). As soon as that was finished, Monroe began composing her autobiography as a scrupulous record of the literary history she had helped to make over a fifty-year career as a writer and editor. She is characteristically direct about her motivations, writing, "The battle which *Poetry,* from its first issue, fought for a 'new movement' . . . is in danger of being obscured by the mists of time and by propaganda for later literary interests." Just as one cannot fully understand Edith Wharton's reticence in *A Backward Glance* without reading it as a silent rebuke to Gertrude Atherton's *Adventures of a Novelist,* one cannot fully appreciate Harriet Monroe's autobiographical methods and motives without counting Margaret Anderson's *My Thirty Years' War* among them. Monroe was particularly concerned about setting the record straight regarding some false and misleading claims that Anderson had made in *My Thirty Years' War.* The facts bear out Monroe's contention that Anderson "makes a blanket claim to most of the poets whom *Poetry* had introduced a year or two before her first issue."[8] Monroe also correctly points out that Anderson's autobiography made use of a speech that William Butler Yeats gave at a *Poetry* awards banquet, implying that the speech was affiliated with Anderson's own journal, the *Little Review.* Because Monroe was so concerned with setting the record straight, critics unanimously agreed that Monroe's autobiography was a "book of importance."[9]

Many of Mary Austin's contemporaries also considered her autobiography the most important book she ever wrote. While it was still in production, Austin's publisher, Houghton Mifflin, mounted a lavish publicity campaign and touted *Earth Horizon* as "the greatest autobiography since Benjamin Franklin's."[10] The Literary Guild named the book to their exclusive list of must-reads, and Austin attended several gala events in the book's honor during and after a prepublication lecture tour on the East Coast.[11] When the volume finally appeared, Hugh Stevenson Tigner told readers of the *Christian Century,* "To say that Mary Austin's autobiography is a worthwhile book would be like saying that the sun is a praiseworthy institution emanating valuable rays of energy."[12] Other reviewers called the book "a biography of genuine distinction," a "worthy record," "a beautiful, clear, noble, illuminating portrait," and a "rich, profound" book of "first-class importance."[13] Isabel Patterson valued the "quality of greatness" in *Earth Horizon,* and R. L. Duffus praised Austin's "artistic discrimination."[14] Readers praised its style, saying *Earth Horizon* had the "dramatic force of a novel."[15] In fact, Austin's powerful use of narrative allowed her to hold readers in thrall with her performance as a storyteller, and the book has met with ongoing attention uncommon for a woman's literary autobiography of the period. Along with Gertrude Stein's *Autobiography of Alice B. Toklas,* which is discussed in chapter 6, *Earth Horizon* has sustained critical inquiry while most of the other women's literary autobiographies of the 1930s have been critically neglected or even dismissed.

However, there was one important group of readers who did not approve of *Earth Horizon.* Austin's characterization of certain people, as well as some "factually inaccurate" versions of events, greatly distressed her family and friends. The controversies had serious repercussions: Houghton Mifflin had to rerun the first printing under threat of a libel suit by H. G. Wells, who objected to Austin's recollection of a conversation they had about the pregnancy of his mistress. Others who knew Austin personally read her book as an act of revenge. It is true that during the time she was composing her autobiography, Austin was involved in a struggle for custody with the rest of her family over the guardianship of her niece, to whom Austin thought she could offer better opportunities than the girl's biological parents. Those involved in the dispute found Austin's version of the custody battle slanderous.[16] Further, family and friends who had known Austin's mother, Susanna Hunter, protested over the injustice *Earth Horizon* did to "such a fine woman."[17]

Whether or not Austin's book does justice to her mother may never be determined; however, early in the autobiography, Susanna Hunter comes across as cold and unresponsive to her imaginative daughter's needs. In one of the first stories in *Earth Horizon,* Austin recalls being left on the sidewalk at the age of three when she fainted on the way home from church, watching her family walk away while her mother accused her of dramatizing herself. In passages painfully similar to those describing Charlotte Perkins Gilman's relationship to her mother, Hunter's apparent emotional rejection of Mary is frequently and painfully described. Austin recalls being pushed away from her mother's knee when she tried to cling to her after both her father's and her sister's deaths. Writing in the third person, she declares that "Mary could have wept over this one voluntary caress" she receives from her mother after returning home from a long absence. Austin further reports that when her mother found out that Mary's only child, Ruth, was developmentally disabled, she implied that Ruth's affliction was "a judgment" on Mary for something she had done. As is the pattern in so many of these autobiographies, the mother figure silences any form of expression considered improper for a young lady. In *Earth Horizon,* Susanna Hunter censors Mary's reading and punishes her for her "wicked" storytelling, just as Margaret Deland's "Mama" does in *If This Be I.* The widespread Victorian belief that publishing was not "womanly" was so strong in Austin's household that when she published her first poem, her mother made her use a pseudonym. When Hunter's only response to Austin's first successful short story is, "I think you could have made more out of it," Austin exclaims, "Where was now the triumph and encouragement that should go to one's first professional adventure!" *Earth Horizon* also contrasts Austin's father's invitation for her to explore his library and his acceptance of her imagination with her mother's disapproval of it.[18]

Nonetheless, because of Austin's novelistic approach to *Earth Horizon,* she also expresses some understanding and admiration of her mother, referred to as "Susie" in the book. Unlike the mother figures in other women's literary autobiographies of the 1930s, Susie is a character whose significance and agency extends beyond her relationship to Mary, a woman who had considered writing herself. Susie Hunter, like Mimi King in *Memories of a Southern Woman of Letters,* is a storyteller in her own right: "Susie had power with an audience . . . an aura of spiritual integrity." Further, Austin hints that her mother may even have taken some pride in her daughter's abilities: "Susie had not been entirely unaware that the girl had possibilities! She had had, as nearly as Mary could make out, a sort of vision of her in a black silk dress, with lace, reading papers at educational conventions, a corollary to the hope she had once had of sending Mary to Mount Holyoke College." Why else would Susie take Mary's poetry to Frances Willard for evaluation? Why else would she scold Mary not to "waste [her college education] on some man?"[19] In passages like these, Austin gives her mother a history and a voice instead of making her into a straw man for conventional Victorian femininity as did Atherton and Anderson, and, to a more limited extent, Edith Wharton, Grace King, Charlotte Perkins Gilman, and Margaret Deland.

In depicting their early family relationships, Austin's and Monroe's texts reveal a common dilemma that many female autobiographers share: shall one express oneself through one's attachments and relationships, which can compromise a narrative trajectory of individual achievement, or shall one insist on detachment in one's autobiographical persona, even though the independence and individuality implicit within a more detached persona can mutilate a text—as it had in both Wharton's and King's autobiographies—and result in what Tara Hart has termed "a paralyzing sense of loss."[20] This has proven incredibly difficult ground to navigate and is especially highlighted in this generation of female authors' depictions of their mothers. Atherton's and Anderson's detachment is so insistent in their life-writings that readers decided they were heartless. In Gilman's, Deland's, and King's autobiographical depictions of their mothers or mother-figures, attachments and detachments are so frequently expressed and then contradicted that the portraits of their families become muddled, their relationships indecipherable. But both Austin and Monroe balance their narratives, trying to be fair to those who hurt them by including not only their personal feelings but also alternative perspectives and reasoned judgments.

These two autobiographers' primary method of achieving balance is the creation of multiple perspectives on the same event or within the same scene. Austin's *Earth Horizon* allows for varied perspectives on her early relationships by mixing the first- and third-person points of view. Austin primarily uses the third person for the first half of the book, referring to herself, her mother, and other family members by their first names. This technique—temporarily removing the autobiographical "I" and utilizing a narrative eye instead—balances Austin's desire to express both attachment to and independence from not just her mother but her whole family and, later, her husband. In some passages, Austin's depictions of Mary—her younger self—are also spilt into two characters with different perspectives on life: Mary-by-herself and I-Mary. Mary-by-herself seeks attachment, affection, and approval; she is hurt by her mother's rejection and frightened by the financial and emotional hardships the family suffers in their move from Illinois to California. Eager to please, this Mary made "endless perforated cardboard book-markers" for her grandfather and "faithfully copied so many times" her father's favorite picture.[21]

By contrast, I-Mary is bold and brave, needing no one and fearing nothing. Representing an urge to detachment, I-Mary is ambitious and confident. Early in *Earth Horizon,* I-Mary surfaces in moments of need. For instance, she has "conviction," "certaint[y]," about things that Mary-by-herself "couldn't have managed. She was but dimly aware of something within herself, competent, self-directive; she meant to trust it." According to Austin, I-Mary, who exhibits "the wish and intention to write," directs Mary's steps with the power of a novelist over a character: "When you were I-Mary, you could see Mary-by-herself as part of the picture, and make her do things that, when you were she, could not be done at all; such as walking a log high over the creek, which gave Mary-by-herself cold prickles even to think about." Later, in an analogous move, I-Mary forces Mary-by-herself to write "two slender little sketches" that mark the beginning of her writing career. I-Mary is also constantly—and vociferously—fighting gender inequity in her family, even protesting when the breakfast eggs are always cooked the way her brother wants.[22] In a previous autobiographical essay in the *Nation,* Austin made it clear that I-Mary knew "it was only by pushing aside all considerations of liking and insisting on whatever fundamental rightness inherent in a particular situation, that [Mary] could secure a kind of factual substitute for family feeling and fair play."[23] Knowing that this insistence on leaving affection and personal relationships out of the equation in her personal activism may have warped her readers' reactions to her, Austin writes, "I have been so much concerned to miss no item of the thoroughly objectionable qualities of a young woman in the late eighteen hundreds making her way to intellectual independence and the forefront of a feminist revolt that I have almost forgotten to record that Mary had a few genuinely good points."[24] Austin's technique here—associating I-Mary with the ego and viewing I-Mary as just one part of her whole self—sheds more light on some of the other less-balanced autobiographical personas in this group of texts, particularly Anderson's and Atherton's. After reading *Earth Horizon,* one almost wishes to go back and rename the personas of *My Thirty Years' War* and *Adventures of a Novelist* I-Margaret and

I-Gertrude. In Austin's case, her explicit narrative detachment from her own ego allows her to sketch a more nuanced self-portrait than either Atherton or Austin did.

As did Austin, Harriet Monroe grew up in a household with complicated allegiances and conflict around traditional gender roles. According to *A Poet's Life,* the Monroe marriage was a "haphazard affair," rife with "clashes" because her parents were mismatched.[25] Harriet's mother, Martha Mitchell Monroe, is portrayed as a lonely representative of conventional femininity in an intellectual household, alienated from her bookish family. While her husband and four children would all routinely gather in Henry Stanton Monroe's library together in the evenings, Martha, interested only in housekeeping and fashion trends, was bewildered by the rest of the family's incessant reading and lively cultural engagement. Harriet recalled her mother "spending countless hours at the sewing machine" making clothes for herself and the family.[26] She also remembers her parents fighting about her mother's trendy but unflattering clothes and hats, observations that may have contributed to Monroe's later editorial bemoaning the fact that "clothes are the only form of artistic self-expression about which nine-tenths of our young girls are keenly aware."[27] *A Poet's Life* explains that Monroe's father had become engaged to Martha when she was a lovely young woman and he was just starting out as a lawyer. He only realized that his fiancée was barely literate when she proved incapable of writing her own letters to him. When he realized this, he offered to pay for her to go to school for two years before they married, but Martha Mitchell was "ashamed" of being so far behind much younger girls and did not complete the course. It was not until much later, when Martha proved unable to write letters whose "defects" would not "shock" her daughters when they went away to school as teenagers, that she set her mind to study and became truly literate. However, with Harriet Monroe's characteristic sense of justice, *A Poet's Life* takes care to ensure that readers understand her mother's lack of education was not her own fault. As the oldest daughter in a nineteenth-century family, Martha Mitchell had helped her mother manage a household that included multiple boarders and three younger children, making her education "a much neglected second thought."[28]

Trying to be fair to both her parents, Harriet Monroe's detached judgment reads thus: "So they lived more or less at cross purposes, neither understanding nor deferring to the other, and united only by the close tie of flesh." Since he and his wife did not have shared interests, Henry shared his intellectual enthusiasms with his children. This meant a great deal to Harriet. A middle child, bossed, bullied, and teased by her older sister, Dora, Harriet "grew up incased in a thick shell of reserve." She only emerged from her shell in her father's library, where he was a "merry playfellow with his children," a man of "very human sympathies" who "lived on equal terms with his children, as with everybody else."[29] Henry's interest in arts and culture probably contributed to Harriet's, and her younger sister, Lucy's, work as art critics for the Chicago newspapers.[30] Henry Monroe was instrumental to the development of his daughter's career in other ways as well. As a lawyer, he helped Harriet win an important 1893 lawsuit against the *New York World* when they printed one of her poems without permission or remuneration. The lawsuit redefined the rights of poets to their work and brought Harriet $5,000, making it feasible for her to travel and pursue her writing career. *A Poet's Life* makes it clear that Henry's love of books and culture, his democratic idealism, and his loyalty to Chicago even after losing almost everything in the Great Fire of 1871, became the same standards that rooted Monroe's own career.

Both Monroe and Austin try to reconcile their tenuous, difficult childhood attachments in narrating their grief at their mothers' deaths. Monroe narrates her mother's passing with more feeling and detail than any other scene in *A Poet's Life*. She narrates her mother's deathbed confession to an enduring jealousy for her husband's books, feeling they "separated" him from her. When Martha Monroe asks for forgiveness from her husband and he replies, "I have nothing to forgive," Monroe muses that she "had never known anything more beautiful than those last days."[31] In *Earth Horizon,* when Austin describes the passing of Susanna Hunter, she suddenly reverts back to the first person. Acknowledging her mother's inestimable importance to her despite their differences, she speaks of her "incalculable ravening" grief, "the psychic wound, the severed root of being."[32] When Austin's "I" speaks, as it rarely does in the first third of her book, the words are all the more striking for the dramatic shift in point of view: as interjections made in a deeply personal voice, they sum up the significance of "Mary's" integrated experiences.

Because of Austin's experiments with point of view in *Earth Horizon,* critics Tara Hart and Anna Carew-Miller have argued that this autobiography accords with traditional "female" life-writing in which identity is relationally determined and represented.[33] Viewing the differentiation between the two Marys in the text as challenges to the conventional notion of a unified self, Carew-Miller argues that Austin tries to silence and erase the voice of Mary-by-herself in her life-story. Austin herself argues in certain passages in *Earth Horizon* that the creation of her character was a collaborative effort, that her own mind was "shaped and sharpened" by perceiving both the virtues and flaws of others, noting that this point "should never be lost to the reader's consciousness."[34] I would also contend that the multiple voices in *Earth Horizon* work collaboratively with one another, allowing Austin the freedom to express the complexity of her relationships, desires, and ambitions.

While Monroe's autobiography does not diverge from the first person, her extensive quotations from diaries, letters, and essays create a similar collaborative combination of voices in *A Poet's Life.* These three voices in the text can be distinguished as (1) Harriet Monroe the woman, (2) Harriet Monroe the writer, and (3) Harriet Monroe the editor. The first invokes Monroe's personal memories and emotions, either directly or through reprinted diary entries, while her persona as a professional writer takes shape in the excerpted voice we hear in the many quotations from her previously published works. The third voice, the editorial voice, is a mediating one that offers commentary to contextualize events and bridge all the different kinds of documents in *A Poet's Life.* When writing about any given event in her life, Monroe typically combines actual artifacts from her past, her present feelings about the memories in question, and a reasoned critical retrospective analysis of what they meant and how they molded her future, addressing each event or topic in at least two of her three different voices. For instance, when she describes her six months of canvassing for pledges to start up *Poetry* magazine, Monroe's voice shifts three times. First, she remembers her personal feelings about some of those who gave: "E. P. Ripley of my beloved Santa Fe Railroad . . . beautiful Helen Birch . . . whose very presence was always a joy. And I felt really touched when groups in three or four women's clubs each pledged fifty dollars for five years in five-or-ten dollar individual subscriptions." Then Monroe, the seasoned editor, intervenes to balance those effusions with the bigger picture, remarking that "of course those . . . were the easiest to get." She then includes a diary entry from January 23, 1912, "No one in but Mr. B—who declined," to bring a feeling of immediacy to a passage that skims over "days of deep discouragement."[35] Rounding out her depiction of the fundraising process, all three voices work together to reveal the highs and lows of her lengthy, painstaking efforts to start up *Poetry.*

Monroe repeats this pattern throughout *A Poet's Life.* In her chapter on World War I, the emotional voice of her memory refers to Rupert Brooke's visit to Chicago in 1914 as "mystically prophetic of agonies to come" and the "sudden shattering of hope" she felt when war was declared. As the diction here indicates, the voice of Monroe's memory is a much more sentimental and florid one than the other two voices. After this dramatic passage, the editorial voice takes over, remarking, "Modern poets, I thought, should enter a protest." Finally, she introduces an excerpt from a September 1914 editorial she wrote called "Remove the Glamour."[36] Monroe's voice as a writer in this excerpt—and all the other excerpts in her autobiography—is distinguished from both the other voices in *A Poet's Life.* Her excerpted professional work is both more disciplined and more sophisticated than that of her memory, and much livelier than her editorial voice throughout *A Poet's Life.* The editorial voice is blunt, almost toneless, and effaced of individuality, which may explain why some reviewers found the book dull.

In Austin's autobiography, the first-person voice is much more engaging, but it still functions like Monroe's editorial voice; it explains the "pattern" of Austin's life, the retrospective meaning behind her lived experience. For instance, the first-person voice is "reluctant" to speak of Mary's painful marriage and divorce, but it "has to be gone through." As Austin says in her preface to *Earth Horizon,* she needed to write the autobiography to reveal her "acutest understanding" of events.[37] In the case of her divorce from Wallace Stafford Austin, this also served as a response to the scandal that still lingered around it decades later. In a 1939 biography, Helen MacKnight Doyle, a doctor who treated Mary's special-needs daughter when Austin lived in Bishop, California, recalled the gossip about Austin: "I heard that she grossly neglected and mistreated her subnormal child, that she avoided her duty to her home and her husband, who was a very fine man, that she was a snob, holding herself superior to the people of the town."[38] Some of the problems Mary Austin had in portraying her husband, to whom she refers simply as "Stafford" in *Earth Horizon,* may stem from the fact that she is one of the first female writers to openly discuss divorce in a literary autobiography. She spends a good number of pages building a case for her decision to divorce, reiterating Stafford's inadequacies as a husband. She describes his distaste for work, explaining that her husband turned down jobs he considered beneath him, even when they were deeply in debt. Mary roots these inadequacies in Stafford's southern upbringing and his assumption of white privilege: "Brought up on a huge carelessly kept plantation, in assumptions of social superiority such as accrue to Nordics living among brown peoples . . . he had never heard of such a thing as budgeting." In her desire to try to see him through a more detached lens, Austin characterizes his refusal of a teaching job when she was in her last trimester of pregnancy as "something less discreditable than it sounded. It did not mean that he had measured his dislike of school teaching against his wife's impending crisis . . . and taken the chance in favor of his own predilection. It meant that he . . . had reacted characteristically," according to his constitution and upbringing. According to *Earth Horizon,* his failure to pay the rent caused them to be evicted from their home during her eighth month of pregnancy; as a result, Mary had to earn the family's keep by cooking at a boardinghouse.[39]

Austin's portrayals of her husband's flaws in *Earth Horizon* function similarly to Charlotte Perkins Gilman's imagery of selfless martyrdom in her depiction of her marriage to Charles Stetson in *Living* and Edith Wharton's subtle renunciations of Teddy Wharton in *A Backward Glance.* All of them attempted to deflect the condemnation they knew would result from having been divorced in order to pursue their literary ambitions. In writing about her divorce, Austin is careful to imply that she did not reject marriage in theory but that her husband was emotionally unavailable. Austin characterizes Mary as having high hopes and "straightforward intention" in her marriage. Stafford, however, is "polite and uninterested" in her attempts to communicate with him, so much so that he is surprised when she finally asks for a divorce. She holds his financial instability and lack of communication responsible: "He was never able to make of our marriage a Thing, a planned, progressive arrangement. In the midst of an agreed-upon activity, suddenly I would be thrown upon my own resources, scrabbling for means, dislocated in my professional career."[40]

In depicting their personal aspirations, it is clear that neither Austin nor Monroe believed that their gender would present an obstacle to having a successful literary career. Although scholar Ann Massa rightly notes that Monroe's "career constituted an effective rejection of gender stereotyping," Monroe's autobiography implies that she always believed her personal life and professional ambitions could be smoothly combined.[41] As did Gertrude Atherton and Mary Austin, Harriet Monroe believed that the western United States offered young women more independence and opportunity than either Europe or the East Coast. A proud Midwesterner, Monroe and her younger sister reveled in "bicycling, alone or unchaperoned" even on a trip to France, to the shock and confusion of the local residents. Although Monroe never married, *A Poet's Life* (a gender-neutral title that provides an interesting contrast to Grace King's *Memories of a Southern Woman of Letters*) explains that she fully expected that men would "fall at my feet" and that she would both get married and follow all "my dreams of fame," for "no lover should win my favor who was not my completely sympathetic affinity." Monroe also emphasizes her "strong desire of motherhood" and devotes pages to describing beaux who proposed and those who did not. Her autobiography even explores the notion of sexual chemistry when she recalls having a literary crush on Robert Louis Stevenson, which ended abruptly when they met and she found him physically unattractive. The book makes mysterious mention of a relationship she describes as the "rapture and agony shared in perfect sympathy . . . a feeling which united for years a man and woman who rarely saw each other."[42] When looking at the trajectory of her career, it is doubtful whether Monroe would have openly written about any of these things until after 1920. She had become more and more open about her life as a single woman as she aged, writing and publishing poems—her own and those of other women—about love, desire, and spinsterhood in her sixties. In *A Poet's Life,* Monroe insists that a rich, full life was available to an unmarried woman, but that she personally would have liked to have been married as well, as were many of her successful professional female friends in Chicago.

Austin's autobiography also expresses a positive view of her gender identity, writing, "Mary was never much taken with the wish of many girls of her acquaintance that they had been boys. She thought there might be a great deal to be got out of being a woman."[43] As Anna Carew-Miller argues, *Earth Horizon* "succeeds in conceiving the artist as a woman, complete with a female body."[44] This attention to the female body in its many life stages was indeed one of the unique triumphs about *Earth Horizon:* Austin appears unafraid to express the mixed feelings that come with each stage. Despite her frustrations with her marriage, Austin explains, "Nobody had wanted children more than Mary did; few intellectuals of her generation have clung more obstinately to the idea of a home, a house, a garden."[45] Austin's openness about childbearing, caring for an infant, and the need for open communication in marriage supports this assertion. However, Austin also edited out some experiences she deemed irrelevant to her career, particularly her affair with Lincoln Steffens, who had published his literary autobiography three years before she published her own. Austin's correspondence with Steffens indicates both the depth of her passion and her rage at his rejection, which she claims damaged her career.[46] Yet in *Earth Horizon,* Steffens goes unmentioned save in a list of people who once lived in Jack London's artist's colony in Carmel, California. Austin knew readers would be curious about her private affairs. She relates, with laconic humor, readers' requests that she "tell the truth about [her] sex life." However, she deflects such requests, saying she would tell the truth about "everything that matters" but that her love affairs made no difference to her work.[47] Since she uses the fact that she is writing a *literary* autobiography to justify this omission, Austin's silence may have as much to do with how she wished to be perceived as an artist than it did with concealing her painful break with Steffens.

While Austin dismisses sex as irrelevant to her career as a writer, housework is treated as both relevant and important in *Earth Horizon.* Austin identifies domestic work, especially cooking, as her earliest form of art, explaining that participating in this "ancestral exercise" helps her to create.[48] Austin promoted the image of herself in the kitchen throughout her life, describing the foods she made to celebrate finished writing projects and taking pride that her chocolate layer cake was a favorite among stagecoach drivers.[49] Although she enjoyed cooking, Austin was no proponent of separate spheres. An open and committed feminist, she wrote a number of articles about women's struggle for equality, including *The Young Woman Citizen,* a 1918 treatise laying out the cultural, social, and political roles for women after World War I. Like many of her essays, her autobiography takes on women's issues, such as the "new psychology," which Austin writes, "seems to Mary no more than another mask for the terror that was in men at any move on the part of women." When a doctor diagnoses Mary's breakdown at college as "the natural incapacity of the female mind for intellectual achievement," Austin links it to the diagnosis of "all illnesses of women." She repeatedly emphasizes the commonalities of women's experiences, such as housework, childbearing, and sexism, in *Earth Horizon,* defending her mother's distaste for the "dull" drudgery of housework, since "the business of ordering the large pioneer household, with exigencies calling forth all a woman's powers of ingenuity and invention, had dwindled to a petty housemaid's round" by the last third of the nineteenth century.[50]

Through her depictions of other women, Austin promotes the power of female solidarity in her autobiography. She specifically recalls Susie's approval when Mary slapped the face of a man who cursed at his wife during a difficult labor and delivery. *Earth Horizon* also expresses Austin's indebtedness to the Native American women who acted as surrogate mothers to her in her early days in California, helping her care for her special-needs child and teaching her how to survive in the desert. Watching them hunt, gather, and weave makes Austin appreciate the creative potential of "women's work," for "it was in this fashion that she began to learn that to get at the meaning of work you must make all its motions, both of body and mind." Austin's fiction often embraced the traditions she learned from Native women; many of her female artist figures can be seen as "chiseras," or medicine women, who possess extraordinary gifts of healing and creativity. *Earth Horizon* also affirms female community when Austin tells of a female secret society she joined in college, a support group based on women's shared ambitions.[51]

A Poet's Life likewise reveals the importance of female solidarity, making it clear that Monroe did not see herself as an exception among women but as one of a community of Midwestern female intellectuals and influencers.[52] Monroe's friends included several strong female leaders in Chicago society, such as Jane Addams of Hull House (which Monroe supported in numerous ways) and art collector and activist Bertha Palmer, referred to in *A Poet's Life* as Mrs. Potter Palmer, as was customary in society at that time. Mrs. Palmer, a businesswoman, socialite, and art collector, was one of *Poetry*'s original sponsors. Monroe acknowledges other women frequently in her autobiography, speaking eloquently of the "intellectual women of strong character" she met while attending convent school from 1877 to 1879. Joining the "Fortnightly—one of the earliest so-called literary women's clubs" gave her training, support, and encouragement to overcome her shyness and learn to "rise and speak" with confidence. Monroe mentions the female poets whose work she printed in the same lists as male poets, including well-known women like H. D., Mary Austin, Amy Lowell, Edna St. Vincent Millay, and Marianne Moore, as well as lesser-known ones like Hilda Conkling. As Mary Roberts Rinehart's autobiography also avers, Monroe points out that marriage, childrearing, and hospitality can coexist with women's professional careers in *A Poet's Life*. However, Monroe wryly acknowledges that she had always assumed that someone else would do the housework, so she would not have to "sacrifice" any time from the pursuit of "my intellectual or vocational needs." In a self-critical moment, looking back as an older woman who was not always able to afford domestic help, Monroe muses, "It never occurred to me that I might not be entitled to all this service," reflecting on her own assumption of privilege.[53]

Fondly referring to *Poetry*'s editors as "we women of the 'staff,'" Monroe's evocation of her female coworkers emphasizes their energy, incisive wit, and ruthless criticism. Her tribute to Alice Corbin Henderson, *Poetry*'s first associate editor, points out that women need not sacrifice marriage and motherhood to career, nor vice versa: Monroe lists Henderson's roles as "poet . . . wife and mother and critic." While Monroe headed up the office, most of the other *Poetry* staff were women, such as Eunice Tietjens, who was not only a contributing poet but also a sort of "business manager" for the magazine, taking over the associate editorship for Henderson when she became ill in 1916. Next was Marion Strobel, associate editor from 1920 to 1925, a poet whom Monroe had published as well as an active matriarch, fun-loving grandmother, influential socialite, and occasional mystery novelist. The text especially highlights *Poetry*'s hospitality, an approach for which Monroe became known and one which she valued deeply, and explicitly links *Poetry*'s famous hospitality to one of the pleasures of domesticity. Speaking of the welcoming "atmosphere" of the magazine offices at 543 Cass Street, Monroe writes, "I had never been the actual mistress of any home . . . but this little kingdom was mine, and I rather enjoyed dispensing its fleeting hospitalities."[54]

Monroe's hospitality was neither a pose nor a hobby: known for an "open-door" policy to which she committed in the magazine's second issue in November 1912, Monroe's democratic editorial inclusivity was and is unique, and she sustained it for her entire tenure. A 1934 article on Monroe in *Studies in English Literature* declared *Poetry* to be "the only distinguished poetry magazine in the English speaking world that is open to every kind of sincere poetic effort, in any style, traditional or revolutionary."[55] According to scholar Harry Hansen, who knew Monroe personally, her "chief quality was hospitality," and this made *Poetry* special: "Unlike other little magazines, she had not become the niche or voice of one movement over others: in her magazine at least all schools and voices have been heard. . . . It is to her credit that she was never heard shouting in enthusiastic abandon over one group or another."[56] Monroe resisted a good deal of pressure over the decades, both in private letters and through public discourse, to narrow her magazine's scope. An "indefatigable colonizer of all the little magazines," Ezra Pound was often frustrated by the stability of Monroe's vision for *Poetry,* as it prevented him from taking control of it the way he took control of many other little magazines.[57] Because of her uniquely inclusive approach, Monroe printed poets in *Poetry* who were complete unknowns, and literary history has vindicated many of her choices. She defended Carl Sandburg from a snobbish attack on his lack of formal education and working-class roots in the *Dial,* after she had taken the risky step of publishing Sandburg's "Chicago" poems when *Poetry* was still trying to establish itself, while simultaneously defending her magazine, which had been labeled in the same editorial as a "futile little periodical."[58] When she felt a writer had potential but that their work was not appropriate for her magazine, Monroe would try to persuade writers to edit their material in ways she thought would improve it—for instance, though she was captivated by the rest of the poem, she never got over the bleakness of the ending to T. S. Eliot's "The Love Song of J. Alfred Prufrock" and tried to get it changed before she printed it in *Poetry.*[59] As in the case of "Prufrock," Monroe often printed work she did not like when she believed the poems had merit, regardless of her personal taste. As she noted in a 1912 *Poetry* editorial entitled "The Open Door" and reiterated in her autobiography more than thirty years later, "one must give the artist his *donnee.*"[60]

Perhaps because of the inclusiveness that resulted from Monroe's open-door policy, *Poetry* is the only little magazine of its era that has survived to the present day. It may well be that Monroe understood sustainability and welcomed diversity in a way that few of her fellow writers and editors did. For instance, her anthology *The New Poetry*—first published in 1917, then revised and reprinted for new editions in 1923 and 1932—was generally well-received, except for one thing. Critics "found fault with the anthology's inclusivity," not feeling that poets like Alice Meynell represented the cutting edge of modernity.[61] But, for Monroe, sincere, gifted poets of all stripes, styles, and formal proclivities would be granted a seat at her table. She was always more inclusive than the highbrow literary establishment would have wished.

By 1920, the mechanisms of modernism had started pressuring Monroe to exclude the voices of female poets who were not composing in the most avant-garde style, women whose innovations were topical rather than technical. Recent volumes such as *Modernist Women Writers and American Social Engagement,* edited by Jody Cardinal, Dierdre Egan-Ryan, and Julie Lisella, have demonstrated how the narrowness of this litmus test for modernism came to exclude many women who were writing in Monroe's time, including those, like Millay, whom Monroe was criticized for publishing.[62] However, when critics tried to belittle Monroe's editorial decisions on the basis of gender, she was ready to engage, not only on her own behalf but on the behalf of other women writers as well. In a column from the June 1920 issue of *Poetry,* Monroe reflects on having been accused in the newspapers of making *Poetry* too feminine. Rather than letting herself be baited on the question of what is "feminine" or "masculine" in literature, she put the reporter's spurious claim that "most of its contributors are feminine" to a statistical test, discovering a 64 percent predominance of male contributors and declaring that she would need to right the "injustice" she had committed "toward my own sex."[63] Throughout the 1920s, when she was publishing love poems and poetic reflections on women's lifecycles rather than exclusively publishing work that we would now term "high modernist," a number of critics accused Monroe and/or *Poetry* of being both too feminine and too feminist. Rather than backing away from these attacks, Monroe went full steam ahead in that direction, happily mocking one accuser's claim that the "powdered feminism" he perceived in the magazine somehow made it disreputable.[64] In the 1920s, Monroe wrote a series of essays on female poets, advocated for a female winner for the Levinson Prize, an annual five-hundred-dollar prize named for donor Salmon Levinson, which Monroe instituted in 1914 and which is still awarded each year for the best poem published in *Poetry.* She also published an all-women's edition of *Poetry* in September 1926.[65] However, Monroe's manuscript for *A Poet's Life* skips over those years, either because the critical pushback she fought against in the 1920s was too painful to recall or because she died before she could go back and tackle those years in her manuscript.

Both Austin's and Monroe's autobiographies also mention their friendships with powerful or famous male writers: for Austin, Charles Lummis, George Sterling, Lincoln Steffens, Henry Canby, Van Wyck Brooks, H. G. Wells, and Sinclair Lewis, and for Monroe most of the poets whose work she introduced to American audiences, as well as the influential Chicago businessmen, architects, and lawyers who helped to build the city's national and international reputation, just as she did. Unlike Monroe's autobiography, however, Austin's does not really acknowledge the importance of fellow female writers. She notes Dr. Frederick Webb Hodge's influence on her work but rarely mentions being similarly guided by scholarly women. In fact, Austin creates female foils for herself in *Earth Horizon.* She denigrates the women who "flung themselves at Jack [London]," referring to their "psychic indolence," "parasitism," and self-delusion regarding their capacity as muses. She also calls Gordon Craig's pursuers "prairie dogs . . . with their fingers drooping and their mouths slightly open." In contrast to other women, Austin explains, she "talked with him about art and the theater."[66] In a rhetorical move similar to Wharton's and King's depictions of their literary friendships with Henry James and Mark Twain, Austin makes it clear that she was not one of the female parasites or pursuers but simply one of two writers having a conversation.

Although Austin wrote letters scolding male contemporaries and friends like Jack London for not capturing "the note of feminine power" in fiction, she does not portray a community of women writers in *Earth Horizon.*[67] Instead, she locates her sense of community in the desert, with its shepherds, stage drivers, ranchers, and Native American women, or, as she terms them, "Mahalas." Yet these relationships, as depicted in the text, are not ones of equally shared subjectivity. Mahalas and other characters like Spanish Lupe flit through the book like ghosts, providing "good material." In telling of these communities, Austin contributes to her sense of self as their champion, pointing out that she was called on by a "committee of ladies" more than once to question her trespasses on social distinctions, such as participating in Indian dances.[68] Benay Blend, reading Austin from an ecofeminist viewpoint, examines Austin's "double status" as an outsider who does not fit into either "white . . . or Indian society."[69] Austin's treatment of characters outside of her race and class in *Earth Horizon* demonstrate this doubleness. For instance, she writes of her gratitude to the Mahala who nursed her baby when she was unable to do so but assures the reader that she had the (white) town doctor examine the woman before she allowed the practice to continue.[70] Biographer Esther Lanigan Stineman has speculated that writing about these peoples and the land in which they lived allowed Austin to escape the "civilized" world in which she felt ostracized.[71] Although Austin's more experimental, nonlinear work focuses on nonwhite cultures and communities, when she wrote semi-autobiographically using white, middle-class characters in books like *A Woman of Genius,* Austin returned to more traditional forms of narrative. And, even in *Earth Horizon,* when Austin writes about her identity as a prominent author, the principles of individuation, hierarchy, and linear development again become important. While Austin clearly placed a high value on participating in and representing the minority communities that had welcomed her and taught her so much, the concepts of linearity, competition, and whiteness appear to have been inextricably related in her imagination.

This pattern may explain why Austin is less kind to famous living white women, especially fellow writers, in the autobiography. This begs the question as to whether Austin only praises nonliterary women or Native American women in *Earth Horizon* because they do not threaten her unique status as a privileged white author. Although Austin had praised Wharton's "intellectual illumination" in print earlier in her career, attended Atherton's salon, and been published in *Poetry*, Austin mentions none of these fellow female authors in her autobiography.[72] Many critics have also noted the uneven treatment of Charlotte Perkins Gilman in *Earth Horizon.* First, Austin identifies Gilman as a model, writing of her "beauty" and defending her from the charges of "unnatural motherhood" for having given up custody of her daughter.[73] According to Melody Graulich, Austin's short story "Frustrate" may be a fictionalized record of one of the first encounters between Gilman and Austin, in which a young, frustrated wife meets an older, wiser woman writer. Gilman, who had ended her marriage and begun a writing career while Austin was still struggling, was probably an important role model for Austin, Graulich asserts.[74] But the autobiography then denigrates Gilman's "almost fanatic" views and her magazine's "terrible sameness." Austin declares, "I could not get her interested in writing," and eventually "left her standing at the old corner, crying the same wares." Instead of representing herself as Gilman's protégé, Austin characterizes herself as Gilman's superior. While we might wish to characterize Gilman's dismissal in *Earth Horizon* as a cruel aberration, not representative of Austin's treatment of women writers, this is not quite true. The same pattern occurs in

Austin's treatment of Ina Coolbrith, whose friendship and advice about writing were instrumental to Austin. As Austin was beginning her career, she sought out Coolbrith, the only western woman poet acclaimed by eastern magazines. Having eagerly taken the advice and used the connections that the older woman generously offered, Austin dismisses Coolbrith in her autobiography as a "minor poet."[75] However, these comments should also be read in light of the fact that Austin was well known for her "caustic" criticism of other writers, both male and female.[76] Her fierce competitiveness may have had more to do with her identity as an artist than her identity as a woman.

Although Monroe was a better advocate for fellow female writers than Austin, both women labored to create and sustain regional literary communities that offered an alternative to the New York literary establishment. Because of their Midwestern regional affiliations, Austin and Monroe had each experienced frustrations with the way the East Coast literati treated them. *Earth Horizon* criticizes the eastern establishment as stodgy and reactionary: "That was how it was with a great many things Mary wanted to write about; when they were new and fresh to her, Eastern editors wouldn't believe them, and by the time the East had become aware, Mary had moved on to something wholly new and unauthenticated by New York."[77]

Austin's complaints about the East Coast literati were based in fact. She largely found herself an outsider in that world. Austin herself told Carl Van Doren, "Once in every seven years . . . New York discovers me."[78] To Mabel Dodge Luhan, she complained, "I grow weary of the attitude of young New York toward my work."[79] In her article "New York, Dictator of American Criticism," originally published in the *Nation,* Austin indicts the literary establishment for its narrow definitions of literature. She resents "the smallness of the group" of prominent critics and the fact that they are "all under forty," and criticizes Waldo Frank for only mentioning two women in "Our America"—the more radical Emma Goldman and more experimental

Amy Lowell.[80] For her part, Austin believed, "It is time for that silly snobbishness of New York to have its quietus."[81]

Monroe similarly struggled for decades to make headway with the East Coast establishment before she founded her own alternative platform. Although she had placed the occasional piece with *Century* or the *Atlantic* before the turn of the century, Monroe had been eking out an insecure living with her writing for nearly twenty years before she launched *Poetry* in 1912, living off of a combination of arts criticism, poetry, and essays. During this period, Monroe suffered from her "recognition of powers within me that seemed to be going to waste," but there seemed no available path.[82] In those years, Monroe realized that not only was poetry undervalued but that she was doubly pigeon-holed by other editors as a woman from the western region of the United States.[83] Her autobiography takes on what she perceived as the East Coast's bias toward its own traditions, its exclusion of other voices, and its assumption that poetry should only be written by independently wealthy dilletantes, not by working artists who needed to earn a living. The roots of her disenchantment with the eastern establishment went back to 1893, when Monroe successfully sued the *New York World* for reprinting her "Ode for the Columbian Exhibition" without permission. She characterizes the pirating of her work as the opening salvo in a lifelong battle with the eastern establishment in *A Poet's Life*. That fateful "Ode" was an important fulcrum in Monroe's career, one that crystalized the values which motivated her to start *Poetry* almost thirty years later. First, her "Ode" boosted Chicago as a vital city of innovation and culture, and second, the unauthorized reprint of her poem brought home the fact that poets were treated differently than other artists, as newspapers of the era would regularly use poets' work with neither permission nor payment and consider that they were doing the poet a favor by doing so.[84]

A loyal Chicagoan who viewed the skyscrapers in her native town as more exciting achievements than the East Coast's reproductions of

European architecture, Monroe saw value in "creating a regional identity" in her editorial work.[85] In 1911, she pitched potential supporters for her magazine by pointing out that her undertaking could finally put Chicago on the literary map. *A Poet's Life* affirms that she achieved her goal, proudly citing Foster Damon's claim that "Harriet Monroe was making a literary center for the continent."[86] *A Poet's Life* reveals that Monroe's vision was mocked from the beginning with headlines like "Poetry in Porkopolis" and other "sarcastic comments" about Chicago. However, the book celebrates the Midwest as an alternative literary community, pointing out that "there were friendly groups of artists in Chicago at this time," and emphasizing that these groups "were less divided by cliques and professional barriers and jealousies than in certain other cities." Monroe routinely claimed that the *Dial*'s constant editorial attacks on *Poetry* stemmed from its allegiance to an East Coast establishment that was inhospitable to other voices. As she reiterates in her autobiography, the *Dial* may have had "residential loyalty to Chicago" but its "literary loyalty" was to the East.[87]

The attacks Monroe's autobiography documents did not stop after *Poetry* was long established. After the *Little Review* left Chicago for New York, Margaret Anderson, egged on by Ezra Pound, reprinted an Edgar Jepson essay called "The Western School" in the September 1918 issue. The essay dismissed Vachel Lindsay, Edgar Lee Masters, and Robert Frost—all of whom were regularly included in *Poetry*—as negligible and inferior artists. Monroe never failed to respond to these attacks and answered the "cheap incompetence" of Jepson's hit job in her next issue. Monroe was unabashed in her belief that American poetry's future lay in the Midwestern and southwestern regions, even penning an enthusiastic invocation of the "prairie muses" for the magazine.[88] According to *A Poet's Life*, by 1916 she was "resisting the Boston verdict" and "searching the Far West for aboriginal poetry and giving its interpreters an issue of the magazine."[89] As the years went by, Monroe became more and more committed to the verse of the Midwest and

Southwest, even more so when other magazines were turning away from them. She never stopped believing that work revealing "the creed of the pioneer" was the truer strain of American verse, the one that her readers needed to hear.[90]

Eventually, Monroe's appreciation for the Southwest brought her into the same publishing arenas as Austin. Both of them contributed to the 1928 project *They Know New Mexico: Intimate Sketches by Western Writers,* an early version of cross-marketing designed to simultaneously capitalize on the challenge southwestern regional literature was presenting to the eastern literary establishment and to promote southwestern tourism.[91] Austin had first made a name for herself with 1903's *The Land of Little Rain,* a book inspired by southwestern landscapes ranging from California's Death Valley to the High Sierra mountain range. Even though she wrote in many other genres and settings, Austin was known as a southwestern regionalist throughout her career. But, like Monroe, Austin was sometimes mocked on the basis of her regional allegiances, and she used *Earth Horizon* to answer remarks that still rankled. For instance, Austin was so offended when a doorbell pull she had made out of "ancient Spanish hair rope" was described as a "cow's tail" in the press that she felt compelled to correct the mistake in her autobiography.[92] Austin argued that Native American culture was the origin of American rhythms in life and art in 1923's *The American Rhythm,* and by then Monroe had come to agree with her that Native American oral tradition represented a crucially neglected root of American poetry.

Deemed the "High Priestess of Regional Literature" by Carl Van Doren in 1933, Mary Austin sometimes found that literary brand that had launched her as a writer limited her when she ventured into other projects.[93] Her "regional priestess" image—which she utilized those famous Ansel Adams photographs of her to promote—was so prevalent that those who wished to devote critical attention to her had to act as apologists. In an analysis of Austin's other work, Henry

Nash Smith argued that she was not "a sort of recluse in the Western deserts" as "critics" may have thought.[94] As the years went by, Austin was perpetually frustrated about the narrow way her work was marketed. She wished to be known for more than her work on Native American cultures and the desert, but she had to keep returning to those topics to earn a living, so the trajectory of Austin's literary career was markedly uneven. It was not so uneven as Gertrude Atherton's, but it was uneven enough—mostly for financial reasons—to befuddle scholars who tried to evaluate it. Stineman describes Austin's oeuvre as "haphazard" including about 250 short stories, novels, essays, and articles.[95] By the time she wrote *Earth Horizon,* her contemporaries were questioning whether Austin had a coherent vision: "She has failed to develop in a direct line, and her career is cluttered with unsuccessful experiments," wrote Van Wyck Brooks.[96] Even critics who were kinder made similar observations. Carl Van Doren observed that her work was deficient in the "cool, hard discipline of the artist," and she "wrote no book like its predecessor . . . leaving behind her a rich detritus which she will perhaps be willing to consider detritus if it helps to nourish future generations."[97] Austin intentionally addresses these critiques in her autobiography, using the central image of the Earth horizon to explain the scattered trajectory of her work. She explains that any "haphazardness" that critics may have perceived in her life or career was merely part of a "quest [for] the Sacred Middle" where the "soul [is] happily at rest." This quest is the unifying vision of *Earth Horizon.* As Austin explains, whenever she felt "desperately displaced" from her Sacred Middle, she made a "search for a new center of personal direction." Perhaps in answer to the criticism of Brooks and Van Doren, Austin writes that her "books have no sequence" because they simply "come out of the arc of the Earth Horizon."[98]

Harriet Monroe's autobiography too focuses on her personal revision of events that were misunderstood or mischaracterized. This motif came through clearly to readers and was noted in several reviews of *A*

Poet's Life: Percy Hutchison refers to "that clarity of vision which was one of Miss Monroe's intellectual characteristics," and John Holmes to her "reach of vision."[99] Monroe's vision always included serving both poets and their readers throughout her career; it was central enough that she revisits it again and again in *A Poet's Life.* She writes that she always "believ[ed] in the existence of 'mute inglorious Miltons' or at least of lesser smothered geniuses," and that it was her goal to serve them by allowing their work to be heard. Monroe believed that poets too had a responsibility to serve something greater than themselves; she believed poetry could—and should—help articulate the imaginative life of the modern world, noting, "The little theaters and the little magazines . . . have greatly served [the artist] by presenting his art to the world, as they have—quite incidentally, greatly served the critic by enabling him to function."[100] In her attempt to serve poetry, Monroe did not take a salary from the magazine for the first two years, working a second job as an art critic to make ends meet. When she was forced to take a salary in 1914, she kept it at fifty dollars per month for the next eleven years. The facts indicate that her motivations for starting and sustaining *Poetry* were as she stated from the beginning: to support poets and to enrich literary community in America, rather than to enrich herself.

Monroe's vision of art was always communal and collaborative—she overtly rejected the notion of the solitary genius. As *A Poet's Life* demonstrates, Monroe believed that "nothing can stand alone, genius least of all."[101] Because of this, she chose Walt Whitman's phrase "To have great poets you must have great audiences too" as the magazine's epigraph. Monroe had discovered the phrase during the six months of library research she conducted before she launched the magazine, and she selected it because it emphasized a reciprocal, collaborative responsibility among artists, readers, editors, and publishers. When it came to collaboration, Monroe practiced what she preached. Although scholars have tended to repeat the angry complaints and accusations made against Monroe by Ezra Pound whenever his will for *Poetry* was thwarted or even merely delayed (comments that often denigrated Monroe's age and gender as the culprits for their disagreements), the truth is that for decades, Harriet Monroe managed to work with some very difficult personalities including Ezra Pound, Amy Lowell, and William Carlos Williams. As *Poetry*'s editor, Monroe was accustomed to dealing with other writers' egos, and *A Poet's Life* confirms that she witnessed "cases almost pathological of hidden or blatant self-belief in genius" during the course of her long editorial career. Since she meant her magazine to be hospitable, she was prepared to calmly manage the vagaries of fellow artists, for "one cannot expect poets to run on an even keel." By keeping her own hand steady at the helm, Monroe tried to build a sense of mutual trust and respect among her contributors by responding to their submissions and questions promptly and by her "insist[ence] on paying" them for their work. While they were imperfect, Monroe's lengthy collaborations with so many of her fellow poets are placed into high relief when you consider their own disastrous attempts to collaborate with each other. For instance, Monroe's autobiography diplomatically sums up the notorious Pound-Lowell contretemps over the establishment of imagism in simple terms: they were "two captains, each accustomed to command, [who] could not get on together in the same boat."[102] Monroe even mastered a collaboration of formats when she created *Poetry,* an unprecedented "publishing format for verse that combined the aesthetic refinement and emotional complexity of 'high art,' the modernized marketing practices of mass culture, and the targeted audience and professionalized demeanor of the disciplinary journal."[103]

Austin's vision of genius was also one of collaboration and service to something greater than oneself. In *Earth Horizon* she writes of the times when she suffered because of her gifts.[104] She also published a semi-autobiographical novel devoted to the notion of female genius, *A Woman of Genius,* in which she explains, "For to be a genius is no such vanity as you imagine. It is to know great desires and to have no will of your own toward fulfillment; it is to feed others, yourself unfed; it is to be broken and plied as the Powers determine; it is to serve, and to serve, and get nothing out of it beyond the joy of serving. And to know if you have done that acceptably you have to depend on the plaudits of the crowd; and the Powers have no sign; many have died not knowing."[105] Collaboration and reciprocity are central tenets of Austin's vision both of genius and of the Earth horizon, "that other splendor of realizing that in the deepest layers of ourselves we are incurably collective. . . . It is not that we work upon the Cosmos, but it works in us." She speaks of the "experiences" when she felt "all the knowledge in the world, hers, aching intolerably to escape through her."[106] Ultimately, Austin defines her own life-story as valuable for its vision of shared experience and characterizes artistic genius as a denial of self, feminizing the term by asserting the "givingness of great women." She observes, "As for the great artist woman, depend upon it, she will be found in the last summing up more interested, as Sara Bernhart is, for example, in making her art contributory than in making it exceptional."[107]

Monroe also characterizes her vision of greatness as "contributory" in *A Poet's Life.* Now known as a sort of midwife to new poetry, in her time she was called a "Priestess of Poetry," an honorific that evokes a sense of her devotion to the art form.[108] When musing in her autobiography on "why was Poetry left out" of the Arts Movement in Chicago, Monroe notes that poetry is a shared art form, not an acquisitive one. As she explains, "A poem cannot be exhibited and bought and possessed by some private or public collector." Like Austin's Mahalas, poets enriched and interpreted life for others but were largely invisible, because, as Monroe explains, "poetry had no one to speak for it." In *A Poet's Life,* Monroe encapsulates her editorial career in these words: "I became convinced that something must be done; and since nobody else was doing anything, it might be 'up to me.'"[109]

In taking on the task of "speaking for" poetry, scholar John Newcombe asserts that "Monroe and her colleagues made their magazine a crucial pioneer."[110] Indeed, pioneering was always at the heart of Monroe's personal and professional vision, and the term continually seeps through in assessments of her work. In her quest to give voice to new poets, Monroe was the first U.S. editor to print Rabindranath Tagore, Carl Sandburg, William Carlos Williams, and Marianne Moore, among others, also bringing new movements like imagism into focus by printing Pound's "Don'ts" in *Poetry.* When she collected some of the best work from the first five years of her magazine into an anthology called *The New Poetry,* she concluded, "We have tried to be hospitable to the adventurous, the experimental, because these are the qualities of the pioneers, who look forward, not backward."[111] *A Poet's Life* underlines this trait in Monroe herself. Again and again, Monroe takes risks, trying to build a new space in which poetry can flourish, to create a literary landmark that will last, just as her beloved Chicago had done for other art forms when it dedicated its Fine Arts Building at the turn of the twentieth century. Monroe reminds readers that "it was a gamble," that "the reader should remember that the name of Ezra Pound [when she first published his work] was then largely unrecognized in his native country, and very little known anywhere."[112]

Austin too reminds the readers of her autobiography that "Mary" was a pioneer as well and is only important because she took a new path: "For the purposes of this book, I have to treat Mary as having at least the significance of a road mark, a pointer on the trail which generations after her were more or less to take. Otherwise, I could not get my consent, nor hers, to spend so much time with her." Their autobiographies demonstrate that Monroe's and Austin's journeys to fame were long and rarely easy. But in looking back, the two authors appear to be most proud that they kept looking forward. Austin writes, "I have suffered in my life, in my means, in my reciprocal relations; but I have this pride and congratulation, that I have not missed the significance of the spectacle I have been privileged to witness. . . . As much as I am able, I celebrate the Earth Horizon."[113] Over and over in their autobiographies, Austin and Monroe emphasize the centrality of their enduring visions, not only in determining the arc of their lives but also as the proper way to interpret their creative and editorial decisions. These unique autobiographies invite their readers in, asking them to understand and to share the way these women see art's role in the world. Including her readers by shifting to the plural pronoun "we" in the final paragraphs of *A Poet's Life,* Monroe asserts that a lack of shared vision is what truly ails the contemporary world. She laments "that we, so grandly born, so mightily endowed, should grope with blind eyes . . . until we can hardly see the blue of the sky or the glory of the seasons, until we can hardly clasp our neighbor's hand or hear his voice." Having clarified her own vision throughout *Earth Horizon,* Austin also calls for readers to join her in her final pages, so that together they can use "our collective power to visualize what has been observed and imagined."[114] Near the end of their life-writings and of their lives, Mary Austin and Harriet Monroe, like the pioneers they so admired, kept their gazes pointing forward, inviting their readers to join them.

Chapter 5

American Everywomen

Middlebrow Professionalism in Mary Roberts Rinehart's *My Story* and Edna Ferber's *A Peculiar Treasure*

WHEN BIOGRAPHERS and critics study the lives of Mary Roberts Rinehart and Edna Ferber, they tend to slip into comparisons to Horatio Alger or reference the American Dream.[1] Both authors came from humble beginnings and built virtual empires with the written word, inspiring their readers through their fiction and through their lives. And, unlike those of most of their female contemporaries, their autobiographies, Rinehart's *My Story* and Ferber's *A Peculiar Treasure,* were enthusiastically received by both reviewers and the public. Fan letters poured into *Good Housekeeping* during *My Story*'s serialization, and Doubleday sold 35,000 copies of Ferber's book in the first few months. The projects represented major milestones for their authors as well. Ferber declared that *A Peculiar Treasure* was the only one of her books she would save from a fire, and one of Rinehart's biographers judges *My Story* to be her finest work.[2] Written to 1930s market demand, these texts were the first of two autobiographies they would each publish. In their fifties, Rinehart and Ferber both still had a major stake in the reputation game when they were composing their texts—they hoped not only to construct an argument for how they should be remembered, as did most of the other autobiographers in this study, but also for how their writing should be understood in the current literary milieu.

As one review of Ferber's *A Peculiar Treasure* observed, "There is a good deal to be said for autobiographies which are written in middle-life, in success, in good health and in the spotlight."[3] The *New York Times* notice proclaimed Ferber's book "intensely interesting in every incident, on every page."[4] Other reviews predicted great success for the "big, generous book" because it lacked "pretense and pose."[5] Rouben Mamoulian noted that "Ferber's vivid, active, sensitive nature" is evident throughout the autobiography as it had been in her fiction.[6] Another reviewer remarked, "Her mind has stored whatever she has seen. And her autobiography is packed with dramatic detail, always and everywhere."[7] As engaging today as in 1939, the casual, conversational voice of *A Peculiar Treasure* and the development of scenes with dialogue (one of Ferber's greatest strengths as a writer) make all the difference. It is fortunate that conditions incentivized Ferber to write and publish an autobiography some thirty years before she died, because her later autobiography, *A Kind of Magic* (1968), does not compare well to *A Peculiar Treasure* in either content or style.

Rinehart's *My Story,* published in 1931 when she was also in mid-career, is just as engagingly written as *A Peculiar Treasure.* As with Ferber's reviews, Rinehart's note that, though she had already written over thirty books, *My Story* was "no swan song," and that the autobiography was a sign that "now she is only beginning to write."[8] Indeed, one reviewer designated *My Story* "a finer story than any she has told before."[9] Rinehart, who was not only deluged with confessional letters from fans and advice-seeking letters from aspiring writers in response to *My Story* but was also in correspondence with a college professor who taught her work, had hopes that the book would alter the critical attitude the literati had expressed regarding her popular work, having noted that they only praised her least-successful books.[10] Rinehart employs a casual, confidential voice in *My Story,* welcoming readers with a persona as unpretentious as Ferber's. Beginning with the caveat that there is no truly honest autobiography, Rinehart acknowledges when there are things she does not clearly remember and speaks spontaneously—or at least makes the prose feel that way—about the things she can recall. At the book's conclusion, she calls the story "as honest as I have been able to make it. It is the truth, but it is not all of the truth."[11] The *New York Times Book Review* found that Rinehart's life-story was "told with an admirable spontaneity, without egotism."[12] Her reviews, all positive, remark on Rinehart's casual, friendly prose; the "patent honesty" of her memories; and her own "engaging modesty."[13] The later, expanded editions of Rinehart's *My Story* (1948 and 1951) are just as engaging as the original and more forthright about some of the most difficult times in her personal life.

Part of the broad appeal of Rinehart's and Ferber's autobiographical personas lies in their insistence on their own ordinariness. Their books imply that everyone else is just as interesting and full of potential as they are, regardless of their success and fame. Ferber starts out by explaining that she's just a "conventional, thrifty, hard-working, respectable" person, and that "the story of any life, told with truth, selection, and a dramatic sense, would make an arresting book. Surely romance and agony, humor, adventure, and tragedy lie within the span of any ordinary lifetime." Ferber claims that she "fought the desire" to write an autobiography for several years before she "gave way." Chapter 1 of *A Peculiar Treasure* concludes with her hope that writing an autobiography might allow her not just "to discover what I am doing at a typewriter in a penthouse apartment" but how she got from Kalamazoo, Michigan, to Park Avenue, New York.[14] Ferber's success and lower-middle-class roots were a big sell to the Depression-era reading public: notices advertised the book as "the success story of an American girl who made good; the mercilessly hardworking, albeit glamourous, career of a popular novelist and playwright."[15] Like Rinehart, Ferber declares her intention to write the truth but not a "tell-all" in *A Peculiar Treasure.*[16] Autobiography, as she sees it, is a work of discovering, after the fact, *how* we happened, since we already know what happened.

Rinehart's *My Story* was also received as a tale of "enviable success . . . American to the core."[17] Rinehart's mastery of a variety of genres as a writer, including plays, mysteries, comedy, journalism, romance, travel writing, and short stories, was well known in her time. Her comic fiction, detective stories, and travel writing are still popular today. She created the "Had I But Known" narrator, and though she does not used the exact words, the oft-repeated old saw "the butler did it" originated from one of her books, *The Door.* A film adaptation of her stage play *The Bat,* coauthored by Avery Hopwood, partially inspired the comic-book hero Batman.[18] It is difficult to overestimate Rinehart's popularity; tallying all the bestseller lists in America between 1895 and 1944, her work comes out on top. Although her reputation is most associated with her genre fiction, Rinehart's serious short fiction of the 1920s has been favorably compared to Edith Wharton's.[19] Nevertheless, Rinehart insists on her ordinariness throughout her autobiography, referring to herself simply as "a woman. Any woman. Every woman" in the final chapter.[20] The *New York Times Book Review*'s reviewer played along, printing the headline "Everywoman in America," and proclaiming that Rinehart's life story was different "in degree, not in kind" from that of any woman.[21]

Like Mary Roberts Rinehart, Edna Ferber was a household name in the 1930s, due to her success not only as a novelist and playwright but because of her prolific production of short fiction, which was perpetually in high demand. As with Rinehart, Ferber had published a lot of her work—especially the funny stuff—in middlebrow magazines for nearly thirty years by the time her autobiography was released. Both Ferber and Rinehart were regular contributors to the *Saturday Evening Post,* which may have been America's most broadly read magazine between 1900 and 1933.[22] One reviewer for *A Peculiar Treasure* quipped that Ferber had written "a hundred short stories that everyone has read and half a hundred that are better than that."[23] Just as Rinehart had done with her mystery novels, Ferber invented a niche for herself that became her own unique brand of fiction: the regional saga. Her multigenerational novels usually focus on powerful individuals or families and how they accumulated their wealth and status from humble beginnings. Ferber had even won the 1925 Pulitzer Prize for one of them: *So Big.* The novel tells the story of a woman who creates a successful agricultural business—a national brand name, in fact—out of a small farm she inherits when her husband dies. In *A Peculiar Treasure,* Ferber defines Americanness as a desire and a drive for continual progress, extrapolating her personal belief that progress was possible through hard work and cultural pluralism.

But Ferber had another purpose for writing the book that had nothing to do with the growing market for autobiography: the rise of Nazism in Europe. While she was composing *A Peculiar Treasure,* Ferber was advocating, arranging for, and personally financing the rescue and relocation of seven Jewish refugees—distant family connections—from Nazi Germany. One of them had already been sent to a concentration camp but was released when Ferber sent an affidavit pledging her sponsorship for him to emigrate.[24] Ferber's title specifically relates to her Jewish heritage, which, along with her American citizenship, she considered a peculiar treasure, calling the book "the story of an American Jewish family in the past half-century."[25] Written a few years before the United States entered World War II, *A Peculiar Treasure* is partially a plea to America to act on behalf of displaced and persecuted Jewish people around the world. The title comes from Exodus 19:5, a combined commandment and blessing from the Tanakh, which many of Ferber's readers who were not Jewish would have identified as part of the Old Testament in the Christian Bible: "Now therefore, if ye will obey my voice indeed, and keep my covenant, then ye shall be a peculiar treasure unto me above all people: for all the earth is mine:

And ye shall be unto me a kingdom of priests, and an holy nation." The importance of the verse is emphasized, as it is placed as the epigraph to the volume. In fact, there are more references to Ferber's Jewish identity in *A Peculiar Treasure* than in any other book she wrote. In its pages, she freely discusses the incidents of racism she had encountered in her career. She mentions her ethnic heritage "repeatedly; otherwise we should forget it; and she does not want us to forget it."[26] Although she was emphatically proud of her Jewish heritage, Ferber's fiction often focuses on the merits and benefits of American pluralism, and her autobiography is no exception. She explains that the reason she has such happy memories of her youth in Appleton, Wisconsin, as opposed to her bleak memories of Ottumwa, Iowa, is because the Appleton community was open to friendships across barriers like "creed, color, race, money." Ferber's examples of this include dating several of her "goy" acquaintances and bonding with an African American classmate who shared her passion for Shakespeare.[27] Many of the fan letters Ferber received after the work was published were from readers who professed that the book had either made them rethink their own prejudices or made them resolve to fight anti-Semitism at home and abroad.[28] *A Peculiar Treasure* even inspired one reviewer to the exhortation, "Here is our peculiar treasure, of democracy and freedom, to be guarded by us all."[29]

In keeping with the inclusive tone of their texts, Rinehart and Ferber reject postures that might alienate them from their readers, instead creating personas that resist the "celebrity" label with which critics sometimes dismissed them and questioning the more highbrow "artistic" template that other writers of this era used to frame their 1930s autobiographies. These two writers were well aware of critical pushback against their popularity. In the 1920s, when high modernism was coming into vogue, their work had not always fared well with the critics. In the years leading up to *My Story,* reviewers were unkind to Rinehart, calling her "old-fashioned" and remarking that her work should find "popular favor," with all the scorn that highbrow modernism could put into that phrase, while Ferber was sneered at as "not a first-rate writer."[30] Although Ferber won the Pulitzer Prize in 1925, the decision had been highly contested with two of the judges—both college professors—ranking her book third among the finalists.[31] Knowing that her prize-winning novel *So Big* was being taught in American literature courses meant a great deal to Ferber, who had never gone to college. She declares, "That alone [was] worth working for" in *A Peculiar Treasure.*[32] Rinehart was well aware that most of the books she wrote were not considered highbrow enough to be "literature," and she acknowledges in *My Story* that it stung when her children went off to college and learned in their "literature classes, that 'mother' was no light of the world, but only a good professional writer."[33] Why, then, when "professional" was a coded put-down within the mechanisms of modernism, would these two autobiographers write texts affirming the "professional" label that had been used against them in literary criticism?

As it turns out, Ferber's and Rinehart's motivations for focusing on the professional template for authorship were probably more rooted in 1930s cultural discourse about working women than in literary critical discourse. Scott Ortolanto has observed that high modernist texts tended to "ignore modernity's impact on women in the working and middle classes."[34] Nonetheless, Rinehart and Ferber were middlebrow authors born into these classes, and as such were both interested and invested in the cultural shifts associated with the rise in the numbers of working women as well as with the public's growing interest in female professionalism. In the 1930s, the numbers of women who held jobs outside the home had already reached a majority. By 1930, half of the women in America had worked at one time, and even more significantly, female-occupied jobs were not mostly held by immigrants anymore.[35] Throughout *A Peculiar Treasure,* Ferber proclaims her focus on "working people . . . of those who got the tough end of life," affirming that "almost every line I have written since my writing days began in 1911 [was] about working men and women."[36] As Ferber observes in her short story "Sisters under the Skin," a humorous story about female garment workers and their interactions with some naive but well-meaning social activists, "Women who know the joys and sorrows of a pay envelope do not speak of girls who work as Working Girls. Neither do they use the term Laboring Class, as one would speak of a distinct and separate race."[37] Unlike their highbrow contemporaries, Rinehart and Ferber paid great attention to working women not only because those women formed part of their immense readership but because they identified with such women personally.

In building this identification with their common readers, Ferber and Rinehart emphasized their own backgrounds. Their autobiographies spend a good deal of time describing the working families in which they grew up. Rinehart's father was a would-be inventor turned traveling salesman, and Ferber's was a Hungarian Jewish immigrant to the United States who ran a struggling general store. Their mothers contributed to the households as well: Ferber's worked in the store, and Rinehart's took in boarders for a while. Looking back on her childhood, Rinehart recalls being "ashamed of [the] work" her Irish grandmother had done at home as a seamstress—work she views as "heroic" by the time she writes *My Story.* Both Rinehart and Ferber had wanted to go to college. However, their families could not afford it, so they started working full-time in their teens, Ferber as a news reporter and Rinehart as a nurse-apprentice. *My Story* depicts the brutal conditions of Rinehart's apprenticeship: nursing training was at the time a matter of making one's own white apron and cap and then having one's stamina and stomach tested by being given the dirtiest jobs in the hospital. On Rinehart's second day, the petite teenager was handed a bucket and looked down to find an amputated foot in it. According to *My Story,* after "two years of this contact with life as it is at its rawest and hardest," Rinehart had witnessed what multiple knife wounds did to the human body, realized that pimps beat the prostitutes who worked for them, and heard the life-stories of patients who, fearing imminent death, revealed their darkest secrets to her. In her autobiography, Rinehart particularly recalls nursing a dying woman who lived alone with her illegitimate daughter, shunned by her community; years later, she wrote a short story based on the scenario, exposing the "cruelty" and "stupidity" she had witnessed. Amid her exhausting, overwhelming nursing work, *My Story* explains that Rinehart found that she "wanted to write it. I wanted to write about the injustices and kindnesses and violence of that life."[38]

Ferber's autobiography also traces both her work ethic and her successful career to her first job. Realizing that she would need to earn her own income, a determined, seventeen-year-old Edna Ferber signed on as the *Appleton Crescent*'s first female reporter. After a year and a half, the paper was sold, and when the new owner decided he did not want a female reporter, Ferber got a new job reporting for the *Milwaukee Journal*, learning the same hard facts of life as Rinehart had—although not in the same intimate, physical proximity—through covering law enforcement stories and courtroom trials. From these experiences, Ferber argues she gained more wisdom than the college she never went to could have taught her. Ferber claims, "I wouldn't swap that year and a half of small-town newspaper reporting for any four years of college education. . . . I learned to read what lay behind the look that veiled people's faces, I learned to sketch in human beings with a few rapid words." Noting that reporters are "likely to be at once hard-boiled and sentimental," *A Peculiar Treasure* explains that Ferber emerged from her three and a half years in journalism with a sense of empathy for people whose stories often went untold, along with a desire for justice akin to Rinehart's—elements that would drive much of their fiction for the next half-century.[39]

Both Ferber's and Rinehart's autobiographies construct their early working years as crucibles of experience that transformed them into the writers they would later become. However, the labor they performed took a toll on their health. Both women suffered physical or mental breakdowns in their twenties, brought on by overwork, and both autobiographies claim that their forced convalescence inadvertently led to their writing careers. Rinehart wrote while she was confined to bed, first from nervous prostration after nursing one of her sons through diphtheria and later after an operation.[40] Ferber wrote her first novel, *Dawn O Hara, the Girl Who Laughed,* a semi-autobiographical tale of a female news reporter recovering from a nervous breakdown while convalescing at her married sister's home, after her work on the *Milwaukee Journal* led to a complete collapse. Open about her financial motives, Ferber notes that once she discovered her knack for fiction had more value in the marketplace than freelance journalism, she abandoned the latter forever. According to her autobiography, Ferber continued trusting in her work ethic all her life. *A Peculiar Treasure* explains that when she lost more than half of her savings in the stock market crash of 1929, she relied on her work ethic to prevent her from panicking over the loss: "I went calmly on finishing my book, and when it was finished I found I had made a lot of money all over again."[41]

Neither of these writers had any highbrow reservations about discussing money in their autobiographies. Ferber quips, "I do not think that money or talk of money in business is vulgar, and I am not among the artist souls who shrink therefrom."[42] Because money mattered to ordinary people like themselves, both women cite the exact dollars and cents they earned as their careers as writers began and acknowledge the times when they took on work with specific financial goals in mind. *My Story* relates that Rinehart earned a dollar each for her first few published stories. While her children were small, she also assisted her husband in his home-based practice as a family doctor. Writing in the odd scraps of free time she could find in her family's busy day, Rinehart notes that once she had earned $1,842.50 for forty-five stories, it seemed like it was time to invest in her new work, so she bought a $20 portable desk.[43]

In a 1936 volume of literary criticism, Professor Margaret Lawrence grouped women writers into different "types," depending on the behaviors they idealized in their fiction. The chapter entitled "The Go-Getters," in which Ferber's work is used as an example, reads like a definition of the American middlebrow. Discussing the "go-getter" woman writer, Lawrence declares, "Most of them stand securely on two feet. One foot is modern and daring; the other foot is safely conventional. . . . They are business women making shrewd use of fiction because it is an excellent business once it is established."[44] Because of the word's affiliation with business, I would suggest that "professional" was a code used by middlebrow authors of the early twentieth century to reframe their writing careers along lines that felt more accessible, more relatable, to the reading public. According to Jennifer Haytock's *The Middle Class in the Great Depression: Popular Women's Novels of the 1930s,* the 1920s and 1930s solidified American middlebrow identity for both authors and readers, while Jamie Harker notes that middlebrow writers of the time were able to combine a "highbrow concern for serious issues" with the "lowbrow's demand for accessibility and entertainment."[45] Both Rinehart and Ferber mastered this combination. Rinehart could probably have had a more highbrow career and reputation had she chosen to do so; according to Jan Cohn, Rinehart's stories in *Married People* (1937) demonstrate "what her gifts might have been, under other stars, as a realist."[46] But both Ferber's and Rinehart's tidy, satisfying, popular plots reflected how much middlebrow American readers wanted novels with resolution. As one critic quipped, "Thank the Lord for Ferb [who] still believes story should have a beginning, middle, and end."[47] This type of clarity and comfort was especially precious to "the middlebrow reader [who] looked to novels for a sense of identity in an increasingly confusing world," novels that safely addressed some of the cultural upheavals of the early twentieth century in areas such as "marriage, . . . clashes over values, wage-earning work . . . and aspirational desire."[48]

These two autobiographies engage particularly heavily with questions of hard work and aspirational desire, questions that were especially relevant for Depression-era readers. But Rinehart's and Ferber's expressed beliefs in hard work were not a 1930s spin-job. Biographer and fellow mystery novelist Charlotte MacLeod referred to Rinehart as "the ultimate workhorse."[49] In *My Story* Rinehart proclaims, "I am increasingly impatient with those people who believe that writing, the art of writing, is an easy and simple thing . . . an easy route to fame and money." Rinehart's work ethic was a constant theme in her interviews, articles, and op-eds. She would not accept advances on future work, even when pressed. Only once she had a completed manuscript in her hand would she negotiate or accept payment for it. *My Story* treats Rinehart's writing like the piecework her grandmother took in as a seamstress: "When a piece of work is completed it is for sale, and such offers as come in are entirely dependent on the work being satisfactory."[50] In a 1922 interview, Rinehart claimed, "I have never had any illusions about the work I do." She further stated, "To my three boys their mother's work has been a matter of course ever since they can remember. . . . They regard it exactly as a banker's family regards his bank."[51] In *My Story,* Rinehart records feeling "tired and empty after a full day of work. On this manuscript, for example, I have been writing steadily for seven to eight hours a day for almost a year."[52] At the end of the Depression, Rinehart's 1939 article "Writing Is Work" mounted a thorough defense of writing as a legitimate form of labor, calling it "a hard, arduous, and highly competitive business."[53] In *My Story,* she outlined the changes in working conditions for writers over the years of her long career. She explained, "Writers who began before [World War I] were trained in a hard school. We sent in our material, complete to the last semicolon, got it back or had it accepted at any price an editor chose to pay, and that was that. But it made troupers of those who survived. . . . It is frequently necessary to work against extremely adverse conditions."[54] The genre fiction for which she had been pigeonholed, Rinehart insisted, was as laborious as any other kind of writing—perhaps more so: "If any readers might be tempted to think writing crime fiction is not hard work and is an easy road to publishing," she invited them to picture "a haggard, wild-eyed woman despairingly searching through mounds of yellow paper for the caliber of a bullet."[55]

Both Rinehart's *My Story* and "Writing Is Work" develop a contrast between the average professional writer—that worker bee who must revise and revise and throw failed stories in the trash, burn bad novels in the furnace, and keep on writing—and the "people with such utter self-confidence that every word they write is precious." As Rinehart tartly observes, "It is usually the dilettante who has the superiority complex."[56] However impatient she is with the egotism of the self-styled genius, *My Story* declares that Rinehart has always "helped wherever possible the literary aspirant, humble and eager, who is willing to work." Rinehart herself hung a motto over her desk in the living room: "Ideas and hard work are the keys to all success" and left it there as a reminder for many years. Aside from hard work, Rinehart's autobiography offers no formula for literary success to her readers, for "when it comes to creation itself, there is little to say."[57]

Ferber also demystifies her own "writing process" in *A Peculiar Treasure.* This would have been expected in an "artist's" autobiography, but Ferber does it sardonically, saying all it means for her is to "go on mumbling my story." Ferber spends three hilarious pages depicting her daily struggle to get words on paper, including all her means of procrastination, frustration, distraction, and self-imposed interruptions, and then caps it off with the clearly ridiculous assumption she has heard so many times: "You writers just work when the inspiration comes to you, don't you?" Both these autobiographers clearly privilege perspiration over inspiration. Ferber refers to herself as a "work-worshipper" in *A Peculiar Treasure,* writing seven days a week, keeping writing hours at home as if she were punching a clock in an office. To achieve a reputation for professional integrity, making deadlines mattered. It was that which causes Ferber to rent a typewriter while on a visit to Florence, Italy: "I had contracts which must be filled," though "it took all one's strength of character to get to work mornings. . . . Just to glance out of the bedroom window was fatal."[58] Ferber also publicly encouraged other writers to have the discipline to behave like professional workers, not feckless celebrities.[59] Maintaining her focus and her work-ethic, even once she was an extremely successful author, was crucial to Ferber's understanding of her life, for according to her, "Writing has brought me friends and fortune and happiness and world-wide interests." *A Peculiar Treasure* sets Ferber up as an exemplar of this hard-work-pays-off philosophy, claiming to "have sat daily for hours with my face in a typewriter" for thirty years.[60] The book implies that, though grit and hard work, any American can also acquire these rewards in any sort of business.

If their writing were merely a matter of earning money and fame, that would place these autobiographers closer to the celebrity template for authorship. But both Rinehart and Ferber reject the celebrity label, mocking it in their autobiographies. Their amusingly self-deprecating remarks about the photos they include in their texts work to debunk their images as celebrities and enhance their "everywoman" appeal. Ferber includes a snapshot of herself mowing a lawn, as well as several embarrassing photos from her teenage years, wryly remarking, "The blouse seems to be in trouble" in her senior high school portrait.[61] Rinehart's selection of photographs for *My Story* similarly satirizes her "celebrity" status: she inserts acerbic commentary under the more glamorous photos, including writing "mostly I found myself doing publicity shots" under a photo of herself in a biplane with Cecil B DeMille. Rinehart pairs photographs strategically in the text, placing a candid with no makeup in the same insert with a publicity photo wherein she points out how heavily she was made up. Remarking under one photo that her dramatic eyebrows were achieved at the photographer's insistence, Rinehart makes fun of all the staged shots included in her story, inserting unglamorous snapshots from family camping trips and in group photos for balance.[62]

Both these autobiographies make it clear that neither celebrity nor wealth were sufficient motivation for their decades of labor as writers. Their definition of their own professionalism dovetailed with changing definitions in the greater labor marketplace, for female professionalism was a hot topic through the 1920s and 1930s. Volumes like Elizabeth Kemper Adams's 1921 manual *Women Professional Workers* were published to define the public dialogue on the issue, and Rinehart's and Ferber's implicit definitions of their own professionalism in *My Story* and *A Peculiar Treasure* clearly align with two of Adams's major claims: women's professionalism involved expanding and developing expertise and authority within a specialized field, and female professionals' personal motivations were primarily "intellectual and moral" rather than financial.[63] Both *My Story* and *A Peculiar Treasure* comport with Adams's first tenet by making it clear that developing personal expertise in their chosen specializations was more important than money. To that end, both authors explain their rejection of lucrative offers that would have stunted their growth as writers. As Rinehart observes about the small sums her early stories brought in, "Money was not important. I was learning a new profession." These autobiographers are also clear about the offers they refused to capitalize on their fame. Rinehart's *My Story* notes that she turned down the editorship of the *Ladies' Home Journal,* offered to her at a princely salary, because if she had accepted it, "I should have to abandon my own work, *in toto.*"[64] Ferber, too, recounts a story of resisting financial temptation in the name of deepening her professional skills. Purportedly, *Cosmopolitan* magazine once sent Ferber a blank contract for more of her popular Emma McChesney stories (a series of comic short stories about a middle-aged traveling saleswoman), asking her to fill in whatever dollar amount she wanted. *A Peculiar Treasure* explains that Ferber sent it back untouched because, "if I had signed that contract I never should have advanced as a writer and probably never would have written a fresh line again in all my life." As a professional, Ferber emphasizes, advancing her skills was far more important than any amount she could have written on that check. When, almost a decade after she started writing the McChesney stories, her first "mature novel," *The Girls,* was published, Ferber was outraged when advertising posters compared the novel to the Emma McChesney stories because *The Girls* "marked a definite advance. . . . I had left Emma McChesney behind me."[65] Mary Shaughnessy, in a book-length study entitled *Women and Success in American Society in the Works of Edna Ferber,* theorizes that Ferber distinguishes two types of success in all her novels, revealing material or social triumph to be the lesser types of success, and socially responsible self-fulfillment as Ferber's true ideal.[66] The reasons Ferber's and Rinehart's autobiographies give for their choices highlight the limited roles money and fame played in their definitions of professionalism. As they became more and more successful as authors, they both passed up tempting opportunities that they felt might detract from their professional development as writers, including Rinehart's refusal of two nominations to serve as a U.S. ambassador.[67] Instead, they focused on advancing their expertise as creative writers.

Rinehart and Ferber each had personal reasons to understand the importance of developing a professional specialization. Ferber had watched her mother step in and assume the management of their floundering family store after her father lost his sight, noting that the store "flourish[ed] under her [mother's] active management." Julia Ferber studied Chicago trends in clothing and housewares before the trends reached small-town Wisconsin and became known for her unique stock, offering what local shoppers could not get elsewhere. Ferber's first real literary success, the Emma McChesney stories, which made her a household name, arose directly from observing her mother's savvy. According to *A Peculiar Treasure,* Ferber too created a specialization in her early fiction, the American businesswoman: "I had created a new character in fiction. The American businesswoman had never been done."[68] Moreover, the character Ferber created succeeded in an arena almost exclusively male at the time: Emma McChesney is a traveling saleswoman who creates her own professional specialization. She sells ladies' suiting and undergarments, an area in which she has an advantage over the rest of the traveling salesmen because, as a woman, she can talk to female customers about how the clothes feel and function, not just how they look.

What Julia Ferber did with the family store, and what Emma McChesney does in the fictional world of women's fashion, Ferber did to the field of fiction: she became a specialist and built a name and reputation on her specialty. The sweeping, regional, multigenerational epic became Ferber's stock in trade, and it remained in demand from the 1920s to the 1960s. Ferber describes her method of creating and developing this specialization in *A Peculiar Treasure:* she finds a region, lifestyle, industry, or people whose story has not yet been told, goes there to research it by seeing the places and interviewing the people, and then writes the story. It was this method, *A Peculiar Treasure* reveals, that produced *So Big,* about poor truck farmers in Illinois; *Show Boat,* about vaudeville on the Mississippi and the malignant enduring racism of the South; *Cimarron,* about the pioneers and Native Americans of Oklahoma; *Come and Get It,* about the rise and fall of a logging magnate; *American Beauty,* about the Polish immigrants who resettled the neglected farms of New England; and eventually *Giant,* an ambitious book that became an even more ambitious movie starring Elizabeth Taylor, Rock Hudson, and James Dean about the ranchers and oilmen of Texas. Keeping her brand of fiction distinct also allowed Ferber to diversify into film with a level of success that exceeded nearly every other author of her generation. Many other writers in this study had their works adapted for film. But none of those films had a famous brand name, whereas the "Ferber Film" meant something to the American public and to the film industry. Ferber even insisted that her name appear on the movie posters for adaptations of her work.

Rinehart likewise reveals that she understood professional branding in *My Story*. Describing the time she met the queen of England, she recalls pausing before signing the guestbook, wondering whether she should write "Mrs. Rinehart," as she did in the hundreds of other guestbooks she signed. Rinehart recalls deciding that on this occasion she would sign "Mary Roberts Rinehart," because, after all, it was her "professional name" that appeared on the covers of her books which had earned her the invitation to that royal reception.[69]

Like Ferber, Rinehart first observed the need to develop and maintain a specialization by witnessing her father's failure in business. *My Story* reveals that Rinehart's father designed and patented an innovation to the sewing machine for which he was offered $10,000 by a manufacturer. He turned the offer down, believing he would start his own sewing-machine business and become rich. However, he could not earn enough sales commissions to pay the fees to maintain his patent, and when it lapsed, the same corporation eventually got to use his invention for free.[70] Rinehart's sadness at her father's impracticality is palpable in *My Story*. He had thrown away a chance for success in his true specialization—innovation—by trying to succeed in a different area—sales—in which he had neither shown nor developed real expertise. His despair was deeper than his family realized, for he eventually committed suicide while he was away from home on a sales trip.[71]

Rinehart's early understanding of specialization and branding crystalized when the same publisher bought her first three completed mystery manuscripts and released them one at a time over the next three years: *The Circular Staircase* (1908), *The Man in the Lower Ten* (1909), and *The Window at the White Cat* (1910). She notes the publisher's strategy in *My Story*, marketing each new book by referring to the success of the previous one. She applied her understanding of professional specialization to help her husband in his career as well. When Dr. Stanley Rinehart started experiencing early onset arthritic pain in his hands, they knew the condition would soon prevent him from conducting successful operations.[72] Together, the couple decided to move to Vienna where he could study and become a specialist, and thus do more consulting than hands-on work in the future. They moved to Europe with their three children in 1908, ignoring mean-spirited rumors that Dr. Rinehart was quitting his practice to live off his wife's money. *My Story* points out that Mary Rinehart had helped her husband in his medical practice for years before she became a successful novelist, and there was no gossip about that—people expected it of a doctor's wife. It was when her support for her husband's profession became overtly financial that people started to gossip, so the book reiterates that "we pooled our resources, at my insistence."[73] As a fellow professional, Rinehart understood her husband's need for specialization. The specialized training paid off: he was eventually appointed to the Veteran's Affairs Bureau as a tuberculosis specialist. *My Story* affirms that the couple made room for each other's work throughout their marriage, both when he gave up his new X-ray room so she could have a private office in which to write, and when she moved to Washington, D.C., to be with him while he held the government job, among other instances. Besides being willing to relocate for one another's careers, they discussed both his medical cases and her novels with each other at home.

Beyond valuing hard work and developing specializations, the third shared element to these two autobiographers' redefinitions of themselves as professionals is an insistence on their writing as a craft, not as the more lofty sounding "art." In *A Peculiar Treasure,* Ferber calls herself a "creative craftsman." To her the term "craftsmanship" is not just a reminder of the labor involved in writing but also a reflection of one's commitment and resilience. "The failure of a playwright, an actor, a novelist, a musician is publicly and scathingly announced . . .

in terms . . . cruel, personal, or even malicious," she observes, "yet next day or next week there he is, writing, acting, singing or playing again. That's being a craftsman." Good habits and good practice make for a good professional, Ferber notes in *A Peculiar Treasure,* so she creates the "everyday storehouse method . . . with the mental films all neatly filed away for future development when needed." Ferber's commitment to her writing keeps her at her desk, even when "everyone else in the world, you feel, is out playing golf or lunching or driving or having fun." As she remarks, "Those critics or well-wishers who think that I could have written better than I have are flattering me. . . . One writes as the opportunity and the material and the inclination shape themselves . . . good or bad, popular or unpopular, lasting or ephemeral, the words I have put down on paper were the best words I could summon at the time."[74] Her diction here conjures up an image of a craftsperson whose commitment to work does not wait on ideal conditions.

Rinehart also upholds craft, commitment, and resilience as ingredients for professional success in her autobiography. In the decade leading up to the publication of *My Story,* Rinehart's mystery stories were studied as mastercrafts of narrative. She received letters from a professor who said he often used her stories to teach his students about plot and characterization, and a *Chicago Daily Tribune* piece noted that "no less than twenty-seven classes of embryo fictionalists ha[d] made their pilgrimages to study the technique of her chill mystery manner" when Rinehart's hit play, *The Bat,* came to town.[75] Rinehart's autobiography defends genre fiction for its craftsmanship, claiming that "a logical crime story requires more concentration than any other type of writing, bar none."[76] Her emphasis on craftsmanship translated well for Depression-era readers. One review noted, "She speaks of her writing as a craft and believes that hard work has taught her to do it well."[77] Like Ferber, Rinehart emphasizes that craftsmanship takes a great deal of practice, and that when she was a busy young mother of three, she also had to develop resilience from interruptions. To

Rinehart, "Writing was only a small part of my world. . . . In such leisure as I had I wrote furiously . . . no fountain pen flowed fast enough." Before she had a devoted study in which to work, she would carry a card table from room to room in her house, looking for a quiet spot to get some writing done. Acknowledging that she never was able to follow Willa Cather's advice to lay away manuscripts for months before revision, she instead "learned, through lack of time, to sit down at my desk, pick up my pen, and go to work."[78] Timing, both these autobiographers argue, could not always be controlled, nor could they afford to rely on inspiration as the artist template for writers dictated. For the artistic ideals of inspiration and perfection, these two writers substitute professional commitment to developing their craft.

Just as Elizabeth Kemper Adams's book explains that truly professional women have intellectual and ethical—rather than just financial—reasons for the kind of work they do, both these autobiographers identify themselves as writers who want to make a positive impact on readers' lives. Rinehart had a deep determination that she "must never fail [her readers]."[79] Rinehart's 1922 *Bookman* article "The Unreality of Modern Realism" delineates her ethical reasons for opting out of what we now call high modernism in more detail. The article critiques the "ruthless iconoclast" modernist writer for spreading a false sense of cynicism among readers. She credits the "mainly young, frankly cynical and disillusioned" writers of the 1920s as "honest in their convictions" but finds them misguided: "If realism be truth, then let us have truth," she demands, "and neither a portion of it nor a distortion of it . . . for life is a fluid thing. It has its high moments and its low. . . . From the standpoint of reality one is as incorrect as the other."[80] One of her biographers sums it up thus: many of Rinehart's stories carried a "double message: Life is Hard; There is Some Hope."[81] In *My Story,* Rinehart explains that she viewed writing crime fiction as a way to fight injustice in real life, by exposing the latent causes for violence and suffering, learned in her nursing days.[82]

Her fictional protagonists generally balance a dogged pursuit of truth and a compassionate response to human foible, and biographies of her imply that she may have aspired to both these qualities personally as well. During her research for a 1914 book, *The After House,* which was based on a famous ax-murder case, Rinehart became convinced that the convicted man was innocent of the crime. Her research caused the investigation to be reopened, and the wrongfully convicted man was eventually released.[83] For Rinehart, the naive, middlebrow claim that the contents of a book have an indelible impact on "real life" was a personal gospel.

The final element in both Ferber's and Rinehart's autobiographical descriptions of their literary professionalism is a respect for the American common reader. In her cogent 1933 op-ed in the *Saturday Review of Literature,* "Message and Middlebrow," Margaret Widdemer asked, "What *is* the reading public but the public that reads? . . . They are not highbrow or lowbrow but middlebrow," and they do "discuss art in [moral] terms," looking for "something constructive."[84] Whether you are reading Rinehart's novels wherein the most serious crimes are often solved by middle-aged spinsters, or Ferber's stories where housekeepers, waitresses, and salesgirls carve justice for others or success for themselves out of struggle, these authors' creative work always offers readers Widdemer's elusive "constructive something"—courage, hope, humor, or justice—that most readers seemed to want. By the time they wrote their autobiographies, both Rinehart and Ferber were bold enough to defy the elitists who criticized them for doing so. Knowing they did not fit into the artist or activist templates, and refusing to settle for celebrity, these two authors utilized *My Story* and *A Peculiar Treasure* to construct an alternative template for their authorship—instead of dancing around their popularity, they anchor their popular success in their personal professionalism.

Rinehart often used the term "critics' book" to refer to work that she wrote to be impressive, rather than to leaven life for readers or understand it better for herself.[85] However, she remained unapologetic for having written fewer "critics' books" than any other kind. In "My Public," Rinehart declares a preference for "the liking of many," not the "praise of the few."[86] Ferber too debunks the notion of the independent, disinterested artist, stating, "Writers write to be read. Only amateurs say that they write for their own amusement."[87] Ferber was deeply pleased to know that she was read by taxi drivers and porters, not just literary critics, and she saved a review that observed, "A new novel by Edna Ferber means a great deal to a public which is immeasurably bigger than the usual book world."[88] According to one publisher's memoir, it was Ferber's "understanding of, and sympathy for, the plain folk she writes about" that set her apart: "She loves humanity, and is unafraid to reveal her love."[89] Even though their fame presented a burden when they were recognized or approached in public, Ferber and Rinehart appreciated their fans. "God bless them, even if they're occasionally maddening," Ferber reflects in her autobiography, "for, though I write as I please, it is pleasant to know that I please others as I write."[90] Rinehart was also besieged by fans throughout her career, but she too reacted graciously and hospitably. In "My Public," she comments, "The crowd that presses forward to shake hands has a collective grip that hurts for days after," but "I would rather be in the hearts of the multitude than in high places where the mighty sit alone."[91] In her old age, when Rinehart's home in Maine was featured on boat tours in Bar Harbor, she would hear the tour guide point out her house and sometimes find the bolder fans on her doorstep. Always gracious and grateful to her readers, she occasionally escorted them on a tour through her home.

Besides appealing to modern professional women, Rinehart and Ferber established their commonality and connection with more traditional readers through an emphasis on their love of domesticity in their life-writings. According to scholar Francesca Sawaya, between the turn of the century and 1940, many working women increasingly utilized discourses of both "domesticity and professionalism to authorize and shape their work." Other women writers of Rinehart's and Ferber's generation, like Willa Cather, "sought to stabilize the opposition between domesticity and professionalism." Cather rejected both domestic identity and female solidarity in order to "insist on [her] professional authority" and distance herself from "best-selling women's writing."[92] However, Rinehart's and Ferber's autobiographies do the exact opposite, again aligning themselves more with popular cultural discourse than with literary criticism. Establishing a cooperative, rather than a competitive, relationship between domesticity and professionalism was key to establishing their relatability for their readers. Aligning their professionalism with domesticity meant that these two authors didn't scorn writing for ladies' magazines the way that some of their contemporaries did. Rinehart contributed a monthly column to the *Ladies' Home Journal* for a while, and Ferber's autobiography expresses her gratitude to editor Gertrude Lane of the *Women's Home Companion* for her good advice and for all the Ferber stories she printed over the years.[93] Ferber also chose to serialize her autobiography in *Women's Home Companion,* and Lane paid her more per installment than she had ever before offered for excerpted memoirs.[94]

Even when they weren't writing for women's magazines, Ferber and Rinehart worked to erase the perceived divisions between women who worked and women who stayed at home. Reviews of *My Story* emphasized Rinehart's domestic professionalism, "marvel[ing]" at her "enjoyment and care of her home" and devotion to her family.[95] Ferber similarly claimed, "I never have wished that I had been born a man, or thought myself handicapped because I hadn't been," and her text celebrates the diversity of women's contributions to society. Rather than making a joke of them as many early twentieth-century writers had, *A Peculiar Treasure* pays tribute to bourgeois women's clubs: "Thousands of women today owe to these clubs such legal, legislative, parliamentary, civic, and national knowledge as they possess. . . . Their work was charitable, educational, intellectual, vicariously political." Ferber's autobiography, like her short stories, is littered with tributes to women whom others overlooked: to the prematurely aged farmers' wives who came into the general store, to the women's rights movement, to a seamstress, to the hotel housekeeper. In *A Peculiar Treasure,* Ferber declares that the American hired girl "should have a rich, colorful, and important book all to herself."[96] Rinehart's work also emphasizes the value of family, the common joys and pains of motherhood. Her husband and all three of their sons served in World War I, and although only one of them was posted overseas, *My Story* describes her agonized fears that he would be killed: "I was only one mother, and my boy came back. My story is the story of millions of women, all over the world."[97]

Other 1930s autobiographers may not have outwardly denigrated sentimental notions of domesticity, home, and family as thoroughly as Willa Cather, Gertrude Atherton, and Margaret Anderson did, but few of them embraced these things as overtly as Edna Ferber and Mary Roberts Rinehart. Mary Austin and Harriet Monroe came the closest to Ferber's and Rinehart's overt appreciation of domestic life, while Edith Wharton practically omitted it from her literary self-portrait. While we know Wharton luxuriated in her domestic comforts and enjoyed restoring and decorating houses as much as Rinehart and Ferber did, Wharton glosses over the connection between her writing, her earnings, and her homes in *A Backward Glance.* Because *My Story* came out before *A Backward Glance*, Wharton may have known that Rinehart successfully combined domesticity and literary professionalism in her autobiography. But Wharton perhaps thought that such frankness and hominess was only appropriate for a "popular" writer, and may have feared that it would detract from her more highbrow, artistic persona. However, as American everywomen, Rinehart and Ferber, writing from the middle to the middle, were openly enthusiastic about spending their earnings on domestic comforts in their autobiographies. Like

Wharton, both Rinehart and Ferber worked toward the purchase and renovation of homes and land with which they fell in love. Rinehart first became enamored of a rambling property outside of Pittsburgh, with room for her three sons to roam around and climb trees. The entire Rinehart family came to call the place "The Bluffs," not merely because it was on a steep hillside but because of the financial bluff involved in purchasing such a huge place in need of major repairs. According to *My Story,* "The Bluffs" turned out to be "much more than a home. It was a constant and heavy expense," and "it was a point of honor" with her to use her writing to pay for the extra expenses for the home she wanted.[98] While the Bluffs was under construction, Rinehart wrote four novels, dozens of stories, and a play.[99] Despite the difficulties of maintaining the Bluffs, it was the first of three large home renovations Rinehart undertook throughout her lifetime, and the profits from her writing kept the renovations moving forward. Wharton did much the same with The Mount, Pavillion Colombe, and Saint-Claire Le Chateau, but she was too much of an artiste to discuss the connection in her autobiography.

Ferber created a domesticized professionalism similar to Rinehart's in her autobiographical persona. Although Ferber never married, her great-niece claimed that Ferber was very domestic, an enthusiastic gardener and cook, and very involved in family life throughout her career.[100] Not only did Ferber's mother live with her, but her letters indicate that Edna also regularly helped out with her sister's children, living with a similar set of distractions as might be found in Rinehart's daily routine. *A Peculiar Treasure* asserts that Ferber began her career as a novelist while staying at her sister's house, writing every day in the bedroom she shared with her mother, "with the family life swirling around me." Ferber purportedly purchased her New York penthouse so she could have a rooftop conservatory to grow fruits and vegetables in her apartment. She glibly calls the Park Avenue conservatory her "farm," having decided years before that spending the early morning in her married sister's garden, and occasionally baking a pie with its fruits, "was good atmosphere for writing."[101] Friends teased Ferber about her obsession with fresh produce and her penchant for serving them sumptuous meals that ruined their diets.[102] For Ferber loved to cook as much as she loved to grow food. She claims, "I've never seen a really dimensional or important human being who was indifferent to good food and its preparation," and *A Peculiar Treasure* records that Eleanor Roosevelt received Ferber's personal approval for offering her late-night snacks at the White House. Although she traveled quite frequently, Ferber declares that she "hated hotels" and "loved my own bed, my own typewriter, my own bureau drawers and bookshelves and homemade popovers."[103] While she was writing *A Peculiar Treasure,* Ferber was simultaneously building a country house in Connecticut that she named, aptly enough, "Treasure Hill."[104]

In keeping with their professional template for authorship, Ferber and Rinehart used the homes they purchased and redesigned for themselves with their earnings as a way of reinvesting in their own corporations. They appear to have viewed the luxury of their later homes as both a reward for their work and as a way to promote the health, strength, and space they needed to maintain their productivity. Yet neither romanticized the home as a perfectly peaceful seat of bliss and concentration. They recognized that a family home, in which there are children running around and soup on the stove, created challenges to the work of the writer, yet they also made domestic chaos a humorous part of their public personas rather than bemoaning it. In an interview, Rinehart confessed that she "learned to use the typewriter with my two forefingers and a baby on one knee."[105] For Rinehart's "Writing Is Work" article, the illustrator brought to life a domestic scene as she had described it. It includes a drawing of a cluttered family room with both Mary Roberts Rinehart and the family dog watching as her sons appear to be about to use their father's medical scalpels to "operate" on a doll. In the same article, and also in *My Story,* Rinehart explained that she received news of her first contract for a novel while grocery shopping. Her husband called her at the local butcher shop when the acceptance letter came, and she "celebrated" her success by baking a cake that afternoon.[106] Once all her children were in school, she could write almost all day, waiting for them to come home. As she tells it in *My Story*, "All day I would work in my study, until the front door began to slam. Then I would stop, for the family was at home. I would think of that, and my very heart would swell. Home. Home at last."[107]

The clear links these authors make between their work and their homes may be part of the reason they had such broad appeal as "everywomen." But their emphasis on home as an environment that can be designed for both professional work and personal leisure is not the only way in which their autobiographies domesticate their professionalism. When accused of writing light formula fiction, they both defend their work using baking analogies. "It takes a light hand to make pastry. . . . The reader can be certain: the more easily anything reads, the harder it has been to write," Rinehart explains.[108] Ferber also frequently uses cooking analogies to describe her creative process, mixing her cooking metaphors in *A Peculiar Treasure:* "Writing hot off the griddle . . . is no good for me. A story must simmer in its own juice for months or even years before it is ready to serve."[109] Ferber once compared her short story technique to a perfectly prepared pancake: "the same deft pouring of the batter, the same expert jerk, the same neat flip of the wrist at the end."[110] In fact, Ferber considered domestic and professional competency as natural compliments to one another, believing "the woman who is domestic is capable in everything she does. . . . Did you ever hear a good, successful businesswoman, earning a thumping big salary, talk about her house and family? She actually loves it! . . . There is nothing so thoroughly domestic as the successful business woman."[111]

Balancing home and work had become more and more common for American women in general between 1920 and 1930. Labor statistics show that the number of American wage-earning women went from 8 to 10 million during the decade, and the number of *married* working women climbed from less than 2 million to over 3 million.[112] Rinehart discusses the impact of her work on her marriage frankly in *My Story*, acknowledging that it requires compromise. She also publicly advised young girls who wanted a career to first choose a husband—presumably one who was willing to support their work as part of their identity.[113] By the time Rinehart wrote her autobiography, work for women was almost as normal a setting as the home, and "to significant numbers of women, marriage and work no longer seemed like mutually exclusive alternatives."[114] Rinehart addresses this directly in *My Story*. When she first started writing, she muses, "There was the tradition of the woman in the home, and of the comparatively few who had emerged from it to make names for themselves, almost all had failed to make the compromise between marriage and a career. The theory was that the true artist lived and expressed herself only in her art. . . . Above all, she must be free." The "theory" Rinehart summarizes here can help us understand the severely edited narratives that other 1930s literary autobiographers wrote when they were trying to claim the artistic template for their literary legacy. However, Rinehart rejects this theory, continuing, "But I felt confident that this compromise could be made." Rinehart was asked for her opinion on the home versus work debate a number of times throughout her career, but as *My Story* explains, "I believe that the matter is automatically self-regulating; that those women who prefer the home . . . will eventually return to it; that others, like myself, will compromise; and that still others . . . will remain in the world to add to its productivity after their own fashion."[115]

Rinehart is vocal in her autobiography that she has a "Profession" and *not* a "career."[116] The emphatic distinction she makes between the two sounds strange nearly a century later. But there was a palpable difference between the two words in American culture, and most definitely in Rinehart's understanding, in the early twentieth century. A woman's career was generally viewed as a private sideline, an identity that no longer exclusively implied she was single but one that she abandoned at home when she was married. The money she earned was usually not pooled with her husband's income, so that he could still be said to "support" the family. Thus, a career for a woman was separate from family relations, removing a woman from the home just as it sequestered her money from the family purse. But a profession, according to both Rinehart's and Ferber's definitions, was an integrated piece of one's identity, not something one stopped being at home.

Although they traveled the world, palled around with presidents and movie stars, and became immensely wealthy, Rinehart and Ferber come across as firmly rooted in the ordinary details of everyday life in their autobiographies. This may be one reason these two writers have come across as infinitely relatable to their millions of readers. Encouraging women that they could expand their lives if they wished, Rinehart's *My Story* points out that if she could find time to write while raising three children and assisting her husband in his medical practice, then "the American woman hardly exists . . . who cannot spare an hour or two a day for the thing she goes through life lamenting that she cannot do."[117] Ferber's book ends with an inclusive expression of gratitude for the privilege "to have been a human being on the planet Earth, and to have been an American, a writer, a Jew."[118] Facing a national financial depression and a potential return to world war, the future looked as uncertain for these two women as it did for everyone else in the 1930s. In the midst of these more universal worries, however, both autobiographies reveal that Ferber and Rinehart were also privately worried about whether their work would ever be accorded a place in the American canon. Although their names have not yet reappeared in textbooks or on syllabi, Ferber's and Rinehart's books have always remained in circulation, on private and public library shelves and in new audio and electronic formats, secure in the enduring esteem of the ordinary readers whom they always appreciated and understood.

Chapter 6

Strategic Diversions

The Veiled Autobiographies of Gertrude Stein and Carolyn Wells

GERTRUDE STEIN'S *The Autobiography of Alice B. Toklas* and Carolyn Wells's *The Rest of My Life* are both books that almost weren't. Stein had repeatedly declined requests for her autobiography before she came up with her text as a "literary joke," based on her love of detective novels where the secret—in this case, her authorship of the book—is revealed at the end.[1] Wells, who may have written some of the detective novels Stein consumed daily, had pitched a memoir to her publisher decades earlier and been turned down. But by the mid-1930s, when everyone was clamoring for her autobiography, Wells was hesitant, feeling the genre was now overdone.[2] Although Stein's text has been labeled a "mock" autobiography, I would suggest that mockery was the process, not the product here, and that Stein's innovations can be better understood when compared to Wells's text, another 1930s autobiography that makes a game of its refusal to comply with convention. This chapter analyzes Stein's *The Autobiography of Alice B. Toklas* and Wells's *The Rest of My Life* as "veiled" autobiographies, which I would define as life-writings that defy autobiographical conventions while still embedding the more serious, intimate aspects of their lives beneath an amusing surface. Both of these authors frame their life-stories through a series of delightful diversions, using humor and deferral to avoid directly addressing important elements of their personal identities: for Stein, her lesbian relationship with Toklas, and for Wells, her deafness. Both of these texts succeed beautifully at amusing their audiences into accepting whatever these autobiographers choose to reveal or conceal.

Wells opens her autobiography with a tale of rejection—she had pitched her memoirs to her publisher, George Doran, "a good many years ago" and received a resounding "no." However, throughout the 1930s, she declares, people were "advising, urging, coaxing, begging, cajoling, entreating, beseeching, nagging and importuning me to write my LIFE."[3] Wells was a prolific author who primarily published formula mystery novels but was equally famous for both her humor and her middlebrow children's fiction. She also assembled a magnificent Walt Whitman collection that she later bequeathed to the Library of Congress. Wells's satires and parodies, including send-ups of cultural trends like the popularity of bridge, automobiles, and the Gibson Girl, and her famous witticisms, such as "the wages of sin is alimony" and "forgive us our Christmases as we forgive those who Christmas against us," were iconic.[4] In her time, Wells was both well-known and well-connected. She was one of only three women to be included in Thomas Masson's 1922 study *Our American Humorists,* and in 1925 she spearheaded a collaboratively written satire about the flapper era entitled *Bobbed Hair,* with chapters by Dorothy Parker, Alexander Woolcott, and Rube Goldberg, among many others. Wells also wrote the first truly definitive historical study of detective fiction, entitled *The Technique of the Mystery Story.*[5] By 1937, when *The Rest of My Life* was published, Carolyn Wells had written an astounding 166 books. All in all, this indefatigable author published an average of three books a year for her entire adult life, assembling a massive fan base in multiple genres. Her lifelong obsession with puzzles and games underlies Wells's equal adroitness in comedy, mystery, and book-collecting.

Both Wells's autobiography and Stein's *The Autobiography of Alice B. Toklas* succeeded in multiple ways: they were generally well-reviewed, with critics using similar verbiage such as "witty," "delightful," and "charming" to describe them. Both texts also sold well—in fact, Stein's was the career breakthrough she needed in America. More recently, Stein's work has prompted critical responses such as Helena Lenart-Cheng's "Autobiography as Advertisement," which charts Stein's use of repetition in the book as a self-promotion and branding technique. Lenart-Cheng estimates that the words "Gertrude Stein" are repeated "more than a thousand times" in the book, even though Toklas referred to her merely as "Gertrude" in Toklas's own writing.[6] If Stein's book was indeed an advertisement, it was a good one: *The Autobiography of Alice B. Toklas* sold out of its first printing in ten days, and Harcourt Brace followed up with two more print runs. Reviews emphasized the book's wit and accessibility, appreciating its "good-humored, amusing, and sensible" anecdotes.[7] One led with the header, "Gertrude Stein Writes a Book in Simple Style."[8] Others appreciated the fact that while most autobiographers "talk only about themselves . . . with Gertrude Stein, this is not the case."[9] The reviewer for *Independent Woman* magazine welcomed it as "more than a mere amusing autobiography," declaring it an "intrinsically important" book.[10] Because of the book's success, some of Stein's unpublished works that had been languishing for decades found a platform—and a readership. *Time* magazine's review of *The Autobiography of Alice B. Toklas,* entitled "Stein's Way," declared that the book had relocated Stein from the "borders of literature into the very marketplace."[11] This claim was factually accurate, as the veiled autobiography made *Publishers Weekly*'s top-ten list in bestselling nonfiction and was selected for the Book of the Month club list.

The way that Wells used the booming 1930s marketplace for women's literary autobiography as a venue for her own narrative ingenuity is also well worth examining. By the mid-1930s, the hopping demand for autobiography was well-known, and both Stein and Wells offer tongue-in-cheek comments on the proliferation and popularity of the genre in their texts. In 1937, Wells remarked on "this poor long-suffering public of ours; even now writhing under an avalanche of multi-paged biographies, taking arms against a sea of memoirs." The specific market for *literary* autobiography does not escape Wells's notice either; early in her book she jests, "Everybody is doing it. . . . Just look at the lists of high-grade writers who have recently let the world in on their ground floors."[12] Wells's sarcastic treatment of the bull market for life-writing even resulted in one review entitled "Carolyn Wells Hates Autobiographies." Noting that it is not exactly a traditional autobiography, the review goes on to term Wells's book a "gallant and amusing series of episodes . . . strung lightly on the thread of Carolyn Wells' life-story."[13] The reviewer for *Books* declared *The Rest of My Life,* "undoubtably one of the best" memoirs of the period, "wise, and very willful," with "laughs by the dozen."[14] Another reviewer noticed that, while Wells's voice is "unassuming and likeable" and the book "entertaining," it "skims merely over the surface of things" and is "disappointing" for the reader looking for insight into Wells's past, personal life, or relationships.[15] While most critics noted the that Wells's book seemed to have more surface than depth, one excused the "scattered" quality because the book was "original and enjoyable" and written with a "valiant, whimsical, laughing spirit."[16]

This chapter analyzes the narrative techniques by which both the likability and the scattered quality of *The Rest of My Life* and *The Autobiography of Alice B. Toklas* were skillfully engineered. Both texts create effective digressions to avoid the "petty" curiosity that Wells publicly disdained, since both of these women had been pressured to write autobiography by publishers and friends.[17] On the last page of *The Autobiography of Alice B. Toklas,* the narrator comments, "For some time now many people, and publishers, have been asking Gertrude Stein to write her autobiography and she had always replied not possibly."[18] Despite this assertion, Stein had been utilizing autobiographical material for years in her writing. Although *Autobiography* is her first of three official self-portraits, critics like Ulla E. Dydo have noted that, read chronologically, Stein's oeuvre makes up a "single spiritual autobiography."[19] Stein was fascinated with the performance and representation of identity in all its mediums throughout her career and wrote many word sketches of friends, acquaintances, and strangers between 1909 and 1933 that were collected and published in the 1934 volume *Portraits and Prayers* after *Autobiography* opened the American market to Stein.

Critics have written extensively on Stein's narrative experimentation in the text, especially on its nonlinear form, locating it as "the first modernist autobiography" and comparing it to modern art forms such as cubism.[20] James Bresslin notes that *The Autobiography of Alice B. Toklas* exhibits "an intense and creative struggle" with the "conventions of memory, identity, and chronological time."[21] While Stein's innovations clearly do relate to modernist art and experimentation, all the 1930s autobiographers in this study struggled against these conventions to some degree. And since so much excellent work has already been done on the modernist elements of Stein's text, this chapter examines Stein's and Wells's autobiographies as complex jokes *within* and *about* the 1930s book market, reading the texts as games that can be played at various levels, depending on the reader's insight. To approach their texts as games is not meant to imply that these autobiographies cannot be taken seriously; rather, it is to acknowledge the authors' textual hints as invitations to join in their play, for not only did Stein speak of her book as a joke, but Wells's text refers to her "jack-in-the-box brain."[22] Although it had been around for centuries, the Jack-in the-Box was repopularized in the 1930s because it could be mass-produced with tin, rather than made of wood, as it had been in previous generations.[23] Indeed, reading these books as a pair conjures up the image of this popular wind-up toy, with the narrative detours leading the reader around and around the same implied questions the way a child would keep turning the handle and hearing the same tune.[24] In these autobiographies, even once the hidden joker pops out of the box, there is still a lot of unexplored material left underneath, inviting the reader to go "round and round" the book again. This material, including a populist view of literary taste and an argument for the pleasures of repetition and formula—both of which were key elements in the popular success of the Jack-in-the-Box—are explored later in the chapter.

The most obvious joke in both these veiled autobiographies is the mockery they make of the traditional "autobiographical pact." There are three key premises to Phillipe Lejeune's original definition of this purported pact: the narrator and subject are same person; memory is a reliable guide to truth, which is the primary value of the genre; and the self is a knowable entity.[25] Avoiding these demands, Stein narrates her book in the voice of her partner, Alice B. Toklas, famously revealing the text as her story, written by herself, in the last line. However, the text implies that there may also be a second layer to the joke due to its reference to Daniel Defoe's fictional autobiography of *Robinson Crusoe.*

Wells's book flouts the autobiographical pact in other ways. Her primary evasive maneuver in *The Rest of My Life* is to repeatedly declare her book merely a memorandum of the plans she has for the future. Two-thirds of the way through her autobiography, Wells inserts a chapter entitled "Me," lamenting, "The blow has fallen. . . . I am informed by a friend in whose opinions I have absolute faith . . . that I must put Me into my book." Characteristically, though, the rest of the chapter consists of a lengthy, insincere resolution to try to become less self-centered for the rest of her life. While reaching page 223 before writing a chapter about herself is an impressively long detour, Wells does not manage to postpone openly referring to herself as the book's author until the last page. Nonetheless, Wells violates the second premise of the autobiographical pact by declaring that her past "would be poor fodder for an autobiography," and the first and third premises by declaring that she intends to be a much different person in the future anyway. Wells's plans for the future, however, may not be terribly sincere either. They include ending sentences with prepositions, not wasting time on fact-checking or looking up references, and finally organizing her desk.[26]

Refusing to comply with a conventional linear timeframe, both these autobiographies eschew presenting a coherent chronology of their authors' lives. Estelle Jelinek, sorting Stein's chapters back into chronological order, determines that chapter 4 of *The Autobiography of Alice B. Toklas* would come first in a conventional autobiography, and that chapters 6 and 7 are the only ones in chronological order.[27] Like Wells's work, Stein's narrative technique consists of a series of deferred promises and productive diversions. One of the most well-known comes in chapter 1, as the narrator says, "but this time I am really going to tell about the pictures," after which she states that "there were pictures of all kinds there," and then lists some artists and styles for about twenty lines before digressing again. The announcement at the end of chapter 2—"And now I will tell you how two americans happened to be in the heart of an art movement of which the outside world at the time knew nothing"—is an acknowledgment of the question the entire chapter begs the reader to ask. However, the next chapter merely states that Stein's brother was in Florence and "heard of a painter named Cezanne." The next sentence reads, "When he and his sister made their home in Paris the following year they went to Vollard's the only picture dealer who had Cezannes for sale, to look at them."[28] Technically, the promise in chapter 2 has been kept. But in the spirit of the pact, it has not. There is no reflection, no discussion, no narrative dive into the circumstances or decisions that led both the Steins and Toklas to make the move to Paris.

As Lenart-Cheng's article points out, *The Autobiography of Alice B. Toklas* uses "almost all these narrative detours to reflect on a positive moment in [Stein's] career."[29] In chapter 3, the narrator again defers reflection, offering a fact the reader likely already knows—that Picasso painted Stein—rather than the backstory readers may have expected, or at least might have hoped for. In reference to the Picasso portrait, the question of *how* things happened (the question Edna Ferber says is the only real reason for autobiography, as what happened is already known) goes begging again, because "they do not either of them know how it came about," although "a great deal happened during that time." Again, in an effort to impose order on the text that the reader begins to suspect is not entirely sincere, the narrator promises "to go back to all the first times," an indefinite direction indeed. On page 63, she appears to realize that she still has not quite fulfilled the promise in chapter 3 and comments, "I am once more running far ahead of those early Paris days." Later, on page 151, she takes readers around the same proverbial mulberry bush again, reminding herself "to come back to the events that were happening."[30] Throughout the text, the deferrals endlessly flow into one another, until one realizes at the end that the entire volume was a deferral of the announcement of Stein's authorship, the moment when "Jack" pops out of the box.

Perhaps this round-and-round technique in *The Autobiography of Alice B. Toklas* illuminates Gertrude Stein's claim that "it is a good thing to have no sense of how it is done in the things that amuse you."[31] Read carefully, this sentence could also be interpreted as a protest against literary autobiography itself, for why would you tell readers who like your work how you did it if that will spoil the fun for them? This sentence simultaneously identifies and resists a foundational principle for literary autobiography, wherein readers who have long enjoyed or admired a famous writer expect to find out how they became successful or famous writers, often with a subtextual expectation that in discovering the writer's secrets, readers might then be able to replicate their success. Ironically, Stein's autobiography reads as if *of course* she is already a success when, in fact, she was not—yet. Since prior success is customarily an author's ticket to publishing literary autobiography, then in writing *The Autobiography of Alice B. Toklas,* Stein managed to slip past the ticket booth and take command of the show. In reality, Stein's ticket to publishing this particular literary autobiography was her notoriety, and her notoriety at that time was almost entirely based on her odd style being used as a popular joke in the marketplace. Stein scholars such as Rod Rosenquist and Karen Leick have demonstrated how Stein's style was widely parodied in the 1920s and early 1930s, so many Americans who had never read a word she wrote knew about her, through popular advertisements such as Bergdorf-Goodman's "A Rose Is a Pose Is a Rose" advertisement, among others.[32] Knowing she was a joke *in* the American marketplace, Stein wrote a book that was a joke *on* it.

Both Stein's and Wells's selections of images for their texts play games that subvert the autobiographical pact as well. Rather than choosing images to illustrate their life-stories, as was expected and traditional within autobiography, Stein and Wells utilize images that lead the reader away from a knowable, visible self, violating visual autobiographical convention as well as the narrative convention that purports to show the trajectory of an artist's development. Rather than illuminating the text, the images themselves demand further illustration in these two books. For instance, much has been said about the revelation of Stein as the author of *Autobiography* in the last sentence of the book. But if you read the original hardcover with images, you see that this verbal revelation is no revelation at all: the visual discourse in the book lets the reader in on Stein's joke from the beginning. Every solo photo in the text is of Gertrude Stein. From page eight, the visual discourse makes clear whose autobiography it really is, if you read it according to the convention that the portraiture in an autobiography is primarily of its author/subject. Yet the verbal discourse in the text continues to deny this premise until the end of the volume. Much has also been made of the Man Ray photograph that serves as the book's frontispiece. The photograph shows Gertrude seated at a shadowed desk and Alice in a lighted doorway, but Paul Alkon points out that the final illustration in the book is the first handwritten page of the manuscript, meant to authenticate the last page's claim that Stein was the author from the beginning.[33]

The visual discourse in Wells's text also refuses the customary disclosure expected in autobiography. In *The Rest of My Life,* while there is the requisite photograph of Wells as a frontispiece (in which Wells is both posed and dressed in what looks like a near-replica of Edith Wharton's frontispiece photograph), all the rest of the illustrations in the book are taken from an autograph album Wells had been adding to since she was a teenager. While she was hugely famous, Wells did not go in much for publicity shots. In fact, one of the fan letters Wells includes in the volume remarks, "I have never seen your picture published in any magazine."[34] Instead of photographs of Wells, pages from Wells's old autograph album were replicated as illustrations in her autobiography: they consist of previously unpublished ephemera given to Wells by other authors and celebrities, and, as several reviewers commented, these images and artifacts alone make the book worth the purchase price. All of them are original sketches, poems, notes, quips, and cartoons from other well-known or accomplished figures of her day, images that can be found in no other book, magazine, or collection. They include a hand-drawn portrait of G. K. Chesterton, an original poem Rudyard Kipling handwrote for Wells and autographed, and a get-well note with a private joke from Mark Twain, among many others. One might argue that Wells hid herself visually behind her autograph album images the way other literary autobiographers avoided too much self-disclosure by filling their pages with written tributes to famous friends.

The digressive images in these two autobiographies, primarily featuring the work of others—sketches and letters for Wells, and paintings for Stein—also provide a demonstration of their personal taste and relationships to these other artists, visually underscoring their own genius. Scholar Amy Feinstein notes that the *Autobiography* is intended to redefine Stein as an "overlooked genius" to the reading public who had not received her work very well, while Lynn Z. Bloom observes that Stein's repeated association of her own name with that of many legendary artists has the effect of embedding her as one of their "coterie."[35] Paul Alkon also notes that the photo of Stein in medical school may be intended to contradict the prevalent criticism of her writing style as simple-minded and/or incoherent.[36] Taken together, Stein's and Wells's collection of images for their autobiographies serve as visual digressions that help them evade embodiment while still establishing a vision of relational creativity and genius.

Besides violating visual autobiographical convention, both writers continually defer readers' expectations that in reading autobiography they will gain an insider's view of history. Carolyn Wells's text avoids it hilariously. Noting that a crony who read her manuscript told her she was doing it "all wrong" and "must have some chronology," and that she "owe[d] . . . her readers" some insight into her family background, she begins in the twelfth century, looking up and inserting information she can find about anyone notable by the name of Welles. She pulls this same sleight of hand to avert other historical/nostalgic readerly expectations: when an editor demands that she write "all about the Nineties," she merely lists three other excellent books written about the decade, declares that to her the 1890s "connote shirtwaists and humor," and launches into an exploration of all the varieties of shirtwaists that were available then, including both retail and sale pricing.[37] Wells's response to her editor's demand is akin to what Stein does when she promises to really "tell about the pictures." Both writers respond with lists that deflect attention onto others; however, each makes their deferral amusing, rather than frustrating, through diversionary substitutions.

While Stein did not have many readers when she wrote the *Autobiography,* Wells had a multitude of readers who were accustomed to being amused. After the turn of the century, Wells was "considered the chief woman humorist" in America, a reputation that lasted until after World War I.[38] *The Rest of My Life* does chronicle her development as a comedienne but again veils Wells herself behind other figures: popular American humorists and cartoonists Gelett Burgess and Oliver Herford. It was through her growing correspondence with Burgess, editor-in-chief of the *Lark,* a little magazine specializing in comic nonsense, Wells declared, that she learned "to distinguish silliness and nonsense." Nonsense, she learned from Burgess, "is organic, well-ordered, and . . . almost mathematical in its precision, and its certainty to hit the reader or listener straight between the eyes."[39] Working for Burgess, she affirms, "I passed through an experience that might be known as *The Wit's Awakening.*" In another deflection, Wells invokes not only Burgess and Herford but her entire hometown library. Her work as an editor of popular anthologies doubtlessly owed some of its brilliance to the years she spent as a librarian in Rahway, New Jersey. Since the town library was only open to patrons two days a week, Wells's work there became her primary means of self-education: "Every book worth having we bought; every periodical worth reading we subscribed to, and the librarian sat in the middle and read her way out," she recalls in her memoirs.[40]

Just as Nora Doyle has convincingly argued that *The Autobiography of Alice B. Toklas* is a parody of the domestic memoir, Wells's autobiography can be read as a parody of other literary autobiographies. Wells's awareness of other literary autobiographies and refusal to comply with their conventions is transparent and intentional from the very beginning of *The Rest of My Life.* Early in the book, Wells apologizes that she cannot "tell of my fame as an Infant Prodigy. I so enjoyed the account of the baby Edith Wharton, hiding under the dining table."[41] In a single sentence, Wells rejects the orthodox autobiographical narrative of incipient literary genius while simultaneously establishing that what she offers is much more original.

Within her parody of literary autobiography, Wells also refuses its standard narrative trajectory, noting that she regrets that she cannot follow the "orthodox" pattern for literary autobiography (the noble, lonely struggle of a talented, misunderstood individual toward self-expression—as seen in the autobiographies of Edith Wharton, Grace King, Margaret Deland, Charlotte Perkins Gilman, Gertrude Atherton, and Margaret Anderson) since she grew up in a friendly, fun-loving household with parents who *encouraged* her preschool efforts in literature; in fact, Anna Wells saved bits of her daughter's literary juvenilia all her life. Further, while almost all the other 1930s literary memoirs promote hard work and/or social purpose as writerly virtues, Wells acclaims "impatience" as her most prized virtue: "I discovered that impatience would achieve things, while patience got me nowhere." The fruits of impatience are many, she explains, including burning her mouth on hot soup. Her autobiography declares her other most important personal virtue to be the opposite of impatience: perseverance. Then, in what has become a familiar move, she undercuts that idea as well, offering a list of things she has quit, like playing the piano, painting, skating, and learning to ride a bike.[42] This anticipatory subversion and parody of traditional autobiography forms a pattern in both Wells's and Stein's texts: genius should mean originality, they imply, not just the standard narrative of progress toward achieving the standard stamps of approval from the same old literary establishment.

Because of the freedom writing in the third person afforded her, Stein's *Autobiography* boldly and repeatedly claims that she is a genius because of her uniqueness. When "Alice" lists the geniuses she has met, she includes groundbreaking figures from three different intellectual disciplines, among which Stein is the only creative writer: "The three geniuses of whom I wish to speak are Gertrude Stein, Pablo Picasso, and Alfred Whitehead. I have met many important people, I have met several great people but I have only known three first class geniuses and in each case on sight something within me rang." The book emphasizes Stein's originality repeatedly throughout the text. In one passage, she comments, "She realizes that in English literature of her time she is the only one. She has always known it and now she says it."[43] The editorship of the *Atlantic Monthly,* which serialized *Autobiography,* clearly perceived this thread in the book as well. In an advertisement for the first installment, published in May 1933, the blurb reads, "Gertrude Stein is one of God's originals."

Wells's autobiography focuses on her originality and brilliance as well. Although her book is written in the first person, Wells uses other voices to make the claim. To establish her uniqueness, she quotes S. S. Van Dine: "Carolyn Wells has done for the mystery story what Planck did for physics, what Copernicus did for astronomy, what Freud did for psychology."[44] Just as Stein's veiled autobiography groups her with Picasso and Whitehead, Wells aligns herself with Max Planck, Nicolaus Copernicus, and Sigmund Freud, geniuses who redefined forms of discourse, in Wells's case the mystery genre. Like the narrator who claims that in literature Stein is "the only one" like her, Wells's chosen quote identifies her as the only one who could have achieved what she did. *The Technique of the Mystery Story,* Wells's only scholarly volume, is still used as a reference work and guidebook for writers today: first published in 1913, it was reissued in 1929, and reprinted again in 2011. Reading *Technique,* one begins to feel that if anyone had read every mystery ever written before 1929, that person would be Carolyn Wells. In his introduction to the original 1913 edition, J. Berg Esenwein praises the work as "a labor of distinction . . . the first exhaustive study of the genre."[45] In this case, Wells's genius in dissecting the mystery came from repetition—she read similar books in the same genre over and over and over until she identified all the patterns within them.

While Wells shows superb scholarly concentration in *Technique,* her literary style in her fiction often lacks polish. Several critics have rightly noted that the concept of many of her detective novels was originally brilliant but that her fiction faltered in its execution. It is true that the writing itself, as well as the stories' denouement, often fail to live up to the riddle generally presented in the first chapter of each mystery. Readers, then and now, most likely keep reading just to find out who did it, and, even more importantly, how it was done, or to see if they can outwit Wells and figure it out before her detective does. In fact, Wells herself believed the primary reason to read mysteries was as a sort of brain exercise.[46] She seems to have been more interested in making the puzzle truly original than in developing the characters and polishing the narrative. In contrast to literary autobiographies like Mary Roberts Rinehart's *My Story* and Edna Ferber's *A Peculiar Treasure,* which depict the labors of writing and the author's development of her craft, Wells simply claims that writing "never seemed like work" in *The Rest of My Life.*[47] Claiming to have debunked Alexander Pope's popular lines from *The Essay on Criticism,* "True ease in writing come from art, not chance / As those move easiest who have learned to dance," Wells declares that "writing is not an art, it is nature. It cannot be learned, it is inborn."[48] While she graduated from Rahway High School as valedictorian, Wells refused to be sent to college to learn what other people thought was important in a manner that she considered a waste of time.[49] Instead, in a uniquely independent gesture that reminds one of Stein's decision to leave medical school, Carolyn Wells simply corralled or corresponded with people whom she thought expert in the areas she wanted to master and kept on reading whatever she liked.

Both these autobiographies bolster their claims to originality by describing their writers' unique aesthetic methods. While Stein's is clearly not the first autobiography written in the third person—her predecessors include Henry Adams and William Butler Yeats, while Mary Austin and Margaret Deland used the technique as well a year or two after Stein did—it is the first one with the narrator unveiled as the subject in the last sentence. However, the volume offers additional commentary intended to set Stein apart from other writers. She discusses writing from 11 p.m. until right before the birds start to sing, or writing "in the automobile while she was waiting in the street," a habit of which she becomes "particularly fond." Stein, in Alice's observer voice, declares, "I do not know whether Gertrude has more genius than the rest of you all . . . but one thing I have always noticed is that you paint and write and are not satisfied and throw it away or tear it up, she does not say whether she is satisfied or not . . . but she never throws away any piece of paper upon which she has written."[50]

Wells's *The Rest of My Life* emphasizes her eccentric methods of composition as successfully as Stein's are highlighted in *The Autobiography of Alice B. Toklas.* Some critics have accused Wells—perhaps not entirely inaccurately—of "never having had an unpublished thought."[51] If there is any truth in the accusation, then Wells, like Stein but unlike everyone else, may have simply been unwilling to waste or discard anything she composed. Wells's autobiography includes jokes about sending her manuscripts to publishers in an empty chocolate box, declaring, "When the chocolate is gone, the book is done." Wells is unabashedly proud to confirm this gossip (true or not) in *The Rest of My Life.* As she tells it, "I was born with no sense of moderation, and I have never acquired one." Back in Rahway, she had had all the publishers' catalogues sent to her, with "no restrictions of expense or judgment" as to what she ordered. Having read everything, Wells uses her "good memory," as well as "time, and [the] liberty to order any book published," and begins writing books nearly as quickly she can read them.[52]

Clearly aware that most of her work was considered frivolous reading, Wells's autobiography further parodies other literary autobiographies that characterize their authors as "serious" artists by mocking "ideals, standards, and aspirations" as "chameleon words [that] take color from their speakers,—often false tints." While other authors quote their best reviews, Wells quotes her most ridiculous fan-mail, including one that reads, "Miss Wells you must be a very queer person or a very wonderful one," and "my friend said probably you are a man, because unquestionably you are the greatest woman writer living." Her autobiography reveals her clear preference for "funny" fan letters over "banal compliments or fulsome flattery." To this end, she also quotes the editor of the *Bookman,* a Dr. Peck, who calls her writing "plenty of fun . . . giv[ing] the effect of being written for the pure pleasure of expressing herself. . . . One should always judge a writer by his or her own standards. If you set out to compose an epic poem, that is one thing. If you merely wish to have some fun with your muse, why that is quite another." Wells turns to her favorite essayist, Thomas De Quincey, to defend her talent from her highbrow detractors, quoting his adage, "None but a man of extraordinary talent can write first-rate nonsense." In *The Rest of My Life,* Wells has the last laugh at critics who chastized her for lack of seriousness, joking that "I've long wanted to do a book on the Deeper Issues of Life. But I don't know what they are, and I can't find out. I've asked a dozen of my friends, the wisest ones, but they either reply with some bit of foolishness or say frankly they don't know."[53] Her book flouts the most common criticisms of her work by exposing them as pretentious and implying that some writers take themselves too seriously.

In fact, both these autobiographies subvert the importance of literary criticism as a whole, denying its relevance to their work. Stein explains that "she never asks anyone what they thought of her work, but were they interested enough to read it." And unlike most of the other autobiographers in this study who respond defensively by offering ire at criticism or explanation for rejection, Stein, like Wells, merely laughs, for after all, "No artist needs criticism, he only needs appreciation. If he needs criticism, he is no artist." Recalling the "long campaign of ridicule" to which *Tender Buttons,* a highly experimental collection of poems that used a great deal of repetition and often violated traditional syntax, was subjected, the narrator comments, "When the columnists are really funny, and they quite often are, Gertrude Stein chuckles and reads them aloud to me." *Autobiography* also reveals Stein's awareness of all the parodies of her that had spread across America, proclaiming that "the real Gertrude Stein was . . . funnier in every way than the imitations, not to say much more interesting." However, as the book acknowledges, after thirty years of writing every day, Stein has become a little bitter about her unpublished manuscripts, which the *Atlantic Monthly* once called "not without interest" although they were unwilling to have their readers "affronted" by Stein's work. How could she get to the readers she craved with American publishers barring the gates, and American critics penning parodies of her instead of serious reviews? Stein hints at her explanation when she repeats the phrase "there is art and there is official art" in a scene that expresses how much an artist's success has to do with their acceptance or lack thereof by the official gatekeepers and arbiters of taste. In effect, Stein uses *The Autobiography of Alice B. Toklas* to write her own literary criticism, giving herself the glowing notices she feels she should have received from others. For instance, she names *Melanctha* (1909) as "the first definite step away from the nineteenth century and into the twentieth century in literature," or *The Making of Americans* as "the beginning, really the beginning, of modern writing." Stein reminds readers that the few things that she has published have been recognized as great, original work by a select few, such as when the editor of *Transition* magazine predicted she "could be a bestseller in France." She clearly craves ordinary readers more than the approval of the establishment, noting that her favorite review of *Three Lives* appeared in the *Kansas City Star* but was unsigned, thus she never found out who it was who had understood her work so well.[54] Stein feels sure that if she could get to the actual readers, she would be recognized. And her appeal for readers worked: *The Autobiography of Alice B. Toklas* increased Stein's American readership, and her follow-up text, *Everybody's Autobiography*

(1937), revels in all the direct contact she has with readers—in lecture halls, on the street, in drugstores, wherever they recognize her. Frankly, Stein's first autobiography is all the better for being written before Stein's success. For both these authors, refusing, parodying, and refuting autobiographical tradition was a smart decision. As Estelle Jelinek observes, Stein's later text *Everybody's Autobiography,* which more resembles traditional women's literary autobiography by telling the story of a "successful writer who has made it in a man's world," comes across as "self-conscious and dull."[55]

Like Mary Austin's and Harriet Monroe's autobiographies, Stein's text establishes her unique form of genius by highlighting her particular artistic vision, including her appreciation for the work of other artists, positioning Stein as one of the first Americans to discover Cezanne, Picasso, and Matisse. *The Autobiography of Alice B. Toklas* further demonstrates the connection between her original taste and vision by pointing out the connection between "looking and looking at [the 'big Cezanne']" and the composition of *Three Lives* (1909), one of the few works Stein succeeded in publishing before 1933. She further validates herself as an extraordinary person when, by no coincidence whatever, it just so happens that most of the famous artists she meets want to paint, sculpt, or photograph her, including Pablo Picasso, Israel "Lippy" Lipschitz, Felix Vallotton, and Man Ray. Both she and Wells build on their claims to genius by creating narrative selves who are clearly visionaries. Stein's best example of this comes early in her text:

> There were Cezannes to be seen at Vollards. Later on, Gertrude Stein wrote a poem called Vollard and Cezanne, and Henry McBride printed it in the New York Sun. This was the first fugitive piece of Gertrude Stein's to be so printed and it gave both her and Vollard a great deal of pleasure. Later on when Vollard wrote his book about Cezanne, Vollard at Gertrude Stein's suggestion sent a

> copy of the book to Henry McBride. She told Vollard that a whole page of one of New York's big daily papers would be devoted to his book. He did not believe it possible; nothing like that had ever happened to anybody in Paris. It did happen and he was deeply moved and unspeakably content. But to return to that first visit.

Before the narrative ever enters into her relationship with Ambroise Vollard, Stein casts herself as a prophet, patron, and aesthetic arbiter: readers are shown the end result of Stein's confident eccentricity before she ever gets to the beginning of it. However, this is not her only correct literary prophecy in the autobiography. She also comments, "She thinks this is equally true about *The Great Gatsby.* She thinks Fitzgerald will be read when many of his well-known contemporaries are forgotten."[56]

Wells uses a similarly roundabout technique to exhibit her unique vision in *The Rest of My Life.* Before she gets to the central question of how and when she started writing, she recounts an ongoing debate with her mother over her tendency to "cross my bridges before I came to them . . . bridges [that were] not even seen in the distance and most likely weren't there at all." This tendency, she explains, "was due to my leaping mind. . . . I always saw . . . ahead."[57] Of course, like Stein, in merely writing her autobiography because of her status as an author, Wells has already proved that her vision was right all along—the bridges she imagined were indeed there, just as the full-page review for Vollard's book was. In another instance of digressive, roundabout narrative, *The Rest of My Life* points out that Wells's mind, like Stein's, must fly into the future before it can even begin to tell of the past. This prescience becomes a pattern in both texts, most famously in Stein's purchase of the "big Cezanne," which was to inspire *Three Lives,* and in Wells's relentless commitment to assembling the Walt Whitman collection.

Since both Stein and Wells were avid collectors who were nearly as famous for the collections they assembled as for their own work, both these autobiographies also offer a treatise on artistic taste. *The Autobiography of Alice B. Toklas* establishes Stein as a visionary art collector, terming the Matisse paintings Leo Stein bought as "the first modern things to cross the Atlantic." Stein repeatedly emphasizes her visionary taste in *Autobiography,* pointing out that at the time she started to buy such art, "negro sculpture had been well known to curio hunters but not to artists."[58] Wells too reveals herself as unashamed to be grouped among the lowbrow "curio hunters" in *The Rest of My Life.* And, like Stein's purchases, what Wells collects ends up having value. Her autographed collection of poems, drawings, and notes is as unique in its own way as Stein's atelier. Wells started out with the ubiquitous autograph album—she called hers the "Mermaid Book" because it had a mermaid on the cover—possessed by every girl in every North American high school between 1870 and 1920. Unlike most high school girls, however, Wells kept adding to the album throughout her life, and by the 1930s it was as impressive in its own way as the Whitman collection she assembled in her sixties. The only literary celebrity Wells met but apparently did not impress was Theodore Dreiser, when she was a young woman trying to get an assignment as a society reporter for the *Delineator.* As told in *The Rest of My Life,* however, Dreiser's decision to deny her the post was rooted in aesthetics rather than intellect. Reportedly, Dreiser took one look at her, her hat and coat bedraggled by a rainstorm, and declared her not right for the job. Despite that setback, Wells never lost her optimistic energy, and she rarely left home without her Mermaid Book in which to collect drawings, signatures, limericks, and the erudite "nonsense" she so treasured from any noteworthy person whom she met. Using her high school autograph album to assemble an unprecedented collection of celebrity ephemera that she ended up publishing in her literary autobiography is so unapologetically lowbrow that—like Stein's signature style—it must indicate either simple-mindedness or a visionary stroke of genius.

Both these literary autobiographers blur the highbrow/lowbrow lines in their collection, appreciation, and production of art. First, they portray Wells and Stein as incessant, omnivorous readers. Stein's text recalls reading all of Queen Victoria's letters aloud to Toklas, and the book substantiates her claim to read one detective story each day. Through their ceaseless, indiscriminate reading, both autobiographies challenge highbrow notions of taste. Stein's extensive reading is not limited to serious texts: the narrator claims that "even now [she] still is always reading and . . . however foolish the book may be no one must make fun of it."[59] Honestly, given her detective fiction habit, some of those "foolish" books Stein reads voraciously are probably formula mysteries written by Wells. By the 1930s, Wells was publishing three mysteries per year. In *The Rest of My Life,* she quips, "I had not read more than a hundred detective stories before I began to write them." Wells repeatedly asserts in her memoir that she was always either reading or writing, claiming she penned detective stories "as fast as I could, because I had to."[60] Her body of work provides continual proof of her voracious reading, and her promiscuity of taste, for both Wells and her fictional characters quote freely and extensively from other writers, ranging from Plutarch to P. T. Barnum.

Both these writers connect their incessant consumption and production of art to what Walter Benjamin called the "Age of Mechanical Reproduction" in which they lived. Interestingly enough, these two veiled autobiographies reveal that both women were fascinated by modern means of industrial reproduction, each evincing an uncanny appreciation and affinity for Henry Ford and his assembly line. Stein's affection for her Ford motorcar and its mechanisms is well-known, and watching mechanics work on its engine inspired her "Composition and Explanation."[61] Wells too admired the new assembly-line efficiency: in *The Rest of My Life,* she refers to her literary oeuvre as "my mass production." Most critics agree that the breakneck speed at which Wells wrote had its consequences, both for the quality of the writing and for the quality of her reputation. However, Wells is unapologetic in her autobiography, though all her critics agree that haste was her biggest weakness, boasting, "I can produce more copy in less time than any other writer in my class," without actually identifying what class that is. Some of her incredible productivity may have stemmed from a combination of the growing mass readership of the early twentieth century and Wells's intrinsic desire to be obliging. Contemplating her diverse, fast-paced publishing history in *The Rest of My Life,* Wells muses, "Why I had so many publishers, I don't know, except that they asked me for books and I was too good-natured to refuse."[62] The same statement can be applied to her relationship with her millions of readers. If they wanted three Carolyn Wells mysteries per year, she was willing to oblige them. It simply meant she had to figure out a method of mass-production. If one is to believe *The Rest of My Life,* Wells managed to mass-produce books with the help of large boxes of mass-produced drugstore chocolates.

The Autobiography of Alice B. Toklas also seems to embrace the production-and-consumption cycles of modernity. The book particularly evidences Stein's desire for a broad, popular readership. While she may seem elitist in her claims to be the first and only writer of truly modern literature, Stein's text asserts a revulsion from elitism, claiming that "she is very grateful not to have been born of an intellectual family, she has a horror of what she calls intellectual people." Indeed, *Autobiography* seems to privilege populism over elitism: "Gertrude Stein wants readers not collectors. In spite of herself her books have too often become collector's books . . . and that does not please her, she wants her books read not owned." It also expresses Stein's wish that her work could be released in "comparatively cheap" volumes, so that "people who have very little money" could purchase them.[63] Stein spent several years and a lot of money—so much that she had to sell a Picasso to keep the project afloat—trying to self-publish all her work that had not yet reached the marketplace, prioritizing strategies to make what she and Toklas called the "Plain Edition" affordable to everyday readers.[64] Georgia Johnston's reading of the *Autobiography* emphasizes the egalitarian nature of Stein's text, asserting that "the reader is . . . parallel to Stein," of equal importance in creating the text.[65] The narrator of *The Autobiography of Alice B. Toklas* also gives the impression of an ideal democracy of taste in describing her Paris salon: "For form's sake and in Paris you have to have a formula," but "really, everybody could come in . . . anybody could come" as long as they were interested in the "pictures." Stein's text claims that "she was democratic, one person was as good as another. . . . You must have deep down as the deepest thing in you a sense of equality."[66]

Interestingly enough, both Stein's and Wells's autobiographies make an implicitly populist argument for a democracy of taste. Wells, a librarian turned author turned book collector, argues that readers are the only real measure of a text, and that they are entitled, like Gertrude Stein, to read what they choose, however "foolish" it may be. *The Rest of My Life* includes a full chapter-length digression on all the public and private libraries Wells has visited throughout her life, including the Bodleian, which she loved; the British Museum library, which she loathed; and the Boston Athenæum, which she ranked the highest for its "coziness." Wells lauds the person who can disregard advice in assembling his or her own library and think only of personal taste, declaring that she herself has discarded "perfectly good sets of Dickens and Thackeray" because they "left . . . space for books that interest me more." She laughs that she has seen too many libraries that "had everything in them except something to read." Wells vehemently defends the right of any reader, high-, low-, or middlebrow, to select their own favorite reading material free of the judgments of others. As she explains in her library chapter, "Your true library is a collection of the books you want. You may have deplorably poor taste or bad judgment. Never mind. . . . The nouveau riche who are said to buy their books by the yard . . . are more true to themselves than those who buy highbrow tomes which they never read."[67] Like Edna Ferber's and Mary Roberts Rinehart's, these autobiographies call out the growing elitism and snobbery of high modernism in their own amusing ways.

Thus, as with Ferber and Rinehart, both Stein's and Wells's veiled autobiographies make a case for a sort of literary populism as a replacement for highbrow critical judgment. In this give-the-people-what-they-want spirit, Wells names P. T. Barnum's memoir as a model for her autobiography.[68] Interestingly enough, the use of "Barnumesque publicity stunts" was one of the few criticisms Stein received for *The Autobiography of Alice B. Toklas.* These critiques were published in a formal pamphlet entitled "Testimony against Gertrude Stein."[69] Stein does seem to apply a Barnumesque aesthetic in her autobiography, noting her efforts to make copies of the bestselling romantic western novel *The Trail of the Lonesome Pine* available to the many wounded American soldiers who requested it in the hospitals in which she and Toklas volunteered in World War I. Because it was so popular, Stein read the book herself but did not understand its strong appeal: "She reads anything and naturally she read this and she was puzzled." However, Stein doesn't entirely disinclude herself from this populist taste, emphasizing that she loved the song based on *The Trail of Lonesome Pine* in the same way the soldiers loved the book, and was forever playing it on her phonograph.[70] According to *The Autobiography of Alice B. Toklas,* Stein listens to that record again and again just as she reads and rereads "foolish" books.

The pleasure of repetition, enabled by modern means of mass production and reproduction, becomes a leitmotif in both these works. Stein and Wells each address repetition and formula as legitimate pleasures, both in their writing processes and in their own consumption of books and other objects. *Autobiography* emphasizes Stein's appreciation for "objects that are breakable, cheap objects and valuable objects . . .

a chicken out of a grocery shop or a pigeon out of a fair . . . she knows that sooner or later they will break and she says that like books there are always more to find."[71] It seems that Stein and Wells, each avid collectors, treasured the repetition of seeking their next "find" for their various ongoing collections.

For these literary autobiographers, readers were of greater importance than authors or even publishers in driving the modern marketplace. Both defend the public's right to enjoy mass-produced consumer goods, a category that included those things for which Stein liked to shop, like ceramic chickens and dime-store fiction. The narrator in *The Autobiography of Alice B. Toklas* clearly associates commercial mass-production and mass-consumption with modernity, claiming that "America created the twentieth century" by its innovation in "commercial conceptions."[72] Modernist scholar Alissa Karl observes, "Although historians and critics may regard with ambivalence the promotion of consumerism as a means of public and self-articulation, that concept was crucial to Stein's . . . delineations of modernism."[73] Both Stein and Wells, admirers of Ford's assembly line, also enjoyed leveraging their own access to mechanical reproduction of their creative work. Sarah Wilson points out that, after the success of Stein's first autobiography gave her the mass-readership she had long hoped for, she particularly loved being on the radio because it could reproduce her voice so that "everybody" could hear it everywhere.[74] Stein's embrace of radio technology once again brings to mind Walter Benjamin's "The Work of Art in the Age of Mechanical Reproduction," which was written two years after *Autobiography,* but Stein flips the script on what would become Benjamin's theory that reproduction devalues art. Instead, Stein embraces the idea of being able to use modern technology to reach more listeners, more readers, than she ever had before.

Wells too reveled in having her words distributed through modern methods of mass production, and her own well-publicized method was to release a new book on a set of predetermined dates each year.

As she developed this routine, her output of mystery books grew from an average of one per year before 1917 to three per year from 1917 to 1940. She was often criticized for publishing so quickly: because of her haste, Bill Pronzini has declared her work to be the "heir apparent to the dime novel."[75] In 1927, though Wells's sales were extremely strong, Dashiell Hammett panned her work in the *Saturday Review of Literature,* referring to her mysteries as not just formula but bad formula.[76] She takes on this accusation, all too familiar to her, in *The Rest of My Life:* "It always seems amusing to me when a caustic reviewer comments on the hackneyed plot of a detective story. Yet he never remembers that all love stories have a hackneyed plot." Wells is unashamed of writing formula and laughingly recommends her work *The Technique of the Mystery Story* in her autobiography, because "anyone who reads it can learn by eye how to write detective stories as good as mine." This statement might just be correct: *Technique*'s twenty-six chapters include commentary on plot, structure, clues, characters, motives, evidence, devices, deductive ratiocination, and subdivisions of the genre such as ghost stories, robberies, riddles, and romantic subplots. These categories are then divided into subcategories, including a section cataloguing times when apples, bitten or unbitten, have served as convenient clues. *The Rest of My Life* advises aspiring writers to use their own judgment when plotting their work, that even "hackneyed devices" can succeed if used in an original way.[77] Wells's unabashed analysis of literary formula was openly intended to provide a template for others to produce mysteries according to her methods. This segment of Wells's autobiography might shed some light on one of Stein's minor essays on detective fiction. Considering the genre, Stein mused, "The detective story . . . is you might say the only really modern novel form that has come into existence."[78] In parsing this quotation, one wonders if Stein was partially referring to the use of formula to mass-produce these novels as a mark of modernity. The pleasure Stein found in reading (and Wells in writing) formula fiction combined the comfort and familiarity of repetition with the anticipation of the new. In her sequel memoir *Everybody's Autobiography,* Stein puts it this way: "I am like any dog out walking, I want it to be the same and I want it to be completely unlike."[79] And she was correct: everybody is and everybody does.

Although there is a good deal of discussion of both their reading habits and their methods for writing and collecting in *The Autobiography of Alice B. Toklas* and *The Rest of My Life,* these two autobiographers include very little about their personal lives. In each case, there is one significant elision; for Wells, it is her deafness. When she was six years old, Wells contracted scarlet fever along with her younger sister, Allie. While her sister died, Wells eventually recovered but lost most of her hearing. She underwent many unsuccessful procedures throughout her life trying to restore it, and she declares her deafness to be "the one cherry in my bowl . . . that ought to be thrown out. . . . It is a hardship, and though I bear it smilingly it is an insincere smile." Because of it, she observes, "I have lost one proposal of marriage, two invitations for trips abroad, three or four worth-while gifts, an airplane ride and a few requests for autographs." She relates a number of amusing stories about it, including an awkward conversation with President Theodore Roosevelt, and concludes that her handicap "hurt [her] most through [her] pride and vanity." Although she jokes about it in *The Rest of My Life,* the pain Wells endures is not just emotional—she briefly describes a series of brutal operations, procedures, and devices she tries to regain her hearing, including one involving "running red hot wires up my nose, and—I think—into my brain," and another, the "excruciating agony" of which "I would not wish it on my worst enemy." That she is willing to undergo "every remedy or cure I heard of" indicates the significant role her sudden deafness may have played in the course of her life and career. It is quite likely that her disability was partially responsible for her omnivorous reading and for her appointment to the post of librarian, which gave her financial access to any book she wanted, before she became a successful writer. Having discussed their mutual deafness several times with her good friend Thomas Edison, Wells quotes him as saying, "It let him shut out all noises and concentrate on his work." Perhaps Edison's advice influenced Wells to allow her omnivorous reading and writing to become coping mechanisms: "I have many resources within myself," she muses, "and it is these that help me bear my deafness with equanimity."[80] Connecting with Edison allowed Wells to understand creativity and invention as a compensation for the loneliness he also understood. The isolation that her deafness caused (and the occasional misunderstandings with others) could be temporarily ameliorated and perhaps even forgotten in the world of reading and writing books and in her copious lifelong correspondence with her many friends, as Edison's was ameliorated through his absorption in his discoveries and inventions.

In Stein's text, it is not a painful but a pleasant part of her life that forms her most significant autobiographical elision. Many scholars have traced the "intimate" text, the one that clearly references Stein's and Toklas's relationship, beneath the public text of *The Autobiography of Alice B. Toklas.* Stein's refusal to disclose any intimate details of their relationship may initially seem like par for the course given the age of the text, but this absence actually marks the book as a part of growing trend toward women's *literary* autobiography in the 1930s. In fact, lesbian encounters had formed a notable part of more "tell-all" 1930s autobiographies like Mabel Dodge Luhan's lengthy, rambling *Intimate Memories,* so there was actually a precedent for the type of autobiography that Stein did not write. Stein's perspicacity regarding her relationship may have been designed to remove her from the less artistically respectable category of celebrity "tell-all." However, scholars note that *Autobiography,* purportedly written for Stein by Toklas, was actually written *by* Stein *for* Toklas, to reassure her of their commitment. In publishing the book, Stein is publicly proclaiming their long-term partnership—that Toklas is her wife. Much attention has been given to the text's depiction of Toklas sitting with the wives of geniuses as evidence that Stein may have assumed that genius was essentially masculine, but scholars often skim past the fact that in these passages, it is not just the word "genius" that gets repeated over and over but also the word "wife," and that this repeated pronouncement may be just as intentional. Reading the marginal notes in the manuscript of the book, Ulla Dydo concludes that the composition process, including the typing (which Toklas typically did) and editing of Stein's texts, was part of their playful and romantic domestic rituals, and that the book is a form of love letter from Stein to Toklas. Dydo's work, as well as Georgia Johnston's, reveals the sections and passages that are about their relationship, which had lasted for over a quarter-century by the time the book was written.[81] These layers in the text offer a choice to readers, who can choose to pass over the intimacy of Toklas and Stein in the book, just as they are invited to skim over and dismiss Wells's deafness in *The Rest of My Life,* which is also a constant and permanent, but in Wells's case unwanted, companion. Alternatively, the reader can slow down, listen, and look for signs—and they are clearly there if one chooses to look—of these essential parts of the authors' identities as both women and writers, each hidden as neatly as Edgar Allan Poe's purloined letter, front and center, in plain sight.

In her mid-fifties, Wells was briefly married. In her autobiography, she gives no details about her married life but briefly claims that their union was "crammed with joyful interest" and their brief time together her "most blessed memory." Her husband, Hadwin Houghton, died less than two years after their wedding. Grieving her loss and seeking a new focus for her limitless energies, Wells's general habit of book collecting focused itself on building the famous Walt Whitman collection. In *The Rest of My Life,* she appears to take on the task as yet another whim, but, reading between the lines, it seems a response to the grief that she was too private a person to express. Her friend Edward Norton recalled encountering Wells in a restless moment when she was looking to start a new collector's quest to use up her "surplus energy." According to him, when he recommended Whitman, whom he felt was destined to "take an important place" in literary history, she replied in her usual flip, populist fashion, "Comics are more in my line, but I believe you are right."[82]

Having always flouted the traditional method of doing anything expected of her, Wells's methods of collecting were as straightforward and formulaic as her writing: she explains that she "adopted the absurdly simple plan of writing to all the dealers I could hear of and asking for lists of their Whitman items," ignoring all the unwritten rules of "diplomacy and canny bartering" and simply paying everyone exactly what they asked. Once she had every book, edition, and autographed copy of Whitman imaginable, she began collecting photographs, canceled checks, contracts, letters, and other memorabilia. The completed collection would have brought an astronomical price if Wells had sold it, but instead she bequeathed it to the Library of Congress. Wells handles this achievement in the text as deftly as she does everything else, revealing her expertise about rare books so humorously that one barely notices it at all. She makes a series of book-collecting jokes, laughing at idealistic "breast-huggers" who want to clasp books to their chest (which she rightly points out would damage a rare, old book). Wells also mocks the highbrow notion that "any real collector" would never think of money, declaring that is really all that collectors do think about, and sighing, "This is opposed to tradition, but it is true." Always wary of both tradition and scholarly posing, Wells declares that her "serious scientific study" of collecting has led to "definite, undeniable, and invulnerable conclusions," but that she has decided not to reveal them, as "non-collectors wouldn't understand, and collectors know them only too well, but refuse to admit them."[83] Addressing her biggest claim to highbrow status, her wonderful Whitman collection, Carolyn Wells defers readers' expectations again, begging the question while pretending to answer it.

Autobiographies like *The Autobiography of Alice B. Toklas* and *The Rest of My Life* illustrate just how serious literary jokes can be, as Stein's and Wells's strategic diversions allow them to mock the marketplace while simultaneously exploiting it. Beyond avoiding the readerly expectations of the autobiographical pact and redefining the notion of genius, both texts resist highbrow aesthetic values and replace them with a people's-choice aesthetic instead. Each book tacitly affirms modern methods of mass-production and mass-consumption through exploring the pleasures of repetition and formula. Yet somehow, despite the remarkably populist tone of their autobiographies, Stein and Wells leave no doubt in readers' minds that their own authorship sprang from their relentlessly digressive energy, authentic individuality, and visionary personal genius, not in any mass-marketed formula for success.

Epilogue

Portraits of the Artist as an Old Woman

IN HER inimitable way, Zora Neale Hurston conjures up an image in her 1942 autobiography, *Dust Tracks on a Road,* that might help us understand the tensions involved in the life-writings of the previous decade: "People are prone to build a statue of the kind of person it pleases them to be. And few people want to be forced to ask themselves, 'What if there is no me like my statue?'"[1] For this generation of female autobiographers, the available templates for authorship must have seemed as forced as the monuments Hurston's words evoke. Some of the templates were as rigid as a statue, and others just as unnaturally posed. For these twelve female autobiographers, writing into the available templates for authorship must have been like trying to fit the natural contours of one's body into a preexisting mold of someone else.

The struggles these writers faced in trying to fit their long and multifarious experiences into the prefabricated molds of the 1930s marketplace were intensified by modernist assumptions about the artist. Modernism as we have canonized it—as these women cannily recognized we would—assumes the *Portrait of the Artist as a Young Man,* but the average age of these female literary autobiographers when composing these texts was sixty-seven. As scholar, novelist, and autobiographer Carolyn Heilbrun has noted, "We must recognize what the past suggests: women are well beyond youth when they begin, often unconsciously, to create another story" about who they are, what they are doing, and why they are doing it.[2] Writing autobiography gave these authors a chance to tell that story as older women. However, they knew that due to both their age and their gender, they were the last in line for both the titles and the entitlements of early twentieth-century American literature. Yet, despite the biases these women faced, these autobiographers became the first generation of American women writers to publicly claim the powerful terms of "artist," "genius," and "professional" for themselves.

According to the experiences recounted in these twelve texts, there is more than one kind of genius and more than one way to be a female artist. These autobiographies demonstrate that women could achieve professional success and significance within almost any domestic arrangement or set of personal circumstances. Many of them did not wait to have a room of their own—they wrote anyway and anywhere, and then designed and defined those rooms for themselves in many different forms. Their autobiographies suggest that you can come from the working classes, the deep South or the Midwest, and still craft a literary brand within or across the high-, low-, or middlebrow. Collectively, these texts expose the questions motivating public curiosity about female authorship in the early twentieth century and offer surprising answers, revealing that artists might also be commercial, and geniuses collaborative, or even formulaic, inventing new systems for making fiction the way Henry Ford invented a new way to build the automobile. A true and complete *Portrait of the Artist as an Old Woman* would include all of these possibilities. In the absence of such a composite portrait, however, we might consider these texts as composing an amalgamation of issues that women writers faced in the early decades of the twentieth century. As a group, these portraits further question our notions of literary history:

1. Is the work of an artistic genius never popular, professional, accessible, or formulaic?
2. Is genius only genius when it is young and "make[s] it new," or is there also a sustainable, visionary kind of genius that emerges only through time and endurance?

The first question has only been partially approached through recent reevaluations of the work of predominantly male modernists, or of male-identified women artists like Gertrude Stein. Exclusionary definitions of genius have already been problematized in Stein studies. In *Gertrude Stein, Modernism, and the Problem of Genius,* Barbara Will contends that "high modernism and its investment in an exclusionary notion of 'artistic genius' . . . is at odds with the radically democratic, anti-subjective, anti-essentialist tendencies in much of Stein's writings."[3] Likewise, Bob Perelman points out that modernism associated genius with "illegible authority," arguing that while modernist authors may have intended their work to make an impact in real life, its heavy focus on technical experimentation and innovation often resulted in an incommunicability that prevented a connection with a broad audience.[4] Given this phenomenon, did these authors—and the critics who have privileged and taught their work—retrospectively construct the binary that genius must be so experimental that it is inaccessible, thus labeling accessibility a sign of inferior art? Autobiographers of the 1930s like Gertrude Stein, Edna Ferber, Mary Roberts Rinehart, and Carolyn Wells clearly attempt to deconstruct the modernist binary regarding genius, professionalism, and popular accessibility, but much work remains to be done in this area. When additional early twentieth-century writers are taken into the equation, we will learn more. Recent books such as *Modernist Women Writers and American*

Social Engagement (2019) have opened up our definition of modernist experimentation, noting that such experimentation in women's writing might be found in content, not just in form, and that women might have embraced modern industrial innovations as a means to express new possibilities for feminine cultural power and engagement.[5] In these female authors' work, modern, industrial innovations became new avenues for the expression of genius, designed with large-scale accessibility in mind.

The second question has also started to open up in Stein studies. According to Amy Feinstein, Gertrude Stein's notebooks include evidence of a variety of types of genius, including a "perceptual rather than creative genius" with which Alice Toklas is endowed in *The Autobiography of Alice B. Toklas*.[6] However, the notion of perceptual genius seeps through the writings of other women in this generation as well. The work of watching and the nuanced literary reenactment of what she observed formed a large part of Zora Neale Hurston's undeniable gifts. Or, as Grace King observed in her journal, "My mind occasionally lets me get a peep into the truth of things."[7] Edith Wharton, trying both to understand and to reconstruct her relationship to modernist discourse in *The Writing of Fiction* (1924), decided that "true originality consists not in a new manner but in a new vision."[8] Through experiencing the collective vision that these writers' depictions of their journeys to authorship reveal, complete with their edits and their fibs, we come to realize that for many of them, genius might be in the seeing, not in the being. It might be perceptual rather than technical. And developing their vision just might have been a marathon for them, rather than a sprint. In their long careers, wherein success could be sampled but never assured, these women often had to rely on their own stamina. Writing in her journal on one New Year's Day, Grace King affirmed, "I have but one resolution to make: to work—to endure."[9] Wharton's 1928 essay, "A Cycle of Reviewing," written when she was one year into her autobiographical project, refers to the "inevitable curve," a "gradual cooling off" of critical enthusiasm that an aging writer must learn to expect.[10] Like King's determination to survive her personal suffering through her commitment to her work, and Harriet Monroe's vision for making *Poetry* into a sustainable venue for verse, Wharton also had to learn to take the long view. It may well be worth employing some of the techniques of the digital humanities to track how career trajectories for women writers have differed from those of men from the same era—I suspect that in many more cases, we might find a slower, more sustainable trajectory of growth and impact.

Emboldened by time, endurance, and the accumulation of experience, these autobiographers propose radical innovations to our understanding of gender and genius. Despite the rigidly enforced narrowness of discourse about modernist art and male genius, some of these women were incredibly confident about both their own genius and their gender identity. Esther Stineman explains that Mary Austin "never doubted her own genius and could not understand how others could miss it."[11] Indeed, throughout her life, Austin invested a great deal of emotional capital into her concept of genius, writing books like *A Woman of Genius,* a provocative work entitled *Everyman's Genius,* and a series of articles explaining the "genius process," and organizing a "genius club" of writers.[12] But Austin was not the only confident woman in the group: Emily Leider notes that when Mary Austin once told Gertrude Atherton "I am the greatest woman writer living," Atherton purportedly replied, "The hell you are, Mary."[13]

However outspoken she was in her relationships with other writers, Austin's definition of genius was more muted in her autobiography, which redefines a woman of genius as neither selfish nor egotistical. Rather, she is a female body that nurtures human wisdom through its own suffering. Harriet Monroe's autobiography also insists that genius can never thrive alone but requires the collaboration of editors and readers. In the spirit of collaboration, Monroe sent Wharton a personal invitation to join with her new venture in 1912; Monroe's autobiography notes that Wharton, whom we know had been encouraged to distance herself from the common herd of women writers, was one of only two authors who sent Monroe no reply.[14] Wharton guarded her image from contamination by association with other women writers like Atherton throughout her career. Her isolation appears to have paid off, for, aside from Gertrude Stein's, only Edith Wharton's artistic image has truly endured into the twenty-first century, standing as solitary as the meticulously molded, inaccurate monument that is *A Backward Glance.* The autobiography most like Wharton's, Grace King's *Memories,* is similarly distorted. King had collaborated all her life with both her sisters, and one of them was her most intimate friend and stalwart supporter, but she treats them practically as amanuenses in her *Memories.* Wharton and King seem to have labored to avoid allowing their readers or critics to see them as anything but solitary, "serious" artists. For some of these women, trying to fit their lives into a template that was gendered male meant losing significant parts of their histories and their personalities in the process. In an attempt to wedge themselves securely into the "safe" category of "serious artist" for posterity, Wharton's and King's autobiographies in particular committed strange self-mutilations.

This is not to disparage their labors—just to reveal how oppressively narrow the definition for "serious artist" was in the late nineteenth and early twentieth centuries, especially for women. There were a number of reasons that the lines were so narrowly and consistently drawn, and some of these autobiographies try to expose both the lines and the reasons. While Monroe exposed some of the gendered—and regionalized—entrenchments of the literary establishment in *A Poet's Life,* Austin also openly addressed it in her fiction. In her 1920 novel *No. 26 Jayne Street,* Austin writes that "between you and your public there is a wall of men, a felted, almost sound-proof wall of male intelligence, male reporters, critics, managers, and advertisers."[15] Some of the women writers from this generation either formulated their own means of resistance to this wall or found their own ways to work around it. While Monroe hired mostly fellow women as her coeditors, Edna Ferber formed a lifelong alliance with female magazine editor Gertrude Lane. Additionally, both Gilman and Austin tried to rally their fellow women into intentionally supporting female writers with their money. In Austin's essay "Women as Audience," she suggests that women have "both privilege and obligation" as "paying members" to make demands on male editors to allow women writers to speak out on women's issues. She criticizes female readers for presuming that as mere women, not "critics," they have no power in literary circles, asserting that, en masse, they may have more power to determine what gets printed than do the women artists themselves.[16] The power Austin identifies here may have manifested itself in ensuring Mary Roberts Rinehart's overwhelming sales, as Rinehart's fiction often depicts ordinary women, who are dismissed, underestimated, or neglected by everyone around them, doing extraordinary, unexpected, and powerful things.

However, when women's "votes" as consumers of literature did propel female writers to dizzying commercial success, the "wall" of male editors and critics that Austin invoked seems to have reinforced itself in an attempt to quarantine them. For instance, Wharton's agent, Rutger B. Jewett, used Rinehart's name as a bugaboo to frighten Wharton away from some profitable decisions that might have endangered her "serious" status as an artist.[17] Yet Wharton had significant shared experiences with some of these other "popular" writers and could have joined forces in working for common causes. For instance, Rinehart was just as serious about conveying the realities of World War I to the American public as Wharton. Rinehart was the first American writer to visit the Belgian front during the war, staying near the trenches and reporting on the atrocities she saw firsthand. As recorded in Ed and Libby Klekowski's 2018 volume, *Edith Wharton and Mary Roberts Rinehart at the Western Front,* Wharton reported on the same atrocities.[18] How unfortunate it is that Rinehart and Wharton worked for the same cause at the same time in isolation from one another.

In terms of their fiction, the distance between Wharton's and Rinehart's oeuvre was largely defined by Rinehart's intentional accessibility—and the financial success that resulted from it. However, even writers who decried the profit motive and denied that business and finance formed a part of their calculations were demonstrably sophisticated business professionals. While Edna Ferber was not terribly shy about this in *A Peculiar Treasure,* other 1930s authors were extremely reticent about business and money in their autobiographies. Editorial records and personal letters reveal that, besides Edna Ferber, Margaret Deland and Edith Wharton drove the hardest financial bargains, but if one only judged by what these two women included in their literary autobiographies, a reader would never guess it. Wharton must have been aware that, in the end, her autobiography and Rinehart's appeared in extremely similar venues, which may be another reason Wharton's autobiographical statue is so very awkward, limited, and rigid. Perhaps she had to draw an even clearer line between her memoir and Rinehart's, as there was little difference between where they were serialized. The really big difference was in their fees—Rinehart received twice as much for *My Story* as Wharton did for *A Backward Glance,* but her text was twice as welcoming to readers as well.

In crafting their brands and building their empires, some women writers were complicit in the notion that financial success disqualified writers from the realm of "art." At the turn of the century, Willa Cather commented on "dear Mrs. Atherton's . . . pretensiou[s attempt to] analyz[e] things that she was once content to admire," and her apparent quest to "produce 'literature' at any cost."[19] After all, in the world of letters, continued Cather, alluding to a biblical parable about how difficult it is to get to heaven, the way to the sacred precincts of art is a narrow way, and "not every man who saith unto me Art! Art! shall enter."[20] Cather's choice of allusion here reveals that modernist discourse separating "literature" from mere "writing" was partially based on an almost religious notion of righteousness—could it be that, in this borrowed discourse, writing for profit was construed as some sort of unpardonable sin for which popular writers would pay most dearly after their deaths? If so, it appears that Cather's prophecy—or perhaps her curse?—has come to pass.

There is no shame associated with women's financial success now. Why was there then? Although Ferber's stories of businesswomen were widely popular, not everyone's work in this vein succeeded. Charlotte Perkins Gilman's, for instance, did not, and one of Hurston's last unpublished works, *The Golden Bench of God,* told the story of the first female African American self-made millionaire. Why did it never appear in print? Many of these autobiographies dismantle modernist notions of *the artist* as financially disinterested by using the template of the self-made man for both marketing and editing their lives, reconstruing writing as a business. Rinehart and Ferber, who did not come from money, proclaim that there is no shame in having it—provided one works for it. Their autobiographical cracks about dilletantes and inspiration may well have been directed Wharton-ward. And there is no guarantee that Wells's snarky comment about "Deeper" issues in *The Rest of My Life* was not made in the same spirit, especially given the parodic elements of her text.

In addition to equating financial success with hard work, writers who, like Wells, were not considered "serious" also questioned the negative associations that accessible writing had taken on in the 1920s and 1930s, reconceiving of accessible writing as a form of perceptual genius in the service of humanity. Ferber's and Rinehart's autobiographies do so through their open affiliation with both a female audience and a working audience, encompassing much of the American public who read fiction for leisure. Both these women equated their popular writing with cooking, positioning their work as pleasurable and nourishing, like a good homemade dinner. Other writers pointed out that the canon has always included popular storytellers: "People want to be amused," Atherton declared in 1929, "told a story, not given the detailed description of a single character. Homer, Shakespeare, none of the great writers of all the ages sat down to write exclusively about character. He would have bored us if he had." After this little jab at the highbrow bastions of the literary world, she concluded, "Our most intellectual magazines today are afraid of a good story of life in its broader aspects; their fiction is limited mainly to character studies."[21] In referring to the popularity of Shakespeare and Homer, Atherton legitimates the idea of writing for a popular audience, defending a "give the people what they want" approach to art, just as do the Barnumesque autobiographies of Stein and Wells.

In the 1920s and 1930s, what the people seemed to want was more and more detailed information about celebrities. In post–World War I youth culture, writers like Atherton and Anderson fit into the popular conceptions of celebrities by emphasizing their good looks and eternal youth via endless, effervescent, flapper-esque backchat. It was their way of maintaining a place in the spotlight. Although Atherton and Anderson are the most glaring examples of the influence of celebrity culture, other writers were by no means immune to it. For instance, though she decries the power of fame in her autobiography, Mary Austin, like Gertrude Atherton, did not hesitate to capitalize on it in her lifetime; indeed, she put her name before the public as often as she could, often merging her own public persona with the characters she created.[22] For example, Austin dressed as a Native American princess at parties and made sure that marketing materials noted she wrote in what she called her "wickiup" in a tree in Carmel, California, even having stationery imprinted with "The Wickiup" as her address.[23] However, Austin drew the line at writing about her sexual history. Female autobiographers of this era who composed their stories along the lines of the activist celebrity templates—Mabel Dodge Luhan and Emma Goldman among them—wrote autobiographies that were significantly more revealing in the area of female sexuality and desire than did any of the novelists. Although she was good friends with Luhan, Mary Austin, like all these autobiographers—with the exception of Atherton and Anderson—disapproved of such candor. After reading other literary autobiographies of the day like Theodore Dreiser's, Austin decided they were "too revealing" for her taste.[24] Further, the review of Austin's work in the *New York Times Book Review* demonstrates that there were still consequences for women writers who revealed more. The reviewer expressed relief that Austin was "not one of *those* candid souls" who "told all."[25]

Although celebrity culture of the 1930s thrived on endless images of female bodies, especially in pre–production code Hollywood, there was as yet no space or precedent to discuss or depict some of the realities of women's bodies—certainly not women's aging bodies—in any public venue, including American literary autobiography. But some of these women made brave attempts to speak about the double-bias they faced as older female authors trying to claim a space for themselves in American literary history. Charlotte Perkins Gilman is the most notable example in this group, and her attempts to speak about such things may well be part of the reason her influential work was practically erased in her own lifetime. In the context of what we now know about Grace King's suffering from a fibroid tumor and Wharton's constant struggle for health and strength, both excised from their life-writings, not to mention Ferber's and Rinehart's recurrent nervous breakdowns, which their texts gloss over, Gilman's groundbreaking honesty about her mental illness is thrown into high relief. The realities of living in a woman's body—especially an aging or suffering woman's body—were so generally ignored in "literature" that Austin's recognitions of the difficulties of childbirth and childrearing, Atherton's openness about undergoing radiation treatments to her ovaries in an attempt to regain her youthful appeal and energy, and Monroe's poetic ruminations about spinsterhood were perhaps more courageous than we now recognize.

It would be nearly a decade after the last of these autobiographies was released before women's health issues were openly addressed in public discourse. In fact, it was Mary Roberts Rinehart who broke the national silence about breast cancer after her own battle with the disease, using her name recognition and national celebrity to publicly exhort women to have regular breast examinations in the July 1947 issue of *Ladies' Home Journal.* By then, Rinehart was seventy years old and about to publish her sequel autobiography, a more forthright and comprehensive version of *My Story,* which revealed more about her own physical and emotional struggles than the earlier memorialized version of herself that she crafted in 1931.

When authors' own attempts to memorialize themselves fail, literary history tends to remember them in other ways instead. T. S. Eliot's seminal text "Tradition and the Individual Talent" imagines literary history as a garden of monuments. Eliot's essay theorizes that the addition of new writers to the canon should displace, rather than replace, previous writers, but it seems that these old ladies of letters were relegated to the fringe of the garden, where the monuments are really neglected tombstones, illegible or unmarked, just as Zora Neale Hurston's grave was when Alice Walker found it and gave her back to American literature.[26] These 1930s autobiographies metaphorically expose other neglected or obscured areas of American literary history to allow us a new view of writers whose names have been buried under dismissive, clinging terms like "women's fiction," "nonexperimental," "genteel," "formulaic," or "sentimental" traditions for nearly a century. They remind us that a frozen, memorialized version of a person cannot really represent that individual, nor can any literary label encompass decades of authorship.

Across the years of their careers, these women faced many of the same fears and obstacles, and fought off some of the same labels. They had many more things in common than they ever knew, and had they but known, they might have spoken out together about gender bias and ageism in American modernism. However, because affiliating with other female authors was tantamount to reputational suicide, they were mostly siloed. It is time to revisit their monuments, study the patterns they form together, dust off their individual statues, and relearn and reinscribe their names into American literary history. In doing so, we will achieve a new understanding of female literary entrepreneurship; the creation of literary brands; the roles of comedy, mystery, and other popular genre fictions as forms of resistance to highbrow elitism; and the rise and fall of empires in print.

NOTES

INTRODUCTION: AMERICAN WOMEN'S LITERARY AUTOBIOGRAPHY IN THE DEPRESSION-ERA MARKETPLACE

1. Peter Conn, *The American 1930s: A Literary History* (Cambridge: Cambridge University Press, 2009), 107.
2. Christopher Morley, "Effendi," *Saturday Review of Literature,* July 17, 1946, 4.
3. John Tebbel, *A History of Book Publishing in the United States* (New York: Bowker, 1978), 3:542, 564.
4. Tebbel, *History of Book Publishing,* 3:427–429, 433, 489.
5. Janet Montefiore, *Men and Women Writers of the 1930s: The Dangerous Flood of History* (London: Routledge, 1996).
6. Arthur Hobson Quinn, ed., *The Literature of the American People: An Historical and Critical Survey* (New York: Appleton-Century-Crofts, 1951), 981.
7. T. J. Jackson Lears, *Fables of Abundance: A Cultural History of Advertising in America* (New York: Basic, 1994).
8. Gordon Hutner, *What America Read: Taste, Class, and the Novel, 1920–1960* (Chapel Hill: University of North Carolina Press, 2009), 117; James D. Hart, *The Popular Book: A History of America's Literary Taste* (Berkeley: University of California Press, 1950).
9. Conn, *The American 1930s,* 8.
10. Mark Longaker, *Contemporary Biography* (Philadelphia: University of Pennsylvania Press, 1934), 3.
11. Conn, *The American 1930s,* 149–150, 127.
12. Ann Lane, *To Herland and Beyond: The Life and Work of Charlotte Perkins Gilman* (New York: Pantheon, 1990), 343.
13. David Welky, *Everything Was Better in America: Print Culture in the Great Depression* (Champaign: University of Illinois Press, 2008), 83, 114, 119.
14. Walker Gilmer, *Horace Liveright: Publisher of the Twenties* (New York: David Lewis, 1970), 97–98; Emily Wortis Leider, *California's Daughter: Gertrude Atherton and Her Times* (Stanford, Calif.: Stanford University Press, 1991), 328.
15. Esther Stineman, *Mary Austin: Song of a Maverick* (New Haven, Conn.: Yale University Press, 1989), 190.
16. Carolyn Wells, *The Rest of My Life* (London: Lippincott, 1937), 13.
17. Arthur Colton, "Mrs. Atherton's Life," *Saturday Review of Literature,* May 28, 1932, 54.

18. Mary Ellen Chase, "A Bright Lady," *Commonwealth,* July 27, 1932, 334.
19. Percy Hutchison, "Mrs. Wharton Recalls an Era: Brownstone New York and Europe Share in Her Backward Glance," in *Edith Wharton: The Contemporary Reviews,* ed. James Tuttleton, Kristin O. Lauer, and Margaret P. Murray (New York: Cambridge University Press, 1992), 514–15; Edward Sackville-West, "War and Peace," in Tuttleton, Lauer, and Murray, eds., *Edith Wharton,* 524; Arvin Newton, "The Age of Innocence," in Tuttleton, Lauer, and Murray, eds., *Edith Wharton,* 522–23.
20. Katherine Woods, "Edna Ferber and Her America," *New York Times Book Review,* February 5, 1939, 30; "Mrs. Deland Recalls," *Saturday Review of Literature,* January 11, 1936, 18.
21. Patricia Meyer Spacks, *The Female Imagination* (New York: Knopf, 1975), 181.
22. Valerie Sanders, *The Private Lives of Victorian Women* (New York: St. Martin's, 1989), 9, 17, 1.
23. Sanders, *Private Lives,* 14.
24. Sidonie Smith, "Resisting the Gaze of Embodiment: Woman's Autobiography in the Nineteenth Century," in *American Women's Autobiography: Fea(s)ts of Memory,* ed. Margo Culley (Madison: University of Wisconsin Press, 1992), 79.
25. Margo Culley, "'What a Piece of Work Is Woman': An Introduction," in Culley, ed., *American Women's Autobiography,* 13.
26. Sanders, *Private Lives,* 6–8.
27. Estelle Jelinek, *The Tradition of Women's Autobiography from Antiquity to the Present* (Boston: Twayne, 1986), 90.
28. Ann Gordon, "The Political Is the Personal: Two Autobiographies of Woman Suffragists," in Culley, ed., *American Women's Autobiography,* 112–113.
29. Jelinek, *Tradition,* 97, 124.
30. Jelinek, *Tradition,* 90–92.
31. Martha Watson, *Lives of Their Own: Rhetorical Dimensions in Autobiographies of Women Activists* (Columbia: University of South Carolina Press, 1999).
32. Jelinek, *Tradition,* 92, 128.
33. Tebbel, *History of Book Publishing,* 3:210.
34. Sanders, *Private Lives,* 138.
35. Jelinek, *Tradition,* 132.
36. Mary Kelley, *Private Woman, Public Stage: Literary Domesticity in Nineteenth-Century America* (Oxford: Oxford University Press, 1984).
37. Susan Ware, *Holding Their Own: American Women in the 1930s* (Boston: Twayne, 1982), 173.
38. Phillipe Lejeune, *On Autobiography* (Minneapolis: University of Minnesota Press, 1989), 160; Georges Gusdorf, "Conditions and Limits of Autobiography," in *Autobiography: Essays Theoretical and Critical,* ed. James Olney (Princeton, N.J.: Princeton University Press, 1980), 28–48; Roy Pascal, *Design and Truth in Autobiography* (Cambridge, Mass.: Harvard University Press, 1960).

39. Smith, "Resisting the Gaze," 81, 83; Domna Stanton, "Autogynography," *New York Literary Forum* 12–13 (1984): 15.
40. Culley, "'What a Piece of Work Is Woman,'" 8.
41. Julia Watson, "Towards an Anti-Metaphysics of Autobiography," in *The Culture of Autobiography,* ed. Robert Folkenfilk (Stanford, Calif.: Stanford University Press, 1993), 71; Helen Buss, "*Bios* in Women's Autobiography," *a/b: Auto-Biography Studies* 10, no. 1 (Spring 1995): 114.
42. Sarah MacDonald, "Relationality in Working Women's Autobiography," *Nineteenth-Century Gender Studies* 8, no. 1 (Spring 2012): 1–19. See also Regina Gagnier, *Subjectivities: A History of Self-Representation in Britain, 1832–1920* (Oxford: Oxford University Press, 1991).
43. Gertrude Stein, *The Autobiography of Alice B. Toklas* (1933; reprint New York: Stellar Classics, 2013), 30.
44. William Howarth, "Some Principles of Autobiography," *New Literary History* 5, no. 2 (Winter 1974): 378.
45. Lejeune, *On Autobiography,* 151, 146.
46. Jeanne Braham, *Crucial Conversations: Interpreting Contemporary American Literary Autobiographies by Women* (New York: Columbia Teachers College Press, 1995).
47. Sally Mitchell, "Frances Power Cobbe's Life and the Rules for Women's Autobiography," *ELT* 50, no. 2 (2007): 131–157, 132 (quotation).
48. Linda Peterson, "Female Autobiographer, Narrative Duplicity," *Studies in the Literary Imagination* 23, no. 2 (1992): 81.
49. Barret Mandel, "Full of Life Now," in Olney, ed., *Autobiography,* 72.
50. Joseph Hergesheimer, "The Feminine Nuisance in American Literature," *Yale Review* 10 (July 1921): 718.
51. Tebbel, *History of Book Publishing,* 3:49.
52. Quinn, *Literature of the American People,* 974–975.
53. Elizabeth Ammons, *Conflicting Stories: American Women Writers at the Turn into the Twentieth Century* (New York: Oxford University Press, 1991), 16; Ann Douglas, *The Feminization of American Culture* (New York: Macmillan, 1998). McGovern's actual words were "virility impulse" in his 1966 work, but Ammons summarizes his findings well with her term "virility response."
54. Elaine Showalter, *Sister's Choice: Tradition and Change in American Women's Writing* (Oxford: Clarendon, 1991), 108.
55. Nathaniel West, *The Complete Works of Nathaniel West* (New York: Farrar, 1957), 82, 83.
56. Catherine Turner, *Marketing Modernism between the Two World Wars* (Amherst: University of Massachusetts Press, 2003).
57. Mary Roberts Rinehart, *My Story* (New York: Farrar and Rinehart, 1931), 111.
58. Ammons, *Conflicting Stories,* 123.
59. Linda Wagner-Martin, "Wharton and Gender," in *Edith Wharton in Context,* ed. Laura Rattray (New York: Cambridge University Press, 2012), 243–245.

60. Leider, *California's Daughter,* 220.
61. Joseph Collins, *Taking the Literary Pulse* (New York: Doran, 1924), 48.
62. Susan Koppleman, "Fannie Hurst's Short Stories of Working Women—'Oats for the Woman,' 'Sob Sister,' and Contemporary Reader Responses: A Meditation," in *American Women Short Story Writers: A Collection of Critical Essays,* ed. Julie Brown (New York: Garland, 1995), 137–152, 141 (quotation).
63. Ammons, *Conflicting Stories,* 127; Grant Overton, *The Women Who Make Our Novels* (New York: Dodd, Mead, 1918).
64. Gertrude Atherton, *Adventures of a Novelist,* 3rd ed. (New York: Blue Ribbon Books, 1932), 544.
65. Bonnie Kime Scott, introduction, in *The Gender of Modernism: A Critical Anthology,* ed. Bonnie Kime Scott (Bloomington: Indiana University Press, 1990), 2.
66. See particularly Atherton's *Tower of Ivory* (New York: Hearst, 1910); Wharton's *The Touchstone* (New York: Scribner's, 1900); and Austin's *No. 26 Jayne Street* (Boston: Houghton Mifflin, 1920).
67. Sandra M. Gilbert and Susan Gubar, *No Man's Land: The Place of the Woman Writer in the Twentieth Century* (New Haven, Conn.: Yale University Press, 1987), 1:188.
68. Hergesheimer, "The Feminine Nuisance in American Literature," 725.
69. Gaye Tuchman's study *Edging Women Out: Victorian Novelists, Publishers, and Social Change* (New Haven, Conn.: Yale University Press, 1989).
70. Susan Albertine, introduction, in *A Living of Words: American Women in Print Culture,* ed. Susan Albertine (Knoxville: University of Tennessee Press, 1995), xiii.
71. Thomas Strychacz, *Modernism, Mass Culture, and Professionalism* (Cambridge: Cambridge University Press, 1993), 27.
72. Rinehart, *My Story* (New York: Farrar and Rinehart, 1931), 383.
73. Showalter, *Sister's Choice,* 117, 125; Howard Mumford Jones and Ernest Erwin Leisy, eds., *Major American Writers* (New York: Harcourt, Brace, 1935).
74. Quinn, *Literature of the American People,* 973, 974.
75. Strychacz, *Modernism, Mass Culture, and Professionalism,* 27.
76. Gilbert and Gubar, *No Man's Land,* 100.
77. Showalter, *Sister's Choice,* 104, 120.
78. Wharton, diary entry, 1924, in *The Unpublished Writings of Edith Wharton,* ed. Laura Rattray (London: Pickering and Chatto, 2009), 2:211.
79. Showalter, *Sister's Choice,* 107.
80. George Hellman, "Of Life and Letters and Margaret Deland," *New York Times,* December 7, 1941, 17.
81. Andreas Huyssen, *After the Great Divide: Modernism, Mass Culture, Postmodernism* (Bloomington: Indiana University Press, 1986).
82. Elizabeth Evasdaughter, "Autobiographical Closure in the Future: Women Constructing Hope," *a/b: Autobiography Studies* 9, no. 1 (Spring 1994): 115–133, 115 (quotation).

83. Marysa Demoor, introduction, in *Marketing the Author: Authorial Personae, Narrative Selves, and Self-Fashioning, 1880–1930,* ed. Marysa Demoor (New York: Palgrave Macmillan, 2004), 6, 8.
84. Grace King, *To Find My Own Peace: Grace King in Her Journals, 1886–1910,* ed. Melissa Heidari (Athens: University of Georgia Press, 2004), 54.
85. King, *To Find My Own Peace,* 54.
86. Timothy Galow, "Literary Modernism in the Age of Celebrity," *Modernism/Modernity* 17, no. 2 (April 2010): 313–329, 314 (quotation).
87. Quinn, *Literature of the American People,* 981.
88. Karen J. Blair, *The Torchbearers: Women and Their Amateur Arts Associations in America, 1890–1930* (Bloomington: Indiana University Press, 1994), 4, 181.
89. Margaret Harriman, *The Vicious Circle: The Story of the Algonquin Round Table* (New York: Rinehart, 1951), 2.
90. Wells, *The Rest of My Life,* 17.
91. Stanley J. Kunitz, *Living Authors* (New York: H. W. Wilson, 1931), 12, 13, 139, 316, 336, 434, 421.
92. Lejeune, *On Autobiography,* 3,161, 29, 22.
93. Augusta Fink, *I-Mary: A Biography of Mary Austin* (Tucson: University of Arizona Press, 1983), 248, 250.
94. Tebbel, *History of Book Publishing,* 3:445, 430.
95. Welky, *Everything Was Better in America,* 153.
96. Martha Banta, *Imaging American Women: Idea and Ideals in Cultural History* (New York: Columbia University Press, 1987), 78, 66.
97. Christopher P. Wilson, *The Labor of Words: Literary Professionalism in the Progressive Era* (Athens: University of Georgia Press, 1985), 193.
98. Stineman, *Mary Austin,* 190.
99. Elaine Showalter, ed., *These Modern Women: Autobiographical Essays from the Twenties* (New York: Feminist Press, 1993), 3.
100. Hutner, *What America Read,* 136.
101. Wilson, *Labor of Words,* 82.
102. Showalter, *Sister's Choice,* 15.
103. Edith Wharton, *A Backward Glance* (New York: Scribner's, 1933), 102.
104. Charles A. Madison, *Book Publishing in America* (New York: McGraw Hill, 1966), 289.
105. Edith Wharton to Gaillard Lapsley, March 2, 1933, *The Letters of Edith Wharton,* ed. R. W. B. Lewis and Nancy Lewis (New York: Scribner's, 1988), 557.
106. Fink, *I-Mary,* 247.
107. Wharton to Rutger B. Jewett, April 29, 1933, Lewis and Lewis, eds., *Letters,* 558–59.
108. Jan Cohn, *Improbable Fiction: The Life of Mary Roberts Rinehart* (Pittsburgh: University of Pittsburgh Press, 1980), 176.
109. Mary Austin, *A Woman of Genius* (New York: Feminist Press, 1985), 3–4.

CHAPTER 1: THE ARTIST'S SOUL OR THE WOMAN'S LIFE

1. Grace Elizabeth King, *Memories of a Southern Woman of Letters* (New York: Macmillan, 1932), 48.
2. Edith Wharton, *A Backward Glance* (New York: Scribner's, 1933), 34, 35.
3. King, *Memories of a Southern Woman of Letters,* 45.
4. Clara Juncker, "Woman-as-Artist," *Southern Literary Journal* 20, no. 1 (Summer 1984): 38.
5. Robert Bush, *Grace King: A Southern Destiny* (Baton Rouge: Louisiana State University Press, 1983), 19.
6. Fred Lewis Pattee, ed., *A History of American Literature since 1870* (New York: D. Appleton Century, 1915); Pattee, *The Development of the American Short Story* (N.p.: Biblo and Tannen, 1923).
7. Edith Wharton, *The Letters of Edith Wharton,* ed. R. W. B. Lewis and Nancy Lewis (New York: Scribner's, 1988), 572, 571.
8. Laura Rattray, "Edith Wharton: Contextual Revisions," in *Edith Wharton in Context,* ed. Laura Rattray (New York: Cambridge University Press, 2012), 8–13.
9. Amy Loveman, "The Life and Art of Edith Wharton," in *Edith Wharton: The Contemporary Reviews,* ed. James Tuttleton, Kristin O. Lauer, and Margaret P. Murray (New York: Cambridge University Press, 1992), 662.
10. E. M. Forster, "Good Society," in Tuttleton, Lauer, and Murray, eds., *Edith Wharton,* 950.
11. Percy Hutchison, "Mrs. Wharton Recalls an Era: Brownstone New York and Europe Share in Her Backward Glance," in Tuttleton, Lauer, and Murray, eds., *Edith Wharton,* 13.
12. Newton Arvin, "The Age of Innocence," in Tuttleton, Lauer, and Murray, eds., *Edith Wharton,* 107.
13. E. K. Brown, "A Backward Glance," in Tuttleton, Lauer, and Murray, eds., *Edith Wharton,* 474.
14. Jonathan Daniels, "Grace's King's *Memories of a Southern Woman of Letters,*" *Saturday Review of Literature,* September 10, 1932, 9.
15. Review in *Springfield [Mass.] Republican,* September 26, 1932, 6.
16. Katherine Capshaw Smith, "Conflicting Visions of the South in Grace King's Memories of a Southern Woman of Letters," *Southern Quarterly* 36, no. 3 (Winter 1988): 133.
17. E. P. Noyes, review of Grace King's *Memories of a Southern Woman of Letters, Books,* October 16, 1932, 11.
18. Smith, "Conflicting Visions," 133.
19. Bush, *Grace King,* 308.
20. Bush, *Grace King,* 29–30.
21. Wharton, *A Backward* Glance, 34, 42–43, 70.

22. Bush, *Grace King,* 35.
23. Pan-Gnostic (pseud.), "Heroines of Novels," *New Orleans Times-Democrat,* May 31, 1885.
24. Louis Auchincloss, introduction, in Wharton, *A Backward Glance,* viii.
25. Wharton, *A Backward Glance,* 1, 2, 3.
26. Edith Wharton, "Life and I," in *Novellas and Other Writings,* ed. Cynthia Griffin Woolf (New York: Library of America, 1990), 2:1071; emphasis added.
27. Wharton, *A Backward Glance,* 1; Judith Fryer, "Edith Wharton's 'Tact of Omission': Harmony and Proportion in a Backward Glance," *Biography: An Interdisciplinary Quarterly* 6 (1983): 149, 150.
28. Shari Benstock, *No Gifts from Chance: A Biography of Edith Wharton* (New York: Scribner's, 1994), 47–48.
29. Wharton, "Life," 1071.
30. Wharton, *A Backward Glance,* 20, 77; emphasis added.
31. Wharton, "Life," 1093.
32. Wharton, *A Backward Glance,* 172–173, 304.
33. Grace King, *To Find My Own Peace: Grace King in Her Journals, 1886–1910,* ed. Melissa Heidari (Athens: University of Georgia Press, 2004), 2.
34. King, *Memories of a Southern Woman of Letters,* 122, 152.
35. Anna Shannon Elfenbein, *Women on the Color Line (*Charlottesville: University Press of Virginia, 1989).
36. Grace King, *The Pleasant Ways of St. Medard* (1916; reprint New York: Wentworth, 2016), 219.
37. King, *Memories of a Southern Woman of Letters,* 236.
38. Ann Goodwynn Jones, *Tomorrow Is Another Day: The Woman Writer in the South, 1859–1936* (Baton Rouge: Louisiana State University Press, 1981), 277.
39. Wharton, *A Backward Glance,* 119, 46, 88.
40. Percy Lubbock, *Portrait of Edith Wharton* (New York: D. Appleton Century, 1947), 11.
41. David Kirby, preface, in *Grace King,* ed. David Kirby (Boston: Twayne, 1980).
42. Helen Taylor, "The Case of Grace King," *Southern Review* 18, no. 4 (Summer 1982), 687.
43. King, *To Find My Own Peace,* 2.
44. Taylor, "The Case of Grace King," 688.
45. Wharton, *A Backward Glance,* 81, 121
46. King, *Memories of a Southern Woman of Letters,* 69, 363.
47. Bush, Robert, "Grace King: The Emergence of a Southern Intellectual Woman," *Southern Review* 13, no. 1 (Winter 1977): 285.
48. King, *Memories of a Southern Woman of Letters,* 204.
49. King, *Memories of a Southern Woman of Letters,* 238, 97, 182.
50. Kirby, *Grace King,* 121.

51. King, *Memories of a Southern Woman of Letters,* 200.
52. Wharton, *A Backward Glance,* 112, 114, 144.
53. King, *Memories of a Southern Woman of Letters,* 261, 248 (emphasis added), 336, 337.
54. King, *Memories of a Southern Woman of Letters,* 99, 1, 183, 191.
55. Wharton, *A Backward Glance,* 15, 58–59.
56. Wharton, *A Backward Glance,* 99, 100, 124, 287, 180, 257, 326, 258 (emphasis added).
57. Zita Zatkin Dresner, "Irony and Ambiguity in Grace King's Monsieur Motte," in *New Perspectives on Women and Comedy,* ed. Regina Barreca (Philadelphia: Gordon and Breach, 1992), 179.
58. King, *To Find My Own Peace,* 95, 40.
59. Through her literary earnings, King was also eventually able to purchase a home for the family, the first house that the Kings had owned since the Civil War.
60. Grace King to Sarah Ann King September 14, 1899, Grace King Papers, Louisiana State University Archives, Baton Rouge.
61. Wharton, *A Backward Glance,* 71, 65–66, 16–17.
62. Benstock, *No Gifts,* 23, xx, xix.
63. Wharton, *A Backward Glance,* 123, 135, 222–223, 269, 130, 144, 206.
64. Susan Goodman, *Edith Wharton's Inner Circle* (Austin: University of Texas Press, 1994), 19.
65. Wharton, *A Backward Glance,* 105, 178.
66. Wharton, *A Backward Glance,* 169, 173, 192.
67. King, *Memories of a Southern Woman of Letters,* 67, 219, 212–222.
68. King, *Memories of a Southern Woman of Letters,* 61, 219.
69. King, *Memories of a Southern Woman of Letters,* 176–178.
70. King, *Memories of a Southern Woman of Letters,* 96.
71. Wharton, *A Backward Glance,* 173.
72. Goodman, *Inner Circle,* 16.
73. King, *Memories of a Southern Woman of Letters,* 188.
74. Smith, "Conflicting Visions," 133.
75. King, *Memories of a Southern Woman of Letters,* 325, 322, 336.
76. Joan Dejean, "Critical Creolization: Grace King and Writing on French in the American South," in *Southern Literature and Literary Theory,* ed. Jefferson Humphries (Athens: University of Georgia Press, 1990), 109–126, 111 (quotation).
77. King, *Memories of a Southern Woman of Letters,* 186, 335, 398.
78. Wharton, *A Backward Glance,* 206, 210, 212, 140.

CHAPTER 2: DARING DENUNCIATIONS

1. Grace King, *To Find My Own Peace: Grace King in Her Journals, 1886–1910,* ed. Melissa Heidari (Athens: University of Georgia Press, 2004), 54.

2. Margaret C. Anderson, *My Thirty Years' War: An Autobiography* (Westport, Conn.: Greenwood Press, 1971), 134.
3. Eleanor Richey, "The Flappers Were Her Daughters: The Liberated, Literary World of Gertrude Atherton," *American West* 11 (1974): 4–10, 62.
4. Emily Wortis Leider, *California's Daughter: Gertrude Atherton and Her Times* (Stanford, Calif.: Stanford University Press, 1991), 240, 137.
5. Gertrude Atherton, *Adventures of a Novelist* (New York: Blue Ribbon, 1932), 218, 219.
6. Leider, *California's Daughter,* 240, 286, 290.
7. "Social Contracts," *Los Angeles Times*, April 17, 1921, III16.
8. Richey, "The Flappers," 63.
9. Atherton, *Adventures of a Novelist,* 321.
10. Leider, *California's Daughter,* 313.
11. Atherton, *Adventures of a Novelist,* 165, 313, 451.
12. Leider, *California's Daughter,* 340.
13. Mary Ellen Chase, "A Bright Lady," *Commonweal,* July 27, 1932, 334.
14. Arthur Waugh, "Autobiographies," *Spectator,* October 1, 1932, 410.
15. Carolyn Anspacher, "Books, Books, Books," *New Yorker,* April 16, 1933, 64.
16. Dorothy Van Doren, "Not Quite Aspasia," *Nation,* June 1, 1932, 629.
17. Louise Mandell Field, "Mrs. Atherton Speaks Her Mind," *New York Times Book Review*, April 1932, 2; Arthur Colton, "Mrs. Atherton's Life," *Saturday Review of Literature,* May 28, 1932, 754.
18. Anspacher, "Books, Books, Books," 64.
19. Isabel Paterson, "A Novelist's Memoirs," *Times Literary Supplement,* September 15, 1932, 1; Colton, "Mrs. Atherton's Life," 754.
20. Lois Palken Rudnick, introduction, in *Intimate Memories: The Autobiography of Mabel Dodge Luhan,* ed. Lois Palken Rudnick (Albuquerque: University of New Mexico Press, 1999), xx.
21. Fanny Butcher, "Heroine Tells Her Own Story, What a Book!" *Chicago Daily Tribune,* June 7, 1930, 12.
22. F. L. Robbins, review of *My Thirty Years' War, Outlook,* May 28, 1930.
23. Anderson, *My Thirty Years' War,* 200.
24. Harriet Monroe, "Personality Rampant," *Poetry* 37, no. 2 (November 1930): 95–96; Babette Deutsch, "Record of an Anti-Realist," *New York Herald Tribune Books,* May 25, 1930, J2; F. B., review of *My Thirty Years' War, Boston Transcript,* June 4, 1930, 2; C. H. Grattan, review of *My Thirty Years' War, New York Evening Post,* May 24, 1930, 24.
25. Butcher, "Heroine Tells," 12; Deutsch, "Record of an Anti-Realist," 2.
26. Louise Kroenenberger, review of *My Thirty Years' War, New York Times Review of Books,* May 25, 1930, 2.
27. Sherwood Anderson, "Real-Unreal," *New Republic,* June 11, 1930.
28. Anderson, *My Thirty Years' War,* 3.

29. *My Thirty Years' War* was the first of the three autobiographies Anderson wrote, all of them capitalizing on her personal notoriety. *The Fiery Fountain* (1951) focuses on Anderson's personal, sexual, and public relationships during her time in France, and *The Strange Necessity* (1969) provides a string of meditative essays on all of Anderson's artistic and personal convictions.
30. Ian Hamilton, *The Little Magazines: A Study of Six Editors* (London: Weidenfeld and Nicholson, 1976), 12; Hugh Ford, *Four Lives in Paris* (New York: Northpoint Press, 1987), 231.
31. Hamilton, *Little Magazines,* 21.
32. Anderson, *My Thirty Years' War,* 146, 270.
33. Anderson, *My Thirty Years' War,* 54, 133, 154.
34. Margaret Anderson, "Dedication," in *The Strange Necessity* (New York: Horizon Press, 1969).
35. Leider, *California's Daughter,* 242.
36. Atherton, *Adventures of a Novelist,* 10–11, 174, 313, 314.
37. Anderson, *My Thirty Years' War,* 34, 154, 86, 115.
38. Anderson, *My Thirty Years' War,* 191, 154.
39. Atherton, *Adventures of a Novelist,* 375.
40. Atherton, *Adventures of a Novelist,* 147.
41. Anderson, *My Thirty Years' War,* 123.
42. Atherton, *Adventures of a Novelist,* 390.
43. Hamilton, *Little Magazines,* 19.
44. Atherton, *Adventures of a Novelist,* 10–11.
45. Van Doren, "Not Quite Aspasia," 629.
46. Paterson, "A Novelist's Memoirs," 1.
47. Atherton, *Adventures of a Novelist,* 16 (emphasis added), 19, 26, 220.
48. Atherton, *Adventures of a Novelist,* 225, 105.
49. Atherton, *Adventures of a Novelist,* 57–61, 82, 112, 129, 79, 226, 114, 539.
50. Francis W. Halsey, *Women Authors of Our Day in Their Homes* (New York: James Pott, 1903), 249.
51. Atherton, *Adventures of a Novelist,* 271.
52. Anderson, *My Thirty Years' War,* 4, 11, 9–10, 17, 91, 131.
53. Atherton, *Adventures of a Novelist,* 84, 104–105.
54. Atherton, *Adventures of a Novelist,* 103–105, 168, 271, 480, 108.
55. Editorial, *Little Review* 10, no. 1 (Spring–Summer 1924); unsigned review of *My Thirty Years' War, Booklist,* September 30, 1930, 27.
56. Ford, *Four Lives in Paris,* 236.
57. Anderson, *My Thirty Years' War,* 31, 231.
58. Atherton, *Adventures of a Novelist,* 289, 241.
59. Atherton, *Adventures of a Novelist,* 438.
60. Anderson, *My Thirty Years' War,* 136.

61. Atherton, *Adventures of a Novelist,* 144, 211, 225.
62. Leider, *California's Daughter,* 249.
63. Atherton, *Adventures of a Novelist,* 469, 470.
64. Anderson, *My Thirty Years' War,* 31.
65. Hamilton, *Little Magazines,* 26, 36.
66. Atherton, *Adventures of a Novelist,* 476, 117, 494, 554, 50, 205, 107, 173.
67. Carolyn Anspacher, "Novelist, Non-Conformist, Intellectual Siren . . . Gertrude Atherton, at 87, Is in Her Prime," *San Francisco Chronicle,* October 30, 1944.
68. Walker Gilmer, *Horace Liveright: Publisher of the Twenties* (New York: David Lewis, 1970), 215.
69. Anderson, *My Thirty Years' War,* 15, 154, 70, 90.
70. Ford, *Four Lives in Paris,* 236.
71. Anderson, *My Thirty Years' War,* 101, 227.
72. Anderson, *My Thirty Years' War,* 75.
73. Ford, *Four Lives in Paris,* 258, 231.
74. Atherton, *Adventures of a Novelist,* 102, 181, 374, 111, 169, 184, 312.
75. Anderson, *My Thirty Years' War,* 189, 249–250.
76. Hamilton, *Little Magazines,* 31.
77. Anderson, *My Thirty Years' War,* 60–61.
78. Atherton, *Adventures of a Novelist,* 170, 181.
79. Anderson, *My Thirty Years' War,* 149, 243–244, 235, 245–247, 39, 259–260, 44.
80. Anderson, *My Thirty Years' War,* 260.
81. Atherton, *Adventures of a Novelist,* 561, 570, 368, 457, 356.
82. Anderson, *My Thirty Years' War,* 266, 267.
83. Anderson, *My Thirty Years' War,* 272.
84. Atherton, *Adventures of a Novelist,* 388, 110, 559, 181.
85. Anspacher, "Novelist, Non-Conformist"; "Gertrude Atherton Assails 'The Powers,'" *New York Times,* December 29, 1907, M2.
86. Anderson, *My Thirty Years' War,* 134.
87. Ford, *Four Lives in Paris,* 275.
88. Anderson, *My Thirty Years' War,* 144.
89. Anderson, *My Thirty Years' War,* 134, 139.
90. Anderson, *My Thirty Years' War,* 269.

CHAPTER 3: REFUSING NOSTALGIA, DENYING DESIRE

1. Ann Lane, *To Herland and Beyond: The Life and Work of Charlotte Perkins Gilman* (New York: Pantheon, 1990), 353.
2. Charlotte Perkins Gilman, *The Living of Charlotte Perkins Gilman* (New York: D. Appleton-Century, 1935), 52, 181.

3. Margaret, Deland, *If This Be I, as I Suppose It Be* (New York: Appleton-Century, 1935), 7, 9.
4. Gilman, *Living,* 181, 44, 52.
5. Patricia Meyer Spacks, *The Female Imagination* (New York: Knopf, 1975), 214.
6. Charlotte Perkins Gilman, *A Journey from Within: The Love Letters of Charlotte Perkins Gilman, 1897–1900* (Lewisberg, Penn.: Bucknell University Press, 1995), 256.
7. Harriet Howe, "Charlotte Perkins Gilman: As I Knew Her," in *Critical Essays on Charlotte Perkins Gilman,* ed. Joanne B. Karpinski (New York: G. K. Hall, 1992), 77.
8. Lane, *Herland and Beyond,* xiii; Martha Bensley Bruere, "Three Women," *Survey Graphic* 25 (1936): 50.
9. Gilman, *Living,* 99, 101, 198.
10. Gilman, *Living,* 102–104.
11. Gilman, *Living,* 103, 181–182.
12. Deland, *If This Be I,* 6.
13. Margaret Deland, *Golden Yesterdays* (New York: Harper, 1940).
14. George Hellman, "Of Life and Letters of Margaret Deland," *New York Times Review of Books,* December 7, 1941, 17.
15. "Margaret Deland," *Time,* January 22, 1945, 68.
16. Lane, *Herland and Beyond,* 343, 352.
17. Polly Wynn Allen, *Building Domestic Liberty: Charlotte Perkins Gilman's Architectural Feminism* (Amherst: University of Massachusetts Press, 1988), 169.
18. Lane, *Herland and Beyond,* 158.
19. Gilman, *Living,* 6–7.
20. Gilman, *Living,* 3.
21. Gilman, *Living,* 171, 143; Lane, *Herland and Beyond,* 169.
22. Alexander Black, "The Woman Who Saw It First," in Karpinski, ed., *Critical Essays,* 56.
23. Lane, *Herland and Beyond,* 197.
24. Black, "The Woman Who Saw It First," 61.
25. Amy Wellington, "Charlotte Perkins Gilman," in Karpinski, ed., *Critical Essays,* 67, 69.
26. Lane, *Herland and Beyond,* 7–8.
27. Black, "The Woman Who Saw It First," 57.
28. Clara Stillman, "Dynamic Woman in the Years of High Hopes: Preacher, Writer, Reformer Blood Ran Hot and Strong in Charlotte Perkins Gilman," *New York Herald Tribune Books,* October 29, 1935, 7.
29. Fred Lewis Pattee, "Recorders of the New England Decline" and "Shifting Currents of Fiction," in *A History of American Literature since 1870* (New York: D. Appleton Century, 1917), 220, 394–396.
30. Alice Parsons, "Some Gentle Memories of Early Girlhood," *New York Herald Tribune Books,* November 24, 1935, 7.

31. Diana C. Reep, *Margaret Deland* (Boston: Twayne, 1985), ii.
32. M. A. DeWolf Howe, "Delandia," *Saturday Review of Literature,* January 11, 1936, 18; "The Child Is Father," *Christian Science Monitor,* December 11, 1935, 10.
33. Deland, *If This Be I,* 44.
34. Pattee, *A History of American Literature since 1870*, 394.
35. Hellman, "Of Life and Letters of Margaret Deland," 17.
36. Deland, *If This Be I,* 22, 20, 77, 48.
37. Deland, *If This Be I,* 15, 179.
38. Deland, *If This Be I,* 27.
39. Deland, *If This Be I,* 105, 170, 92 164, 165.
40. Gilman, *Living,* 5.
41. Carol Ruth Berkin, "Private Woman, Public Woman: The Contradictions of Charlotte Perkins Gilman," in Karpinski, ed., *Critical Essays,* 17.
42. Gilman, *Living,* 15, 30, 70.
43. Gilman, *Living,* 6, 10–11.
44. Deland, *If This Be I,* 41, 42, 44, 227.
45. Gilman, *Living,* 21, 23–24.
46. Deland, *If This Be I,* 154, 156.
47. Gilman, *Living,* 42, 43, 101.
48. Deland, *If This Be I,* 102, 101, 103.
49. Gilman, *Living,* 34, 36.
50. Gilman, *Living,* 59, 58; Charlotte Perkins Gilman, *The Diaries of Charlotte Perkins Gilman* (Charlottesville: University Press of Virginia, 1994), 15.
51. Gilman, *Living,* 60, 40–41.
52. Deland, *If This Be I,* 68, 74.
53. Spacks, *The Female Imagination,* 217.
54. Gilman, *Living,* 21, 71, 73.
55. Gilman, *Living,* 83, 85.
56. Deland, *If This Be I,* 208–209, 19, 20.
57. Gilman, *Living,* 85.
58. Charles Walter Stetson, *Endure: The Diaries of Charles Walter Stetson,* ed. Mary Armfield Hill (Philadelphia: Temple University Press, 1985), 274.
59. Gilman, *Living,* 91, 97, 87.
60. Gilman, *Living,* 181, 246, 88, 92.
61. Gilman, *Diaries,* 327–338, 374.
62. Gilman, *Living,* 67, 163.
63. Gilman, *Living,* 180.
64. Gilman, *Living,* 83, 281, 297, 287, 327.
65. Mary Ross, "A Pennsylvania Marriage with New England," *New York Tribune Review of Books,* November 16, 1941, 5.
66. Deland, *Golden Yesterdays,* 39, 179, 180, 188, 317, 268.
67. Gilman, *Living,* 31, 47, 207, 64, 86, 74.

68. Helen Gray Cone, *Pen-Portraits of Literary Women* (New York: Cassell, 1887).
69. Gilman, *Living,* 304, 305, 308.
70. Gilman, *Living,* 284–285.
71. Frederick Wegener, "Charlotte Perkins Gilman, Edith Wharton, and the Divided Heritage of American Literary Feminism," in *The Mixed Legacy of Charlotte Perkins Gilman,* ed. Catherine J. Golden and Joanna Schneider Zangrando (Newark: University of Delaware Press, 2000), 135–159, 136 (quotation).
72. Jill Rudd, "'Once There Was a Pig . . . Does Not Interest' Gilman's Desire for Narrative Control," in *A Very Different Story: Studies on the Fiction of Charlotte Perkins Gilman,* ed. Val Gough and Jill Rudd (Liverpool: Liverpool University Press, 1998), 158.
73. Black, "The Woman Who Saw It First," 63.
74. Gilman, *Living,* 306, 54, 55, 135, 162, 277, 279, 296, 285, 308, 113, 169, 118–120, 201, 249, 284, 307.
75. Gilman, *Living,* 273, 312, 169.
76. Joanne B. Karpinski, "The Economic Conundrum in the Lifewriting of Charlotte Perkins Gilman," in Golden and Zangrando, eds., *The Mixed Legacy of Charlotte Perkins Gilman,* 36–37.
77. Lane, *Herland and Beyond,* 171.
78. Gilman, *Living* 119, 130, 168–169, 298.
79. Gilman, *Living,* 186, 185, 306.
80. Charlotte Perkins Gilman, "Apropos of Literature," in *Charlotte Perkins Gilman: A Study of the Short Fiction,* ed. Denise D. Knight (New York: Twayne, 1997), 104, 105.
81. Gilman, *Living* 303.
82. Gilman, *Living,* 333, 318, 361.
83. Gilman, *Living,* 166, 334, 335.
84. Deland, *If This Be I,* 105, 121.

CHAPTER 4: WOMEN OF VISION

1. Augusta Fink, *I-Mary: A Biography of Mary Austin* (Tucson: University of Arizona Press, 1983), 240, 247.
2. Given the nature of women's autobiography in the 1930s, we cannot be sure that Monroe intended to write about those years at all. Many other women's literary autobiographies in the decade, such as Grace King's and Margaret Deland's, skimmed, skipped, or just plain erased decades they didn't want to discuss.
3. John Holmes, review of *A Poet's Life, Boston Transcript,* March 12, 1938, 1.
4. Percy Hutchison, "Harriet Monroe and Her Service to Poetry," *New York Times Book Review,* March 13, 1938.

5. "Chicago Poetry," *Time,* March 14, 1938; Burton Rascoe, "*A Poet's Life* by Harriet Monroe," *Saturday Review of Literature,* March 19, 1938, 11.
6. M. M. Colum, review of Harriet Monroe's *A Poet's Life, Forum,* May 1938, 280; Eda Lou Walton, review of *A Poet's Life, Nation,* March 12, 1938, 305.
7. Hutchison, "Harriet Monroe and Her Service to Poetry."
8. Harriet Monroe, *A Poet's Life: Seventy Years in a Changing World* (New York: Macmillan, 1938), 362, 363.
9. Holmes, review of *A Poet's Life,* 1.
10. Karen S. Langlois, "Marketing the American Indian: Mary Austin and the Business of Writing," in *A Living of Words: American Women in Print Culture,* ed. Susan Albertine (Knoxville: University of Tennessee Press, 1995), 151.
11. Fink, *I-Mary,* 247–249.
12. Hugh Stevenson Tigner, "God and the Medicine Man," *Christian Century,* March 1, 1933, 295.
13. Michael Williams, "Mary Austin Remembers," *Commonweal,* January 25, 1933, 363; "Pattern for a Life," *Theatre Arts Monthly* 17 (May 1933): 400–401; William Allen White, "A Woman of Genius," *Saturday Review of Literature,* November 12, 1932, 236.
14. Isabel Patterson, "Mary Austin's Story, the Story of America," *New York Herald Tribune Books,* November 6, 1932, 2, 3.; R. L. Duffus, "Mary Austin, Who Found God under a Walnut Tree," *New York Times Book Review,* November 13, 1932, 3, 14.
15. White, "A Woman of Genius," 236.
16. Esther Lanigan Stineman, *Mary Austin: Song of a Maverick* (New Haven, Conn.: Yale University Press, 1989), 214, 165.
17. Helen MacKnight Doyle, *Mary Austin: Woman of Genius* (New York: Gotham House, 1939), 173.
18. Mary Austin, *Earth Horizon* (Boston: Houghton Mifflin, 1932), 41, 47, 86, 238, 257, 104, 42, 55, 150, 240, 51.
19. Austin, *Earth Horizon,* 23, 145, 220, 162.
20. Tara Hart, "Serving Suspended Sentences: Mary Austin's Compositions and Explanations," in *Exploring Lost Borders: Critical Essays on Mary Austin,* ed. Melody Graulich and Elizabeth Klimasmith (Reno: University of Nevada Press, 2000), 95.
21. Austin, *Earth Horizon,* 67, 71.
22. Austin, *Earth Horizon,* 74, 231, 158, 128.
23. Dudley Wynn, "Mary Austin: Woman Alone," *Virginia Quarterly Review* 13 (1937): 113.
24. Austin, *Earth Horizon,* 208.
25. *Monroe, A Poet's Life,* 23–26.
26. Monroe, *A Poet's Life,* 14.
27. Harriet Monroe, "Comment: What Are They Doing?" *Poetry* 17 (January 1921): 204.

28. Monroe, *A Poet's Life,* 8–14, 7.
29. Monroe, *A Poet's Life,* 23, 12, 24, 15, 18, 19.
30. Harriet Monroe's columns can be found in the *Chicago Tribune* between 1891 and 1914.
31. Monroe, *A Poet's Life,* 16, 27.
32. Austin, *Earth Horizon,* 273.
33. Hart, "Serving Suspended Sentences: Mary Austin's Compositions and Explanations," and Anna Carew-Miller, "Between Worlds, Crossing Borders: Mary Austin, Liminality, and the Dilemma of Women's Creativity," in Graulich and Klimasmith, eds., *Exploring Lost Borders,* 87–104, 105–28.
34. Austin, *Earth Horizon,* 246.
35. Monroe, *A Poet's Life,* 246–247.
36. Monroe, *A Poet's Life,* 340, 341.
37. Austin, *Earth Horizon,* 243, vii.
38. Doyle, *Mary Austin,* ix.
39. Austin, *Earth Horizon,* 239–242, 235.
40. Austin, *Earth Horizon,* 220, 228, 241, 350.
41. Ann Massa, "Form Follows Function: The Construction of Harriet Monroe and *Poetry: A Magazine of Verse,*" in Albertine, ed., *A Living of Words,* 115.
42. Monroe, *A Poet's Life,* 155, 56, 58, 186.
43. Austin, *Earth Horizon,* 157.
44. Carew-Miller, "Between Worlds, Crossing Borders," 108.
45. Austin, *Earth Horizon,* 274.
46. Karen S. Langlois, "Mary Austin and Lincoln Steffens," *Huntington Library Quarterly* 49 (1986): 357–382.
47. Austin, *Earth Horizon,* 114–115.
48. Austin, *Earth Horizon,* 68, 252.
49. Doyle, *Mary Austin,* 168.
50. Austin, *Earth Horizon,* 147, 152, 144.
51. Austin, *Earth Horizon,* 142, 223, 247, 174–175.
52. Elinor Frost to Harriet Monroe, March 22, 1936, Monroe Papers, University of Chicago.
53. Monroe, *A Poet's Life,* 48, 78, 55.
54. Monroe, *A Poet's Life,* 324, 317, 323.
55. Uchiye Hayakawa, "Harriet Monroe as Critic," *Studies in English Literature* 14 (1934): 565.
56. Harry Hansen, *Midwest Portraits* (New York: Harcourt Brace, 1923), 257.
57. Ian Hamilton, *The Little Magazines: A Study of Six Editors* (London: Weidenfeld and Nicholson, 1976), 48.
58. Edward Everett Hale, "New Lamps for Old," *Dial,* March 16, 1914, 231–233.

59. Ezra Pound to Harriet Monroe, May 1915, *Poetry* correspondence files, Harriet Monroe Archives, Joseph Regenstein Library, University of Chicago.
60. Monroe, *A Poet's Life,* 293.
61. Craig Abbott, "Publishing *The New Poetry:* Harriet Monroe's Anthology," *Journal of Modern Literature* 11, no. 1 (March 1984): 95.
62. Jody Cardinal, Dierdre Egan-Ryan, and Julie Lisella, eds., *Modernist Women Writers and American Social Engagement* (Lanham, Md.: Lexington, 2019).
63. Harriet Monroe, "Comment: Men or Women" *Poetry* 16 (June 1920): 146–147.
64. "News Notes," *Poetry* 5 (December 1924): 179.
65. Abby Arthur Johnson, "A Free Foot in the Wilderness: Harriet Monroe and *Poetry,* 1912–1936," *Illinois Quarterly* 37, no. 4 (1975): 28–43.
66. Austin, *Earth Horizon,* 291, 303, 309.
67. Stineman, *Mary Austin,* 46.
68. Austin, *Earth Horizon,* 252, 286.
69. Benay Blend, "Building a House of Earth: Mary Austin, Environmental Activist and Writer," *Critical Matrix* 10, no. 11 (1996): 81.
70. Austin, *Earth Horizon,* 246.
71. Stineman, *Mary Austin,* 40–54.
72. Stineman, *Mary Austin,* 130.
73. Austin, *Earth Horizon,* 279, 293.
74. Melody Graulich, "I Thought at First She Was Talking about Herself: Mary Austin on Charlotte Perkins Gilman," *Jack London Journal* 1 (1994): 154.
75. Austin, *Earth Horizon,* 326, 232.
76. Doyle, *Mary Austin,* 248.
77. Austin, *Earth Horizon,* 213.
78. Carl Van Doren, *Many Minds* (New York: Knopf, 1924), 8.
79. Stineman, *Mary Austin,* 167.
80. Mary Austin, "New York, Dictator of American Criticism," in *Beyond Borders: The Selected Essays of Mary Austin,* ed. Reuben J. Ellis (Carbondale: Southern Illinois University Press, 1996), 56–61.
81. Mary Austin to Louise Untermeyer, November 12, 1930, Austin Collection, folder HM 41066, Huntington Library, San Marino, California.
82. Monroe, *A Poet's Life,* 203.
83. Reuben J. Ellis, introduction, in Ellis, ed., *Beyond Borders,* 20.
84. Harriet Monroe, *The Columbian Ode,* designs by Will H. Bradley (Chicago: W. I. Way, 1893).
85. Claire Badaracco, "Writers and Their Public Appeal: Harriet Monroe's Publicity Techniques," *American Literary Realism* 23, no. 2 (Winter 1991): 35–51.
86. Monroe, *A Poet's Life,* 295.
87. Monroe, *A Poet's Life,* 287–291, 197, 315.

88. Hamilton, *The Little Magazines,* 34, 54.
89. Monroe, *A Poet's Life,* 414.
90. Harriet Monroe, review of "The Wasteland," *Poetry* 21 (March 1923).
91. Elizabeth Lloyd Oliphant, "Marketing the Southwest: Modernism, the Fred Harvey Company, and the Indian Detour," *American Literature* 89, no. 1 (March 2017): 91–119.
92. Austin, *Earth Horizon,* 302.
93. World Celebrities Publicity Flyer, Austin Collection, box 23A, Huntington Library.
94. Henry Smith, "The Feel of the Purposeful Earth: Mary Austin's Prophecy," *New Mexico Quarterly* 1 (1931): 17.
95. Stineman, *Mary Austin,* 1; Ellis, introduction, in Ellis, ed., *Beyond Borders,* 2.
96. Stineman, *Mary Austin,* 311.
97. Stineman, *Mary Austin,* 149.
98. Austin, *Earth Horizon,* 274–275, 367.
99. Hutchison, "Harriet Monroe and Her Service to Poetry"; Holmes, review of *A Poet's Life,* 1.
100. Monroe, *A Poet's Life,* 249, 409.
101. Harriet Monroe, "The Audience," *Poetry* 5 (October 1914): 32.
102. Monroe, *A Poet's Life,* 397, 418, 295, 277.
103. John Newcombe, *How Did Poetry Survive? The Making of Modern American Verse* (Champaign: University of Illinois Press, 2012), 26.
104. Austin, *Earth Horizon,* 60, 167, 291.
105. Mary Austin, *A Woman of Genius* (New York: Feminist Press, 1985), 234.
106. Austin, *Earth Horizon,* 368, 154.
107. Mary Austin, "Greatness in Women," in Ellis, ed., *Beyond Borders,* 89–94, 92–93 (quotation).
108. Hansen, *Midwest Portraits,* 253.
109. Monroe, *A Poet's Life,* 242.
110. Newcombe, *How Did Poetry Survive?* 26.
111. Harriet Monroe and Alice Corbin Henderson, *The New Poetry* (New York: Macmillan, 1917), xiii.
112. Monroe, *A Poet's Life,* 249, 258.
113. Austin, *Earth Horizon,* 279, 368.
114. Austin, *Earth Horizon,* 458, 368.

CHAPTER 5: AMERICAN EVERYWOMEN

1. Mary Shaughnessy, *Women and Success in American Society in the Works of Edna Ferber* (New York: Gordon Press, 1977), 13.

2. Julie Gilbert, *Ferber: Edna Ferber and Her Circle* (New York: Applause, 1978), 291; Jan Cohn, *Improbable Fiction: The Life of Mary Roberts Rinehart* (London: University of Pittsburgh Press, 1980), 181–183.
3. Culkin Banning, "Edna Ferber's America," *Saturday Review,* February 4, 1939, 5–6.
4. Katherine Woods, "Edna Ferber and Her America," *New York Times Book Review,* February 5, 1939, 1.
5. Culkin Banning, "Edna Ferber's America," 5.
6. Rouben Mamoulian, "An American Life," *Theatre Arts Bookshelf,* April 1939, 311.
7. Woods, "Edna Ferber and Her America," 30.
8. "A Full Life," *Christian Science Monitor,* April 18, 1931, 10.
9. "Books in Brief," *Forum and Century,* May 1931, xvi.
10. Cohn, *Improbable Fiction,* 149, 158, 181.
11. Mary Roberts Rinehart, *My Story* (New York: Farrar and Rinehart, 1931), 429.
12. Uffington Valentine, "Mary Rinehart Halts and Looks Back: In *My Story* the Novelist Sets Down an Engagingly Honest Autobiographical Record," *New York Times Book Review,* March 15, 1931, 5.
13. Mary Ross, review of *My Story, Survey,* June 1, 1931; "A Full Life," *Christian Science Monitor,* April 18, 1931, 10.
14. Edna Ferber, *A Peculiar Treasure* (New York: Doubleday, Doran, 1939), 4, 5, 13.
15. Woods, "Edna Ferber and Her America," 1.
16. Ferber, *A Peculiar Treasure,* 5.
17. "Books in Brief," *Forum and Century,* May 1931, xvi.
18. Diana Hunter, "The Woman Who Crossed the Cascades and Inspired Batman," *Scientific American,* May 2, 2013, https://blogs.scientificamerican.com/rosetta-stones/the-woman-who-crossed-the-cascades-and-inspired-batman/.
19. Cohn, *Improbable Fiction,* 203; Catherine Ross Nickerson, *The Web of Iniquity: Early Detective Fiction by American Women* (Durham, N.C.: Duke University Press, 1999), 119, 120.
20. Rinehart, *My Story,* 428.
21. "Everywoman in America," *New York Times Book Review,* March 15, 1931, 1.
22. David Welky, *Everything Was Better in America: Print Culture in the Great Depression* (Champaign: University of Illinois Press, 2008), 85–89.
23. Mamoulian, "An American Life," 311.
24. Ines Asher to Edna Ferber, December 20, 1938, Ferber Papers, box 3, folder 3, Wisconsin Historical Society, Madison.
25. Ferber, *A Peculiar Treasure,* 6.
26. Woods, "Edna Ferber and Her America," 1.
27. Ferber, *A Peculiar Treasure,* 114–121.
28. Edna Ferber Papers, box 3, folder 3, Wisconsin Historical Society.
29. Woods, "Edna Ferber and Her America," 30.

30. Cohn, *Improbable Fiction,* 149; Gilbert, *Ferber,* 313.
31. Edna Ferber Papers, box 3, folder 1, Wisconsin Historical Society.
32. Ferber, *A Peculiar Treasure,* 389.
33. Rinehart, *My Story,* 383.
34. Scott Ortolano, "Liberation, Degeneration, and Transcendence: The Promise and Paradox of the 'New Woman' in Edna Ferber's Dawn O Hara and Dorothy Parker's Big Blonde," *Women's Studies* 45, no. 3 (April 2016): 231.
35. John L. Rury, *Education and Women's Work: Female Schooling and the Division of Labor in Urban America, 1870–1930* (Albany: State University of New York Press, 1991), 91–93; Alice Kessler-Harris, *Out to Work: A History of Wage-Earning Women in the United States* (New York: Oxford University Press, 2003), 119.
36. Ferber, *A Peculiar Treasure,* 170, 364.
37. Edna Ferber, "Sisters under the Skin," in *Emma McChesney and Co.* (New York: Frederick A. Stokes, 1915), 178.
38. Rinehart, *My Story,* 5, 53, 55, 76, 64.
39. Ferber, *A Peculiar Treasure,* 101, 103, 110.
40. Rinehart, *My Story,* 83.
41. Ferber, *A Peculiar Treasure,* 339.
42. Ferber, *A Peculiar Treasure,* 173.
43. Rinehart, *My Story,* 86.
44. Margaret Lawrence, *The School of Femininity: A Book for and about Women as They Are Interpreted through Feminine Writers of Yesterday and Today* (New York: Frederick A. Stokes, 1936), 187.
45. Jamie Harker, *America the Middlebrow: Women's Novels, Progressivism, and Middlebrow Authorship between the Wars* (Boston: University of Massachusetts Press, 2007), 119.
46. Cohn, *Improbable Fiction,* 210.
47. Gilbert, *Ferber,* 141.
48. Jennifer Haytock, *The Middle Class in the Great Depression: Popular Women's Novels of the 1930s* (New York: Palgrave Macmillan, 2013), 4–6.
49. Charlotte MacLeod, *Had She But Known: A Biography of Mary Roberts Rinehart* (New York: Warner, 1994), 18.
50. Rinehart, *My Story,* 412, 141.
51. Grant Overton, *When Winter Comes to Main Street* (New York: George H. Doran, 1922), 54, 110.
52. Rinehart, *My Story,* 408.
53. Mary Robert Rinehart, "Writing Is Work," *Saturday Evening Post,* March 11, 1939, 82.
54. Rinehart, *My Story,* 11.
55. Rinehart, "Writing Is Work," 84.
56. Rinehart, "Writing Is Work," 82.
57. Rinehart, *My Story,* 113, 413.

58. Ferber, *A Peculiar Treasure,* 167, 226, 11, 205.
59. Gilbert, *Ferber,* 314.
60. Ferber, *A Peculiar Treasure,* 102, 3.
61. Ferber, *A Peculiar Treasure,* photographic insert between pages 104–105.
62. Rinehart, *My Story,* photographic inserts between pages 330–331, 250–251, 90–91, 218–219.
63. Elizabeth Kemper Adams, *Women Professional Workers* (Chautauqua, N.Y.: Chautauqua Press, 1921), 15.
64. Rinehart, *My Story,* 86, 286.
65. Ferber, *A Peculiar Treasure,* 174, 265.
66. Shaughnessy, *Women and Success in American Society.*
67. Cohn, *Improbable Fiction,* 215.
68. Ferber, *A Peculiar Treasure,* 93, 172.
69. Rinehart, *My Story,* 178.
70. MacLeod, *Had She But Known,* 42.
71. Rinehart, *My Story,* 77.
72. MacLeod, *Had She But Known,* 124.
73. Rinehart, *My Story,* 113.
74. Ferber, *A Peculiar Treasure,* 243, 345, 46, 226.
75. Genevieve Forbes, "Informally," *Chicago Daily Tribune,* May 14, 1921, 7.
76. Rinehart, *My Story,* 92.
77. Ross, review of *My Story,* 1.
78. Rinehart, *My Story,* 95, 132, 91.
79. Cohn, *Improbable Fiction,* 204.
80. Rinehart, "The Unreality of Modern Realism," 463.
81. Cohn, *Improbable Fiction,* 204.
82. Rinehart, *My Story,* 89–91.
83. Martha Hailey Dubose, *Women of Mystery: The Lives and Works of Notable Women Crime Novelists* (New York: St. Martin's Minotaur, 2000), 72.
84. Margaret Widdemer, "Message and Middlebrow," *Saturday Review of Literature,* February 18, 1933, 433–434.
85. Cohn, *Improbable Fiction,* 174.
86. Mary Roberts Rinehart, "My Public," *Bookman* 54, no. 4 (1920): 291.
87. Ferber, *A Peculiar Treasure,* 5.
88. Elyse Vigiletti, "Edna Ferber and the Problems of the Middlebrow," *Studies in the Novel* 48, no. 1 (2016): 70.
89. John Farrar, *The Literary Spotlight* (New York: George H. Doran, 1924), 141.
90. Ferber, *A Peculiar Treasure,* 176.
91. Rinehart, "My Public," 290.
92. Francesca Sawaya, *Modern Women, Modern Work: Domesticity, Professionalism, and American Writing* (Philadelphia: University of Pennsylvania Press, 2004), 16, 17.

93. Ferber, *A Peculiar Treasure,* 303.
94. Gertrude Lane to Edna Ferber, February 17, 1938, Ferber Papers, box 6, folder 7, Wisconsin Historical Society.
95. Valentine, "Rinehart Halts and Looks Back," 5.
96. Ferber, *A Peculiar Treasure,* 19, 119, 97–98, 118, 33.
97. Rinehart, *My Story,* 252.
98. Rinehart, *My Story,* 126–127.
99. Dubose, *Women of Mystery,* 39.
100. Gilbert, *Ferber,* 317, 55, 409.
101. Ferber, *A Peculiar Treasure,* 166, 156.
102. Gilbert, *Ferber,* 54.
103. Ferber, *A Peculiar Treasure,* 197, 164.
104. Gilbert, *Ferber,* 208.
105. Overton, *When Winter Comes,* 109.
106. Rinehart, *My Story,* 95.
107. Rinehart, *My Story,* 130.
108. Mary Roberts Rinehart, *My Story: A New Edition and Seventeen New Years* (New York: Rinehart, 1948), 521.
109. Ferber, *A Peculiar Treasure,* 209.
110. Edna Ferber, preface, in *They Brought Their Women* (New York: Doubleday Doran, 1936).
111. Gilbert, *Ferber,* 409.
112. Kessler-Harris, *Out to Work,* 229.
113. Grant Overton, *The Women Who Make Our Novels* (New York: Moffat, Yard, 1918), 54, 56.
114. Kessler-Harris, *Out to Work,* 228.
115. Rinehart, *My Story,* 111, 330.
116. Rinehart, *My Story,* 86.
117. Rinehart, *My Story,* 112.
118. Ferber, *A Peculiar Treasure,* 398.

CHAPTER 6: STRATEGIC DIVERSIONS

1. Janet Hobhouse, *Everybody Who Was Anybody: A Biography of Gertrude Stein* (New York: G. P. Putnam's Sons), 161.
2. Carolyn Wells, *The Rest of My Life* (Philadelphia: Lippincott, 1937), 13.
3. Wells, *The Rest of My Life,* 13–14.
4. Zita Zatkin Dresner, "Carolyn Wells," in *American Humorists, 1800–1950: Dictionary of Literary Biography,* ed. Stanley Tractenberg (Detroit: Gale, 1982), 1:559.

5. Thomas Masson, *Our American Humorists* (New York: Moffat, Yard, 1922); Carolyn Wells, *The Technique of the Mystery Story* (Springfield, Mass.: Home Correspondence School, 1913; reprint, N.p.: Ramble House, 2011).
6. Helena Lenart-Cheng, "Autobiography as Advertisement: Why Do Gertrude Stein's Sentences Get under Our Skin?" *New Literary History* 34, no. 1 (Spring 2003): 117–132, 129 (quotation).
7. Theodore Hall, "Miss Stein Looks Homeward," *Washington Post,* October 8, 1933.
8. Fanny Butcher, "Gertrude Stein Writes a Book in Simple Style," *Chicago Daily Tribune Books,* September 2, 1933, 1.
9. *Newsweek,* September 9, 1933, 29.
10. Ann MacDonald, "The Business Woman's Bookshelf," *Independent Woman,* November 1933.
11. James Agee, "Stein's Way," *Time,* September 11, 1933, 57–60.
12. Wells, *The Rest of My Life,* 14–15.
13. K. W., "Carolyn Wells Hates Autobiographies," *New York Times Book Review,* December 5, 1937, 7.
14. Will Cuppy, review of *The Rest of My Life, Books,* October 31, 1937, 6.
15. John Merton, "A Pleasant Person," *Commonweal,* November 12, 1937, 80.
16. K. W., "Carolyn Wells Hates Autobiographies," 7.
17. Wells, *The Rest of My Life,* 17.
18. Gertrude Stein, *The Autobiography of Alice B. Toklas* (New York: Harcourt Brace, 1933; reprint New York: Stellar Classics, 2013), 176.
19. Ulla E. Dydo, "Stanzas in Meditation: The Other Autobiography," *Chicago Review* 35, no. 2 (985): 6.
20. Carolyn A. Barros, "Getting Modern: *The Autobiography of Alice B. Toklas,*" *Biography* 22, no. 2 (Spring 1999): 177; Karla Murphy, "The 'Convincing Lies' of Gertrude Stein: Cubism in *The Autobiography of Alice B. Toklas,*" *Platte Valley Review* 22, no. 2 (1994): 5–20.
21. James Bresslin, "Gertrude Stein and the Problems of Autobiography," *Georgia Review* 33, no. 4 (Winter 1979): 901.
22. Wells, *The Rest of My Life,* 75.
23. Retro Staff, "Classic Toys: Jack-in-the-Box," Planet Retro, August 4, 2009, https://blog.retroplanet.com.
24. Many Jack-in the-Boxes play the song "Pop Goes the Weasel" in which the characters go around the Mulberry Bush.
25. Phillipe Lejeune, *On Autobiography* (Minneapolis: University of Minnesota Press, 1989), 160, 22.
26. Wells, *The Rest of My Life,* 223, 23, 28, 110, 236–237.
27. Estelle Jelinek, *The Tradition of Women's Autobiography: From Antiquity to the Present* (Boston: Twayne, 1986), 197.

28. Stein, *Autobiography of Alice B. Toklas,* 7, 19, 20.
29. Lenart-Cheng, "Autobiography as Advertisement," 128.
30. Stein, *Autobiography of Alice B. Toklas,* 31, 63, 151.
31. Stein, *Autobiography of Alice B. Toklas,* 53.
32. Rod Rosenquist, "Copywriting Gertrude Stein: Advertising, Anonymity, Autobiography," *Modernist Cultures* 11, no. 3 (Nov 2016): 331–350, 335 (quotation); Karen Leick, *Gertrude Stein and the Making of an American Celebrity* (New York: Routledge, 2009).
33. Paul Alkon, "Visual Rhetoric in *The Autobiography of Alice B. Toklas,*" *Critical Inquiry* 1, no. 1 (June 1975): 852.
34. Wells, *The Rest of My Life,* 268.
35. Amy Feinstein, "Gertrude Stein, Alice Toklas, and Albert Barnes: Looking Like a Jew in 'The Autobiography of Alice B. Toklas,'" *Shofar* 25, no. 3 (2007): 47; Lynn Z. Bloom, "Gertrude Is Alice Is Everybody: Innovation and Point of View in Gertrude Stein's Autobiographies," *Twentieth Century Literature* 24, no. 1 (Spring 1978): 81–93, 84 (quotation).
36. Alkon, "Visual Rhetoric in *The Autobiography of Alice B. Toklas,*" 849.
37. Wells, *The Rest of My Life,* 74–75, 119–120.
38. Sondra Fishinger, "Carolyn Wells," in *Past and Promise: Lives of New Jersey Women* (New York: Syracuse University Press, 1997), 206.
39. Dresner, "Carolyn Wells," 557.
40. Wells, *The Rest of My Life,* 147, 193.
41. Nora Doyle, "Gertrude Stein and the Domestication of Genius," *Feminist Studies* 44, no. 1 (2018): 43–69; Wells, *The Rest of My Life,* 31.
42. Wells, *The Rest of My Life,* 31, 96, 105, 94, 103.
43. Stein, *Autobiography of Alice B. Toklas,* 4, 53.
44. Wells, *The Rest of My Life,* 160.
45. J. Berg Esenwein, introduction, in Wells, *The Technique of the Mystery Story* (1913 edition), xiii.
46. Wells, *The Technique of the Mystery Story,* 21.
47. Wells, *The Rest of My Life,* 170.
48. Gelett Burgess, ed., *My Maiden Effort: Being the Personal Confessions of Well-Known American Authors as to Their Literary Beginnings* (New York: Doubleday, 1921), 255.
49. Wells, *The Rest of My Life,* 36.
50. Stein, *Autobiography of Alice B. Toklas,* 28, 143, 35.
51. Barrie Hayne, "Carolyn Wells," in *St. James Guide to Crime and Mystery Writers,* ed. Taryn Benbow-Pfalzgraf, Jay Pederson, and Kathleen Klein (Detroit: St. James Press, 1996), 1036.
52. Wells, *The Rest of My Life,* 123, 158, 193, 48.
53. Wells, *The Rest of My Life,* 70, 268, 270, 163, 176, 171.

54. Stein, *Autobiography of Alice B. Toklas*, 35, 164, 109, 119, 135, 22, 37, 61, 39, 77.
55. Jelinek, *The Tradition of Women's Autobiography*, 211.
56. Stein, *Autobiography of Alice B. Toklas*, 34, 20, 152.
57. Wells, *The Rest of My Life*, 53.
58. Stein, *Autobiography of Alice B. Toklas*, 5, 44.
59. Stein, *Autobiography of Alice B. Toklas*, 143, 114, 51.
60. Wells, *The Rest of My Life*, 50, 52.
61. Hobhouse, *Everybody Who Was Anybody*, 131.
62. Wells, *The Rest of My Life*, 170–171, 69.
63. Stein, *Autobiography of Alice B. Toklas*, 48, 171.
64. Bryce Conrad, "Gertrude Stein in the American Marketplace," *William Carlos Williams Review* 35, no. 1 (2018): 23.
65. Georgia Johnston, "Narratologies of Pleasure: Gertrude Stein's *The Autobiography of Alice B. Toklas*," *MFS: Modern Fiction Studies* 42, no. 3 (Fall 1996): 600.
66. Stein, *Autobiography of Alice B. Toklas*, 9, 121.
67. Wells, *The Rest of My Life*, 194, 201, 205, 200.
68. Wells, *The Rest of My Life*, 30.
69. Alissa Karl, "Modernism's Risky Business: Gertrude Stein, Sylvia Beach, and American Consumer Capitalism," *American Literature* 89, no. 1 (March 2008): 97.
70. Stein, *Autobiography of Alice B. Toklas*, 167.
71. Stein, *Autobiography of Alice B. Toklas*, 60.
72. Stein, *Autobiography of Alice B. Toklas*, 54.
73. Karl, "Modernism's Risky Business," 91.
74. Sarah Wilson, "Gertrude Stein and the Radio," *Modernism/Modernity* 11, no. 2 (April 2004): 261–278, 263 (quotation).
75. Bill Pronzini, *Gun in Cheek: A Study of "Alternative" Crime Fiction* (Toronto: Coward, McCann, and Geoghegan, 1982), 43.
76. Jon Breen, introduction, in Wells, *The Technique of the Mystery Story*, 12–13.
77. Wells, *The Technique of the Mystery Story*, 52, 159, 201.
78. Gertrude Stein, "What Are Master-Pieces and Why Are There So Few of them," in *The Gender of Modernism*, ed. Bonnie Kime Scott (Bloomington: Indiana University Press, 1990), 497.
79. Gertrude Stein, *Everybody's Autobiography* (New York: Knopf Doubleday, 2013), 100.
80. Wells, *The Rest of My Life*, 54, 56, 57, 55.
81. Dydo, "Stanzas in Meditation," 4–20; Johnston, "Narratologies of Pleasure," 590–606.
82. Wells, *The Rest of My Life*, 223–224, 248.
83. Wells, *The Rest of My Life*, 256, 254, 255.

EPILOGUE: PORTRAITS OF THE ARTIST AS AN OLD WOMAN

1. Zora Neale Hurston, *Dust Tracks on a Road* (New York: Harper Perennial, 1991), 26.
2. Carolyn Heilbrun, *Writing a Woman's Life* (New York: Norton, 1989), 109.
3. Barbara Will, *Gertrude Stein, Modernism, and the Problem of Genius* (Edinburgh: Edinburgh University Press, 2000), 135.
4. Bob Perelman, *The Trouble with Genius* (Berkeley: University of California Press, 1994), 1.
5. Jody Cardinal, Dierdre Egan-Ryan, and Julie Lisella, eds., *Modernist Women Writers and American Social Engagement* (Lanham, Md.: Rowman and Littlefield, 2019).
6. Amy Feinstein, "Gertrude Stein, Alice Toklas, and Albert Barnes: Looking Like a Jew in 'The Autobiography of Alice B. Toklas,'" *Shofar* 25, no. 3 (2007): 49.
7. Grace King, *To Find My Own Peace: Grace King in Her Journals, 1886–1910*, ed. Melissa Walker Heidari (Athens: University of Georgia Press, 2004), 65.
8. Edith Wharton, *The Writing of Fiction* (New York: Charles Scribner's Sons, 1924), 17.
9. King, *To Find My Own Peace*, 2.
10. Edith Wharton, *The Uncollected Critical Writings of Edith Wharton,* ed. Frederick Wegener (Princeton, N.J.: Princeton University Press, 1996), 159–163, 160 (quotations).
11. Esther Stineman, *Mary Austin: Song of a Maverick* (New Haven, Conn.: Yale University Press, 1989), 4.
12. Augusta Fink, *I-Mary: A Biography of Mary Austin* (Tucson: University of Arizona Press, 1983), 231.
13. Emily Wortis Leider, *California's Daughter: Gertrude Atherton and Her Times* (Stanford, Calif.: Stanford University Press, 1991), 220.
14. Harriet Monroe, *A Poet's Life: Seventy Years in a Changing World* (New York: Macmillan, 1938), 253.
15. Mary Austin, *No. 26 Jayne Street* (New York: Houghton Mifflin, 1920), 6.
16. Mary Austin, "Women as Audience," *Bookman* 55 (March 1922): 2.
17. R. W. B. Lewis, *Edith Wharton: A Biography* (New York: HarperCollins, 1975), 471–472.
18. Ed and Libby Klekowski, *Edith Wharton and Mary Roberts Rinehart at the Western Front* (Jefferson, N.C.: McFarland, *2018).*
19. Willa Cather, "Four Women Writers: Atherton, Ouida, Chopin, Morris," in *The World and the Parish: Willa Cather's Articles and Reviews, 1893–1902,* ed. William M. Curtin (Lincoln: University of Nebraska Press, 1970), 694–697.
20. Matthew 7:21 reads, "Not everyone who saith Lord, Lord to me shall enter" the gates of heaven. Cather, "Four Women Writers," 696.

21. William E. Harris, "Contemporary Writers XI—Gertrude Atherton," *The Writer* 39 (1929): 63.
22. Stineman, *Mary Austin*, 52.
23. Karen S. Langlois, "Marketing the American Indian: Mary Austin and the Business of Writing," in *A Living of Words: American Women in Print Culture,* ed. Susan Albertine (Knoxville: University of Tennessee Press, 1995), 154.
24. Louis Adamic, *My America, 1928–1938* (New York: Harper, 1938), 477–478.
25. R. L. Duffus, "Mary Austin, Who Found God under a Walnut Tree," *New York Times Book Review,* November 13, 1932, 3.
26. T.S. Eliot, "Tradition and the Individual Talent," in *The Sacred Wood* (London: Methuen, 1920), 42–53.

INDEX